RIVERSIDE CITY & COUNTY PUBLIC LIBRARY

P9-DNF-956

Reel ELVIS

ALSO BY PAULINE BARTEL

The Complete Gone with the Wind *Sourcebook*
The Complete Gone with the Wind *Trivia Book*

UPCOMING:

Everything Elvis!

Reel ELVIS!

The Ultimate Trivia Guide To The King's Movies

Pauline BARTEL

Taylor Publishing Company

Dallas, Texas

To Elvis Aaron Presley
and to the fans who love him.

Copyright © 1994 Pauline Bartel

All rights reserved

No part of this book may be reproduced in any form without written permission from the publisher.

Published by Taylor Publishing Company
1550 West Mockingbird Lane
Dallas, Texas 75235

Designed by David Timmons

Library of Congress Cataloging-in-Publication Data

Bartel, Pauline C.
    Reel Elvis! : the ultimate trivia guide to the king's movies /
Pauline Bartel.
        p.   cm.
    Includes bibliographic references.
    ISBN 0-87833-852-7
    1. Presley, Elvis, 1935–1977. 2. Motion picture actors and
actresses—United States. I. Title
ML420.P96B42   1994
791.43'75—dc20

93-4876
CIP
MN

Printed in the United States of America

10   9   8   7   6   5   4   3   2   1

CONTENTS

ACKNOWLEDGMENTS

I am indebted to the following individuals for their assistance, support, and encouragement during the preparation of this book: Lynne Alpern; my mother, Mary F. Bartel; Terry Brown; Debbie Casale; Karen DeMartino; Mary Ellen Dugrenier; my editors, Jim Donovan and Holly McGuire; Shelby Harrison; Jennifer Jones; Sheila Levine; Katherine MacGregor; Joanne McFadden; members of The Arnold Madison Writers Group (Jackie Craven, David Lee Drotar, Joyce Hunt, Kate Kunz, Peg Lewis, Marie Musgrove, Jane Streiff, Donna Tomb); Carol and Alice Michon; Janet Nardolillo; Ellen O'Connor; Maggie Oldendorf; Julia Payne; Doreen Shea; Carole Stallone; Sean Sullivan and the staff of The Waterford Public Library; Lynne Van Derhoof; Dave Van Slyke; Mary Jennara Wenk; and most especially, my own Tiger Man, George.

ALL ABOUT ELVIS

His music and his personality, fusing the styles of white country and black rhythm and blues, permanently changed the face of American popular culture.
—President Jimmy Carter

1935–1953
DID YOU KNOW THAT ELVIS . . .

- **W**as born on January 8, 1935, in East Tupelo, Mississippi? His parents were Vernon Elvis Presley and Gladys Love Smith Presley. Vernon struggled to support his family by working as a farmer, truck driver, painter, and laborer, while Gladys worked as a sewing-machine operator and a nurse's aide.

- Was a twin? His brother, Jesse Garon Presley, was delivered stillborn at 4:00 A.M. Elvis followed at 4:35 A.M., kicking and fussing. The next day, Jesse was buried in the Priceville Cemetery near East Tupelo.

- Attended church services with his parents at the First Assembly of God Church in East Tupelo? Elvis was baptized there in 1944, and he enjoyed singing along with the choir during services.

- Impressed his fifth-grade homeroom teacher at East Tupelo Consolidated School with his singing ability? During morning chapel, before the start of classes, Mrs. J. C. (Oleta) Grimes asked her students if one of them would begin the devotions. Elvis raised his hand, said a prayer, then sang "Old Shep." Mrs. Grimes was so impressed, she had Elvis sing the same song to the prin-

cipal, J. D. Cole. Mr. Cole listened and promptly entered Elvis in the annual talent contest at the upcoming 1945 Mississippi–Alabama Fair and Dairy Show.

• Took second place in the talent contest at the Mississippi-Alabama Fair and Dairy Show? Ten–year–old Elvis stood on a chair to reach the microphone, sang "Old Shep," and captured second prize—five dollars and free admission to the fair's amusement rides.

• Received his first guitar from his mother as a present for his eleventh birthday? In 1946, Gladys took Elvis to shop at the Tupelo Hardware Company store on Main Street in Tupelo, Mississippi. There Elvis saw a .22–caliber rifle that he wanted, but Gladys refused to buy it for him. She had a more suitable purchase in mind—a guitar. Elvis threw a tantrum but was persuaded by Gladys and the proprietor, Forrest L. Bobo, to look at a guitar that was in a glass showcase. Elvis was persuaded to accept the guitar which cost $7.75.

• Graduated from L. C. Humes High School in Memphis, Tennessee, in June 1953? The Presleys had moved to Memphis in 1948, and while in high school Elvis was involved with ROTC, Biology Club, English Club, History Club, and Speech Club. While other boys sported crew cuts, Elvis kept his hair long and greased back into a ducktail. He also favored sideburns and wearing flashy clothes in his favorite colors, pink and black. He spent his spare hours on Beale Street listening to the black singers and musicians in the blues clubs. During Elvis's senior year, his history and homeroom teacher, Mrs. Mildred Scrivener, persuaded Elvis to perform in the school's annual variety show. He sang "Cold, Cold Icy Fingers" and received tumultuous applause from the audience. Mrs. Scrivener invited him to do an encore song, which was greeted with even more applause. One week before graduation, Elvis hitchhiked to Meridian, Mississippi, to participate in a talent show at the first Jimmie Rodgers "The Father of Country Music" Festival. Elvis took second place and won a guitar.

• Was a factory worker at the Precision Tool Company, then became a truck driver for Crown Electric? He earned about forty-one dollars a week driving for Crown (a Memphis electrical contracting firm) delivering materials to job sites, and sometimes stocking the warehouse. During breaks, he entertained his fellow workers by singing and playing his guitar.

• Drove the company truck past the Memphis Recording Service on Union Avenue during his deliveries? Elvis knew that for four dollars anyone could record a two-sided, ten-inch acetate at the studio, operated by record producer Sam Phillips. Elvis also knew that he had to be absolutely ready before he parked the truck by the curb and walked through the door. He would be doing more than just cutting a demo record; he would be auditioning for Sam Phillips, who was also the head of Sun Records.

- Recorded "My Happiness" at the Memphis Recording Service in the summer of 1953? During a Saturday lunch hour, Elvis stopped by the Memphis Recording Service and found the office packed with other aspiring singers waiting to cut records. However, Sam Phillips wasn't in. Elvis began a conversation with Marion Keisker, the studio manager, and told her he was there to make a record as a present for his mother. When his turn came, Elvis sang for the first side of the record one of his favorite songs by the Ink Spots, "My Happiness." About halfway through the recording, unbeknownst to Elvis, Keisker began taping the recording session. She captured the last third of the first song and all of the second song, "That's When Your Heartaches Begin." At the end of the session, Elvis left the studio with his ten-inch acetate. Marion Keisker couldn't wait to have Sam Phillips listen to the white kid who sang with the sound and feel of a black man.

ELVIS IS DISCOVERED

According to Marion Keisker, Sam Phillips always said that if he could find a white man who sang with the sound and feel of a black man, he could make a billion dollars.

Phillips had grown up around that special sound on his father's plantation in Florence, Alabama. An elderly black farm worker, Uncle Silas Payne, bounced young Sam on his knee and sang blues songs to him. Phillips grew to love music, especially the blues, and this love led him to work as a radio station engineer and a disc jockey in Muscle Shoals, Alabama; Decatur, Alabama; Nashville; and Memphis.

In 1950, Phillips opened the Memphis Recording Service and began recording some of the premiere black artists in Memphis, including B. B. King, Bobby "Blue" Bland, Joe Hill Louis, and Chester "The Howlin' Wolf" Burnett, and offering their demo records to other independent record companies. In 1952, Phillips began Sun Records as a place where rhythm and blues artists and country and western singers could record their music.

When Phillips returned to the office that summer Saturday afternoon, Keisker played the tape she had made of Elvis singing. Phillips liked what he heard, although he admitted that the delivery was rough and needed work. Phillips wanted to know who the boy was. Keisker showed him the piece of paper on which she had written Elvis's name, address, and the phone number of a friend, since the Presleys didn't have a home telephone. The piece of paper and the tape went into a file.

On January 4, 1954, Elvis returned to the Memphis Recording Service with another four dollars to cut another record. This time Phillips was in the studio, and he listened as Elvis recorded two country songs, "Casual Love Affair" and "I'll Never Stand in Your Way." Phillips wrote down information about Elvis, including his work number, for the files and told Elvis he would call if something came up.

Something came up a few months later. Phillips had received from Nashville a demo of the song "Without You." He wanted to release the record, couldn't locate the artist, and decided to have someone else record the song. Marion

4 Keisker suggested Elvis, and Phillips agreed. After Keisker called him, Elvis was at the studio in a flash.

However, Elvis had difficulty singing "Without You" as perfectly as he wanted to. Phillips asked to hear what else Elvis could do, and for the next several hours, Elvis sang everything he knew, from gospel, country, and blues, to some songs made popular by Dean Martin. At last, Elvis had the audition he had been wanting, and Sam Phillips had found a raw talent that he thought had definite possibilities.

BILL BLACK, SCOTTY MOORE, AND ELVIS

Elvis told Sam Phillips that he needed a band to help him with his musical ideas. Phillips contacted guitarist Scotty Moore, who, along with bass player Bill Black, was a member of a local Memphis band, Doug Poindexter's Starlight Wranglers. Would Scotty be willing to rehearse with Elvis? Scotty invited Elvis to his apartment, Bill joined them, and the three rehearsed a number of songs. After that, the trio met regularly at Sun Records's studio to rehearse and to develop a distinctive style.

On the evening of July 5, 1954, Elvis, Scotty, and Bill were set to rehearse, but Sam Phillips turned the rehearsal into a recording session. They had taped "Harbor Lights" and "I Love You Because." Nothing so far had impressed Phillips, so they took a break.

During the break, Elvis grabbed his guitar, played a few chords, and—just to goof around—belted out "That's All Right (Mama)," a song written and recorded in 1946 by Arthur "Big Boy" Crudup. Scotty and Bill picked up their instruments, joined in the jam session, and the sounds they made caused Sam Phillips to come running out of the control room.

He had heard sounds that were fresh and exciting, so Phillips asked the trio to do the song again. Various takes were put on tape, and by the end of the evening Elvis had the A side of his first record. (The B side, "Blue Moon of Kentucky," emerged several evenings later in a similar fashion.) And Sam Phillips knew just the right disc jockey to approach with "That's All Right (Mama)."

DEWEY PHILLIPS: FIRST DJ TO PLAY AN ELVIS SONG

Dewey Phillips was a former partner of Sam Phillips's (no relation). In 1950, the two had launched the record label Phillips Records. Now Dewey was on Memphis radio station WHBQ hosting a show called "Red Hot and Blue" that featured records by black blues artists. Dewey had often debuted Sam's new releases on his show. When he listened to the dub made by Elvis, Dewey liked the riotous blending of black rhythm and blues with country and western (a style soon to be called "rockabilly"). He told Sam he'd give the platter a spin on his show.

On July 7, 1954, Dewey debuted "That's All Right (Mama)" and received forty-seven phone calls from listeners asking him to play it again, all of them presuming that Elvis was black. Dewey played the record fourteen times during his show.

Dewey wanted to interview Elvis on the program but had difficulty locating him. Nervous at having his first song played on the radio, Elvis had gone to see *The Best Years of Our Lives* at the Suzore No. 2 in Memphis. His parents had to search the theater to find him and get him to the radio station.

Once at the station, Elvis had misgivings about being interviewed. Dewey simply told him not to say anything dirty, then asked him where he went to high school. When Elvis replied that he had attended Humes, the all-white high school, that told the audience that Elvis wasn't black. At the time, mixing black and white music wasn't done, yet here was a new singer who had done just that, and the audience had loved it. The questions continued, but Elvis didn't realize that the mike was open or that Dewey was conducting the interview. When Dewey told him that the interview was over, Elvis became drenched in a cold sweat.

In only days after the interview, Sun Records was deluged with five thousand orders for "That's All Right (Mama)."

1954-1955
DID YOU KNOW THAT ELVIS...

- Signed a managerial contract with Scotty Moore on July 12, 1954? The terms of the contract guaranteed fifty percent for Elvis and twenty-five percent each for Scotty Moore and Bill Black. Later that week, Elvis signed a recording contract with Sun Records. "That's All Right (Mama)," which was released on July 19, became a top-five hit for him on the country and western sales chart in Memphis.

- Made his first professional appearance at the Overton Park Shell in Memphis? Country singer Slim Whitman was the featured performer for the July 30, 1954, concert, but Elvis stole the show. He made other appearances through the summer and fall.

- Had hits in the Memphis area with "Good Rockin' Tonight," backed with "I Don't Care If the Sun Don't Shine"? Sam Phillips released the record, Elvis's second, in September 1954. Although the songs were popular in Memphis, they did not chart nationally.

- Bombed when he appeared on the Grand Ole Opry in Nashville? The Hillbilly Cat and the Blue Moon Boys, as Elvis, Bill, and Scotty were billed for a short time, were scheduled to appear on The Grand Ole Opry on October 2, 1954. For the performance, Elvis sang "That's All Right (Mama)" and "Blue Moon of Kentucky" to a nonreceptive audience. Afterwards, the Opry's talent coordinator, Jim Denny, suggested that Elvis return to driving a truck. Elvis was crushed.

- Was asked to become a regular on the "Louisiana Hayride"? On October 16, 1954, Elvis debuted on the radio program "Louisiana Hayride" and was a smash. Elvis appeared regularly on the program through 1955.

- Gained a new manager in January 1955? Scotty Moore could no longer balance managing Elvis and playing in the band. So Scotty turned over the managerial reins to Bob Neal, a Memphis disc jockey on radio station WMPS and promoter who remained Elvis's manager until 1956. Neal's cut was fifteen percent.

- Failed an audition for "Arthur Godfrey's Talent Scouts" (1948–1958)? In March 1955, Elvis, Scotty, and Bill flew to New York City to audition for the CBS–TV series which was the hottest showcase for new talent. "Arthur Godfrey's Talent Scouts" said "no thanks."

- Had his first national hit with "Baby, Let's Play House"? The song hit number ten on *Billboard*'s Country Best-Seller chart and number five on the Country Disc Jockey Chart in July 1955.

- Scored two more national hits with "Mystery Train" backed with "I Forgot to Remember to Forget"? "Mystery Train" peaked at number eleven on *Billboard*'s Country Disc Jockey chart. The flip side was number one for five weeks on *Billboard*'s Country Juke Box chart and number one for two weeks on the Country Best-Seller Chart. "I Forgot to Remember to Forget" had a thirty-nine-week stay on the charts.

- Had his Sun Records contract purchased by RCA Victor? In 1955, Sam Phillips sold the contract to RCA for forty thousand dollars which included a five thousand dollar bonus for Elvis. This bonus represented royalties Elvis would have received from Sun. Col. Tom Parker had helped negotiate the deal.

COLONEL THOMAS A. PARKER

Dutch-born Thomas A. Parker (real name Andreas Cornelius van Kuijk) first became aware of Elvis in late 1954. Parker, a former carnival barker, dogcatcher, and honorary Louisiana colonel, officially became Elvis's manager in 1956. Parker had formerly guided the careers of Eddy Arnold and Hank Snow. Under the terms of the Parker–Presley managerial contract, the Colonel received twenty-five percent of Elvis's earnings.

Through the years, Parker's keen ability to wheel, deal, and promote made Elvis the highest paid entertainer in history. For example, Parker established the going rate of one million dollars plus fifty percent of the profits for Elvis to star in a movie. Parker kept in touch with fan clubs, made sure that the Presley merchandising machine operated at peak efficiency, and included information about upcoming films in each piece of outgoing mail from MGM and RCA. When Elvis's RCA contract was up for renewal, company executives grumbled that the deal Parker negotiated included everything but the dog in the company trademark.

In January 1967, Parker renegotiated his contract with Elvis, and his share of Elvis's earnings rose from twenty-five percent to fifty percent. Parker continued as manager until Elvis's death.

THE JORDANAIRES

"If I ever cut a record, I want to use you guys singing background with me," Elvis said to the Jordanaires when he met them at the Memphis Cotton Carnival in early 1954. Elvis had that opportunity in a RCA recording session in New York on July 2, 1956. Backed by Jordanaires members Gordon Stoker (first tenor), Neal Matthews (second tenor), Hoyt Hawkins (baritone), and Hugh Jarrett (bass), Elvis recorded "Hound Dog," "Don't Be Cruel," and "Any Way You Want Me (That's How I Will Be)." Ray Walker took the place of Hugh Jarrett beginning with the recording session on June 10–11, 1958. The Jordanaires were often called "The Sound behind the King."

1956-1968
DID YOU KNOW THAT ELVIS...

- Had all of his Sun singles re-released by RCA Victor? Elvis also went into the studio in January 1956 to record new material. D. J. Fontana joined the band as the drummer. The first song Elvis recorded was "I Got a Woman." Another song recorded during that session, "Heartbreak Hotel," was Elvis's first national number one song.

- Made his national television debut on "Stage Show"? Elvis appeared on the Tommy and Jimmy Dorsey CBS variety series for the first time on January 28, 1956. He made three additional appearances on the show. Elvis also appeared on "The Milton Berle Show," "The Steve Allen Show," "Hy Gardner Calling," "American Bandstand," and "The Ed Sullivan Show." On the last of three appearances on "The Ed Sullivan Show," Elvis was shown on camera only from the waist up.

- Bombed in Las Vegas? For his four-week engagement at the New Frontier Hotel in the spring of 1956, Elvis was booked as the "The Nation's Only Atomic Powered Singer." But the middle-aged crowd failed to appreciate him, and the New Frontier canceled the remainder of the engagement after two weeks.

- Began his film career with *Love Me Tender*? Elvis went on to star in thirty other films and two documentaries.

- Became the target of the wrath of clergymen, teachers, and parents? Those critics accused Elvis of being vulgar and obscene. Elvis always asserted that "when I sing I just start jumping" and that he didn't know what all the fuss was about.

- Saw his hit singles certified gold in 1956? The singles included "Heartbreak Hotel," "I Was the One," "I Want You, I Need You, I Love You," "Hound Dog," "Don't Be Cruel," "Love Me Tender," and "Anyway You Want Me (That's the Way I'll Be)."

- Bought a pink Cadillac for his mother? Elvis bought his mother a 1957 Cadillac in September 1956 despite the fact that she didn't drive.

- Bought Graceland in March 1957? Elvis paid one hundred thousand dollars for the two-story mansion and its surrounding 13 3/4 acres of land in the Memphis suburb of Whitehaven. During the Civil War, Graceland was the site of a farm owned by the publisher of the *Memphis Daily Appeal*, S. E. Toof. Toof named the estate after his daughter, Grace. The house was built in 1939 by the niece of Grace Toof, Ruth Moore. Before Elvis bought Graceland from Moore's daughter, Ruth Marie Moore, the house had been used as a church by the Graceland Christian Church.

- Recorded his first stereo record after his discharge from the Army? In 1960, "Stuck on You" sold more than two million copies and was number one for four weeks on *Billboard*'s Hot 100 chart.

- Had a 1960 Cadillac Series 75 sedan limousine customized? George Barris customized the car for Elvis, and the vehicle became known as the Gold Cadillac because it was painted with diamond-dust gold pearl paint.

- Enjoyed a string of number-one hits from 1960 to 1962? In addition to "Stuck on You," the songs included "It's Now or Never," "Are You Lonesome Tonight?," "Surrender," and "Good Luck Charm." ·

- Surrounded himself with close friends, business associates, and employees that the news media in the 1960s called the Memphis Mafia? Some of the members of the Memphis Mafia included Joe Esposito, Lamar Fike, Alan Fortas, Larry Geller, Charlie Hodge, George Klein, Marty Lacker, Red and Sonny West.

- Was made an honorary colonel? Elvis appeared before the General Assembly of the Tennessee Legislature for a special ceremony held on March 8, 1961. Governor Buford Ellington extolled Elvis's accomplishments in the entertainment field, praised his sense of values, and conferred upon Elvis the title of honorary colonel.

- Gave a benefit concert for the USS *Arizona* Memorial Fund in March 1961? Elvis helped raise sixty-two thousand dollars for the memorial, which was dedicated on May 30, 1962. This concert was his last live performance for the next eight years.

- Met the Beatles? During their second U.S. tour, the Beatles visited Elvis in his Bel Air home on August 27, 1965. They spent four hours exchanging stories, telling jokes, listening to records, and jamming.

SOLDIER BOY

Monday, March 24, 1958, dawned cold and rainy in Memphis, and at 6:35 A.M. a sleepy-eyed Elvis reported to local Draft Board number eighty-six for the start of his military duty. "I'm kinda proud of it," he had told reporters. "It's a duty I've got to fill, and I'm gonna do it." He and twelve other recruits then boarded a bus that took them to Kennedy Veterans Hospital on Jefferson Avenue to undergo blood tests, mental examinations, and to take loyalty oaths. By 5:00 P.M. that day, Elvis had been sworn in as a recruit with the serial number US 53310761 and had hopped aboard a Greyhound bus bound for Fort Chaffee, Arkansas.

There Elvis was welcomed into the army with a haircut, inoculations, and the issuance of uniforms and gear. His stay at Fort Chaffee lasted until March 28 when he boarded yet another bus for Fort Hood, Texas, where he was to begin his eight weeks of basic training—just like any other GI

At Fort Hood, Elvis learned he had been assigned to A Company, Second Medium Tank Battalion, Second Armored Division. He also discovered the pay cut he would take working for his Uncle Sam. Instead of the four hundred thousand dollars a month he had earned as a civilian, soldier boy Elvis would now be making seventy-eight dollars a month.

When Elvis completed basic training, he was granted a fourteen-day leave, which he spent in Memphis with his parents and his girlfriend, Anita Wood. Elvis reported back to Fort Hood on June 14 for eight weeks of advanced individual training and six weeks of unit training. He learned that in September 1958 he would be shipped out to Bremerhaven, West Germany.

Five hundred screaming teenagers greeted the troop ship that brought Elvis and more than one thousand other soldiers to West Germany. An international press corps descended upon Elvis's new post near Frankfurt to learn that he had been assigned as a jeep driver, that he was living off post, and that mail call generally meant nearly ten thousand letters a week for Elvis.

For Elvis, army life settled into a routine of marching, worrying about inspections, and pulling various duties. The routine sometimes included taking Dexedrine, supplied by the sergeants, to stay awake during night guard duty. This was Elvis's first exposure to drug use. In November 1958, he joined the 32nd Tank Battalion for two weeks of maneuvers near the border separating West Germany from Czechoslovakia.

While serving in West Germany, Elvis made private first class in 1958, then specialist fourth class in 1959. By the time he was discharged on March 5, 1960, he held the rank of buck sergeant.

Army life may have been uneventful for Elvis, but his personal life was like a roller coaster because of two significant events: the death of his beloved mother and his meeting with the girl who would eventually become his wife.

ELVIS LOSES GLADYS

Elvis and his mother, Gladys, had a special bond. He was her only living child. His twin brother, Jesse, had been stillborn; Gladys had lost another child through miscarriage in 1942. Elvis was her "little darling"; Gladys was his "Sattnin." She encouraged and supported his dreams; he adored her.

When he became successful, Elvis bought her houses, cars, clothing, jewelry and lifted the shroud of poverty that had haunted the family for generations. But as Elvis's popularity increased, Gladys grew more and more unhappy. She missed her son when he was on the road touring. She feared the fans who stormed the stage wherever he appeared, screaming to touch him and tearing his clothes to shreds. She felt wounded by the letters from parents of fans who accused Elvis of being a moral menace or worse. To cope with the abandonment, the anxiety, and the hurt, Gladys began to drink.

By 1958, the effects of the alcohol—and the diet pills she had taken over the years to lose weight—had taken their toll. Gladys was in the grips of a liver disease, hepatitis. Her doctor urged her to enter the hospital for tests, but she refused. At Graceland, a depressed Gladys painfully shuffled through her day, wearing only the pink housecoat that had been a Christmas present from Elvis.

Gladys endured another separation from Elvis when he was inducted into the army in March. He was so alarmed by her deteriorating condition that when he completed his basic training, he arranged for Gladys and Vernon to settle into a comfortable three-bedroom house in Killeen, Texas, a town near his army post. If Elvis could keep her close, he thought, Gladys would be all right.

Adjusting to the new house, the strange surroundings, and the loss of her routine caused additional stress for forty-six-year-old Gladys. Her drinking increased. By the beginning of August 1958, her skin was jaundiced, but the local doctor could not pinpoint the cause of her illness. The family then decided that Gladys must return to Memphis immediately for treatment by her own doctor. On Friday, August 8, Elvis drove Gladys and Vernon to Fort Worth to board the train to Memphis. Her fear of flying had kept her from taking a plane.

On August 9, her doctor admitted Gladys to Methodist Hospital where tests were run and specialists consulted. The cause of her hepatitis was still a mystery. Sunday and Monday brought more serious reports of her condition, which prompted Elvis to apply for emergency leave. The leave wasn't granted until Tuesday, August 12, and only because strings were pulled when Elvis threatened to go AWOL.

When Elvis arrived that evening, he was told by doctors that Gladys was in critical condition with acute hepatitis and severe liver damage. He visited her and had tears in his eyes when he left her room to talk to the waiting reporters. "Mama's not doing well right now," he told them. "Not well at all."

Elvis kept a vigil at his mother's bedside until the next evening, Wednesday, August 13, when she convinced him to go to Graceland for some rest. He was asleep at home when a phone call broke the stillness of August 14 and shattered his heart. Vernon called to report that Gladys had died at 3:15 A.M.

The cause of death was listed as a heart attack, but that was not confirmed, since Vernon and Elvis refused to permit an autopsy. On the afternoon of August 14, distraught father and son waited at Graceland for the arrival of the hearse bearing Gladys's body. Reporters with questions intruded. "She's all we lived for," Elvis sobbed. "She was always my best girl."

Gladys's silver casket was placed in the living room of Graceland and remained there until the August 16 funeral service, which was held at the National Funeral Home. Gladys's favorite gospel group, the Blackwood Brothers, sang her favorite hymn, "Precious Memories," while outside nearly three thousand fans stood in respectful silence. Following the services, Gladys Presley was laid to rest in Forest Hill Cemetery as the crush of fans, reporters, and photographers bore down on Elvis.

His grief was palpable. "Oh, God! Everything I have is gone," he cried out. And the Elvis Presley that emerged from that cemetery on that day was forevermore a changed man.

ELVIS FINDS PRISCILLA

In 1959, while he was stationed in Germany, Elvis met a pretty fourteen-year-old girl at a party at his home. As he talked to Priscilla Beaulieu, he probably thought that her navy-and-white sailor dress and white socks were sweet. He tried to impress her by playing the piano and singing "Rags to Riches" and "Are You Lonesome Tonight?" Later, in the kitchen, Elvis and Priscilla talked about music, what singers were popular with the kids, and his concern about his fans accepting him when he returned to the United States. Elvis was lonely, vulnerable, still grieving for his mother, and he felt a special closeness to the brown-haired, blue-eyed ninth grader who had come to visit. Elvis dated Priscilla for the remainder of his tour of duty in West Germany.

Phone calls spanned the geographic distance between them. Elvis's relationship with Anita Wood had ended, and Elvis invited Priscilla to visit him in Los Angeles for two weeks in the summer of 1962. Her parents, Ann and Joseph Paul Beaulieu, (a United States Air Force captain stationed in West Germany) reluctantly agreed. Priscilla also visited Graceland for Christmas in 1962, then Elvis convinced her parents to let her come to live at Graceland.

Elvis enrolled her in the all-girl Catholic school in Memphis, Immaculate Conception Cathedral High School. He encouraged Priscilla to dye her hair black and to wear heavy makeup. After she graduated in June 1963, Priscilla attended

Patricia Stevens Finishing School and waited for Elvis's next move in their life together.

The next move came before Christmas 1966, when Elvis popped the question to Priscilla. They were married on May 1, 1967, and their daughter, Lisa Marie, followed on February 1, 1968.

But as the years went by, telltale cracks in the marriage became wide fissures. Elvis was on the road more and more; when he was home, his dependence on drugs made him virtually unreachable. Priscilla found she wanted a life of her own. Soon the emotional distance between them was greater than the geographic miles that separated them.

1968–1977
DID YOU KNOW THAT ELVIS...

- Became disenchanted with making movies? He returned to performing music with the NBC television special, "Elvis" on December 3, 1968. This was the highest-rated program for the week and among women ages eighteen to forty-nine was the most watched television special of the year. Elvis was not only back, but he was raw, powerful, and better than ever.

- Set a Las Vegas record during his first four-week engagement at the International Hotel? During Elvis's engagement from July 31 to August 28, 1969, 101,509 customers paid to see him in his first live concert performances in eight years. The gross take amounted to $1.5 million.

- Scored his last number one record with "Suspicious Minds"? In October 1969, the song spent one week at the top spot on *Billboard*'s Hot 100 chart. Total time on the chart was fifteen weeks. On May 21, 1971, "Suspicious Minds" was honored with the designation of Outstanding Single Recorded in Memphis.

- Received an award from the U.S. Jaycees? Because of his philanthropic service to the community, Elvis was named one of Ten Outstanding Young Men of America by the U.S. Jaycees. He accepted the award in person on January 16, 1971.

- Was honored by the renaming of the stretch of highway that runs past Graceland? Vernon Presley, Mayor Wyeth Chandler, and Sheriff Roy Nixon dedicated a ten-mile section of U.S. Highway 51 South in Memphis to be renamed Elvis Presley Boulevard on January 19, 1972.

- Scored his last top twenty hit with "Burning Love"? In October 1972, the song reached number two on *Billboard*'s Hot 100 chart. Total time on the chart was fifteen weeks. On October 27, 1972, "Burning Love" was certified as a million seller.

- Was seen by more than one billion people during the telecast of "Elvis: Aloha from Hawaii"? The January 14, 1973, television special that was broadcast via satellite to more than forty countries was seen by more people than had witnessed the first moon landing by Apollo 11. Elvis performed at the Honolulu International Center Arena in a benefit concert for the Kuiokalani Lee Cancer Fund and helped raise seventy-five thousand dollars.

- Was divorced from Priscilla in October 1973? In February 1972, Priscilla had left Elvis for her karate instructor, Mike Stone. Elvis filed for divorce on August 18, 1972, and the divorce was granted on October 9, 1973.

- Received his third Grammy award in 1974? Elvis received a Grammy for Best Inspirational Performance for the track "How Great Thou Art" from the album *Elvis Recorded Live On Stage in Memphis.* His two previous Grammy awards were for Best Inspirational Performance of 1972 for the album *He Touched Me* and for Best Sacred Performance of 1967 for the album *How Great Thou Art.*

- Died on August 16, 1977? Elvis was preparing to go on tour and was spending time at Graceland, relaxing and visiting with his daughter, Lisa Marie. After a game of racquetball that ended at 4:00 A.M., Elvis and his girlfriend, Ginger Alden went to bed. Elvis awoke late in the morning to go to the bathroom to read. "Don't fall asleep," Ginger cautioned. "Okay, I won't," Elvis said.

Ginger woke up around 2:00 P.M. and noticed that Elvis had not returned to bed. She entered the bathroom and discovered his body slumped on the floor. He was rushed to Baptist Memorial Hospital, but resuscitation efforts were in vain. Doctors pronounced him dead at 3:30 P.M. Although the official cause of death was listed as cardiac arrhythmia (irregular heartbeat), many believed that Elvis's numerous health problems and his overreliance on prescription drugs may have contributed to his death. No matter—the world had lost the King of Rock and Roll.

On August 18, private funeral services were held at Graceland, and Elvis was buried next to his mother at Forest Hill Cemetery. On October 2, the bodies of Elvis and Gladys were moved to the Meditation Gardens at Graceland.

Long live the King!

LOVE ME TENDER

(TWENTIETH CENTURY-FOX, 1956)

PLOT

*A*fter stealing a Union payroll at the end of the Civil War, three Confederate brothers, thought dead, return home to face the results of their absence and their actions. Their youngest brother (Elvis), who remained at home, has married the eldest brother's girl, and the paymaster can identify the thieves.

CAST

Richard Egan	Vance Reno
Debra Paget	Cathy Reno
Elvis Presley	Clint Reno
Robert Middleton	Mr. Siringo
William Campbell	Brett Reno
Neville Brand	Mike Gavin
Mildred Dunnock	Martha Reno
Bruce Bennett	Major Kincaid
James Drury	Ray Reno

CREW

David Weisbart	Producer
Robert D. Webb	Director
Robert Buckner	Screenplay
Lyle R. Wheeler and	
Maurice Ransford	Art Directors
Lionel Newman	Music
Ken Darby	Vocal Supervision
Edward B. Powell	Orchestration
Col. Tom Parker	Technical Advisor

SONGS
"We're Gonna Move" • "Love Me Tender" • "Let Me" • "Poor Boy"

THE FANS LOVE "LOVE ME TENDER"

Singer and composer Ken Darby wrote the four songs that Elvis sang in his first film. However, ɔecause of copyright difficulties, Elvis and Darby's wife, Vera Matson, were credited with the tunes.

The title song, "Love Me Tender," was based on "Aura Lee," a ballad written in 1861 by W. W. Fosdick and George R. Poulton. Popular with the Union Army during the Civil War, "Aura Lee" was later given new lyrics, retitled "Army Blue," and used by the 1865 graduates of West Point as their class song.

Elvis crooned "Love Me Tender" on his three appearances on "The Ed Sullivan Show." During the first appearance, Elvis announced that he was about to sing the title song from his first film, and he hoped fans would like the tune.

Fans loved the tune and afterwards clamored to buy the record, so much so that RCA reported that advance sales of the single had exceeded one million copies—a history-making milestone in the recording industry.

"Love Me Tender" debuted on *Billboard*'s Top 100 chart at the number twelve position. The song shot to number one where it remained for four weeks. On the Country Best-Seller chart, "Love Me Tender" was a number three hit, and on the Rhythm & Blues chart, the song was a number four hit.

ELVIS'S "BIG BROTHER"

Known in Hollywood for his leading-man roles in action films and westerns, Richard Egan was cast in *Love Me Tender* as Vance Reno, Elvis's older brother. His previous screen credits included *The Damned Don't Cry* (1950), *Demetrius and the Gladiators* (1954), *The Untamed* (1955), *Violent Saturday* (1955), and *The View from Pompey's Head* (1955).

Following *Love Me Tender*, Egan had parts in the films *Slaughter on 10th Avenue* (1957), *A Summer Place* (1959), and *Pollyanna* (1960). He also took his talents to television and starred as a rancher in the series, "Empire" (1962–1963) and its spinoff, "Redigo" (1963).

Memories of working with Elvis in *Love Me Tender* probably flashed through Egan's mind as he sat in the audience at the Las Vegas Hilton on February 23, 1972 listening to the King close his concert. While Elvis sang "Can't Help Falling in Love," Egan stood and started an ovation that spread throughout the entire room. Just what a "big brother" ought to do.

LOVE ME TENDER PREMIERES

The date circled on the 1956 calendar of practically every teenage girl in the New York City area was November 15. At 8:00 that morning, three thousand fans converged on the Paramount Theater on Broadway not only to purchase tickets for the premiere of *Love Me Tender* but to be among the first two thousand to receive their choice of an Elvis scarf, hat, lapel button, or charm bracelet.

As a gigantic cutout of Elvis above the marquee of the Paramount observed the noisy, jostling crowd, the theater manager called out for reinforcements. Thirty-five police officers and twenty extra ushers were needed to maintain order.

That scene was no doubt repeated in other cities when *Love Me Tender* opened nationally on November 21. Twentieth Century–Fox had made certain that the film would be shown in as many cities as possible by upping the normal print order of 200 or 300 copies to a staggering 550 copies.

Critics who reviewed *Love Me Tender* were not kind to Elvis and his performance in the western drama. *The New York Times* noted that Elvis's "dramatic contribution is not a great deal more impressive than that of one of the slavering nags." *The Los Angeles Times* stated that Elvis "pales in comparison when pitted against the resonant inflections of Egan, of course, but who came to watch Elvis act?"

Thousands upon thousands of fans came to watch Elvis act, and they were perhaps more forgiving of the fledgling actor's debut than the critics. The support of Elvis's fans at the box office was staggering, enabling Twentieth Century–Fox to recoup its nearly one-million-dollar investment in the film within the first three days.

DID YOU KNOW THAT...

- *Love Me Tender* was originally titled *The Reno Brothers*? The film was renamed because of the popularity of Elvis's song, "Love Me Tender."

- Elvis's leading lady, Debra Paget, had appeared with him on the June 5, 1956, broadcast of "The Milton Berle Show"? On the show, Paget participated in a gag in which she screamed and threw herself at Elvis upon meeting him on stage. Besides *Love Me Tender*, Paget had roles in *Cry of the City* (1948), *Broken Arrow* (1950), *Les Miserables* (1952), *Prince Valiant* (1954), *Seven Angry Men* (1955), *The Ten Commandments* (1956), *The River's Edge* (1957), *From the Earth to the Moon* (1958), and *Haunted Palace* (1963).

- Elvis received $100,000 for his work in *Love Me Tender*? Colonel Parker had negotiated the flat fee for Elvis's first movie role. For later films, Elvis would not only receive a hefty salary but a percentage of the profits as well.

- Producer David Weisbart produced three other Elvis films? The films are *Flaming Star*, *Follow That Dream*, and *Kid Galahad*. He is best remembered for his work on the James Dean film *Rebel Without a Cause* (1955).

- Two *Love Me Tender* crew members had connections to classic films from 1939? Art director Lyle Wheeler was the art director for *Gone With the Wind*. Vocal supervisor Ken Darby created the voices of the Munchkins in *The Wizard of Oz*.

- The real name of actor Bruce Bennett, who played Major Kincaid, was Herman Brix? Brix won the silver medal in the shot put in the 1928 Olympics. He became Hollywood's seventh Tarzan when he appeared in *The New Adventures of Tarzan* (1935) and *Tarzan and the Green Goddess* (1938). As Bruce Bennett,

he appeared in *Mildred Pierce* (1945) and *The Treasure of the Sierra Madre* (1948).

• Actor Neville Brand received his share of hisses and boos when he "killed" Elvis in *Love Me Tender*? Brand was the fourth-most-decorated American soldier in World War II. He made his film debut in *DOA* (1950), and his other movie credits include *Riot in Cell Block 11* (1954), *The George Raft Story* (1961), and *The Scarface Mob* (1962). He played Texas Ranger Reese Bennett in the television series "Laredo" (1965–1967).

• After filming ended, word leaked out that Elvis dies at the end of the picture? The protest of the fans was so vigorous that the studio called Elvis back to film a new ending in which he lives, but the revised version was not used.

• Elvis received a "Worst Supporting Actor Award" for his performance in *Love Me Tender*? The *Harvard Lampoon* bestowed the dubious distinction.

• *Variety* listed *Love Me Tender* as the number two top-grossing film on its weekly list? For the year, *Love Me Tender* ranked number twenty-three.

• *Love Me Tender* was the first Elvis film to be broadcast on television? The film premiered on the home screen on December 11, 1963.

LOVE ME TENDER TRIVIA QUIZ

1. What was Vance Reno's rank in the Confederate Army?

2. Who was the general under which the Reno brothers served?

3. Where were the Reno brothers from?

4. From what state did Mike Gavin hail?

5. What present did the Reno brothers buy for their mother?

6. How much did the Reno brothers spend at the store?

7. How long had Clint and Cathy been married when the Reno brothers returned?

8. Where did the Reno brothers bury the robbery money?

9. Who said: "I waited for you just like I promised."

10. How much money did Vance plan to take on his trip to California?

11. Who said: "Clint thinks the sun rises and sets in you."?

12. According to Mr. Siringo, what was the length of the jail sentence facing the Reno brothers?

13. What was the name of the Renos' neighbor?

14. After Vance retrieved the money, where was he to meet his brothers and his friends?

15. In what year was Clint Reno born?

3.

LOVING YOU

(Paramount, 1957)

PLOT

Singing truck driver Elvis is discovered by a publicist and her partner, a country-western musician, who promote him to stardom.

CAST

Elvis Presley	Deke Rivers
Lizabeth Scott	Glenda Markle
Wendell Corey	Walter "Tex" Warner
Dolores Hart	Susan Jessup
James Gleason	Carl Meade
Ralph Dumke.	Jim Tallman
Paul Smith.	Skeeter
Ken Becker	Wayne
Jana Lund.	Daisy Bricker
Skip Young.	Teddy

CREW

Hal B. Wallis.	Producer
Hal Kanter..	Director
Herbert Baker and Hal Kanter.	Screenplay
Mary Agnes Thompson	Story
Edith Head	Costumes
Charles O'Curran	Staging of Musical Numbers
Walter Scharf	Conducting and Arranging of Music
The Jordanaires	Vocal Accompaniment
Col. Tom Parker	Technical Advisor

SONGS
"Got a Lot o' Livin' to Do" • "(Let's Have a) Party" •
"(Let Me Be Your) Teddy Bear" • "Hot Dog" • "Lonesome Cowboy" •
"Mean Woman Blues" • "Loving You"

PRODUCER EXTRAORDINARE: HAL B. WALLIS

"Star quality is almost impossible to define," wrote Hal B. Wallis in his 1980 autobiography, *Starmaker*. "But when you see brilliant talent, it registers immediately. It's magic."

Producer Hal B. Wallis first noticed the Presley magic in early 1956 during one of Elvis's appearances on the Tommy and Jimmy Dorsey CBS-TV variety series, "Stage Show." The next morning, Wallis called Colonel Tom Parker to offer Elvis a film contract.

On April 1, 1956, Elvis arrived on the Paramount lot to film a screen test for Wallis. While the camera rolled, Elvis displayed his acting ability by expressing a range of emotions then displayed his vocal ability by singing "Blue Suede Shoes." Last, he was paired with veteran actor Frank Faylen, and the two performed a scene from *The Rainmaker* which the studio was planning to film. Best remembered for his role as harried grocer and harassed father Herbert T. Gillis on the series "The Many Loves of Dobie Gillis" (1959–1963), Faylen let Elvis carry the scene.

Disappointed with his test performance as the character Jimmy Curry, Elvis requested another test, which was probably filmed the following day. Wallis viewed the test, confirmed his feelings about the Presley magic, and offered a seven-year, three-movie contract that guaranteed $100,000 for the first film, $150,000 for the second, and $200,000 for the third. On April 6, Elvis signed on the dotted line.

Hal B. Wallis built a half-century career by recognizing "star quality." He was credited with discovering many actors, including Burt Lancaster, Kirk Douglas, and transforming into stars Edward G. Robinson, Paul Muni, Humphrey Bogart, Bette Davis, Dean Martin, Montgomery Clift, and James Cagney.

Chicago-born Wallis had his first taste of the film industry in 1922 when he

moved to Los Angeles and took a job as the manager of the Garrick movie theater. The following year, twenty-five-year-old Wallis joined Warner Bros. as assistant to the head of publicity. Three months later he was head of the department. In 1928, he was promoted to executive producer and found success producing an eclectic array of films from gangster movies to Busby Berkeley musicals.

He struck out on his own in 1944, leaving Warner Bros. to form Hal Wallis Productions. His independently produced films were released through Paramount and later through Universal. Among the more than four hundred films he produced during his career are some of the most popular movies in film history: *Little Caesar* (1930), *Anthony Adverse* (1936), *Dark Victory* (1939), *The Maltese Falcon* (1941), *Casablanca* (1942), *Yankee Doodle Dandy* (1942), *Barefoot in the Park* (1967), *True Grit* (1969), and *Mary Queen of Scots* (1971).

LOVING YOU: PRODUCTION NOTES

In July 1956, Hal B. Wallis bought the rights to a story by Mary Agnes Thompson that had appeared in the June issue of *Good Housekeeping*. Wallis thought the tale would be a perfect rags-to-riches film vehicle for Elvis.

The working title of the film was *The Lonesome Cowboy*, which was changed to *Running Wild* in fall 1956. Director Hal Kanter yelled "Action!" on the Paramount studio set in January 1957 as production began, and the final "Cut!" was heard in March 1957. The only location filming involved moving the cameras to a rural setting to shoot the scenes at the Jessup farm. Elvis's second film—his first of nine for Wallis—was at last titled *Loving You*, and Elvis looked forward to the Memphis premiere in July 1957.

LOVING YOU PREMIERES

The Strand Theater in Memphis was the selected site for the July 9, 1957 premiere of *Loving You*. Elvis, his girlfriend, Anita Wood, and Vernon and Gladys Presley sat side by side in the theater for the midnight showing, watching Elvis in glorious Technicolor rise from delivery man to a man who could deliver electrifying music to an ecstatic audience. The Presley contingent also saw that he could deliver in the love-making department and watched as Elvis enjoyed his first on-screen kiss. As the song "Loving You" filled the film's Freegate Civic Auditorium, those in the auditorium of the Memphis Strand Theater knew that Elvis had a hit on his hands.

"LOVING YOU"

Jerry Leiber and Mike Stoller wrote the title tune for Elvis's 1957 movie. Elvis recorded "Loving You" in February 1957, and when the record was released in June, it began a twenty-two-week love affair with *Billboard*'s Top 100 chart, peaking at number twenty-eight. On the Country Disc Jockey chart, "Loving You" hit number fifteen. On the Rhythm & Blues chart, the song reached number one.

"(LET ME BE YOUR) TEDDY BEAR"

Recognizing Elvis's love for teddy bears, two songwriters from Philadelphia, Kal Mann and Bernie Lowe, wrote "(Let Me Be Your) Teddy Bear" for Elvis's second film. The song, known simply as "Teddy Bear," was backed with "Loving You."

"Teddy Bear" was a growling success for Elvis. The song hit number one in July 1957 on *Billboard*'s Top 100 chart, where it remained for seven weeks. "Teddy Bear" had a total chart run of twenty-four weeks. On both the Country Best-Seller chart and the Rhythm & Blues chart, "Teddy Bear" was number one for one week, making the song one of only three recorded by Elvis to reach the top of all three *Billboard* charts. ("Don't Be Cruel" and "Jailhouse Rock" were the other two.)

DID YOU KNOW THAT...

- Vernon and Gladys Presley made their film debuts in *Loving You*? The pair participated as audience extras in the Freegate television broadcast scene. They were seated in the fourth row, Gladys in the aisle seat and Vernon next to her.

- *Loving You* marked the screen debuts of Bill Black, Scotty Moore, D. J. Fontana, and the Jordanaires? The Jordanaires provided vocal accompaniment, as they would in other Elvis films. Scotty Moore played a guitar player, and D. J. Fontana played a drummer. Bill Black portrayed Eddie, the bass player, and even had two lines of dialogue: "Hey, Deke. See the picture in the paper of the gals fighting over you?" and "Yeah. From what it says in here, Deke's just about—."

- Actress Lizabeth Scott, who played press agent Glenda Markle, made one more film after *Loving You*? She had a part in the 1972 British film *Pulp*, which starred Michael Caine and Mickey Rooney. Scott's earlier films included *You Came Along* (1945), *Desert Fury* (1947), *Easy Living* (1949), and *Two of a Kind* (1951).

- *Loving You* reunited actor Wendell Corey, who played band leader Tex Warner, with actress Lizabeth Scott? The two had costarred in 1947's *Desert Fury*. Corey's other films include *Sorry, Wrong Number* (1948), *Any Number Can Play* (1949), *Rear Window* (1954), *The Rainmaker* (1956), and *Blood on the Arrow* (1964).

- Actress Dolores Hart, who played Deke's love interest, Susan Jessup, made her film debut in *Loving You*? Hart had a similar role in a later Elvis film. In *King Creole* (1958), she played Nellie, a five-and-dime-store clerk and girlfriend of Danny Fisher (Elvis). In *Loving You*, Hart's character was a singer, and the actress had the opportunity to sing "Dancing on a Dare" and "Detour." Hart's other films include *Wild Is the Wind* (1957), *Where the Boys Are* (1960), and *Sail a Crooked Ship* (1962). *Come Fly with Me* (1963) was her last film after which she left the movie industry to become a nun.

- Actress Jana Lund, who played Daisy Bricker, gave Elvis his first on-screen kiss in *Loving You*? Many think Debra Paget did the honors in *Love Me Tender* (1956), but Jana Lund takes the credit for her pucker power. Lund's other film credits include *Don't Knock the Rock* (1956), *Frankenstein 1970* (1958), *High School Hellcats* (1958), *Hot Car Girl* (1958), and *Married Too Young* (1962).

- Actor Skip Young, who played Teddy, Deke's delivery buddy, portrayed the friend of a rock-and-roll singer in a television series? Young had the role of Wally Dipple, friend of Ricky Nelson, on "The Adventures of Ozzie and Harriet" (1952–1966). Young's other film roles include *The Spider* (1958), *Cold Wind in August* (1961), *WUSA* (1970), and *Smokey and the Hotwire Gang* (1980).

- *Loving You* was Elvis's first color film? Poster art for the film proclaimed that the production was in Technicolor and VistaVision.

- *Loving You* performed well on *Variety*'s weekly list of top grossing films? On the list *Loving You* was ranked number seven.
- In July 1959 *Loving You* was re-released? The film was double billed with *King Creole* in selected theaters.

LOVING YOU TRIVIA QUIZ

1. For what company did Deke Rivers work as a delivery man?

2. How much did Deke earn a week?

3. What was the name of the politician for whom Glenda Markle worked?

4. What was the name of Tex Warner's band?

5. In what town did Deke Rivers first sing professionally?

6. What did Susan Jessup present to Deke as a gift from the band?

7. What was the name of Daisy Bricker's boyfriend?

8. At which theater in Amarillo was Deke scheduled to perform?

9. For which Texas newspaper did O'Shea and Grew work?

10. Who was Tex Warner's booking agent?

11. Under the terms of the contract signed by Deke, what percentage of earnings was Glenda entitled to?

12. Near what town was the farm owned by Susan's parents?

13. What was the name of the rooster on the Jessup farm?

14. What was Deke's real name?

15. What were the call letters of the television station from which Deke's live special was broadcast?

JAILHOUSE ROCK

(METRO-GOLDWYN-MAYER, 1957)

PLOT

*E*lvis kills a man in self-defense in a barroom brawl and is sent to prison where he realizes his talent as a singer. When released from jail, he teams up with a woman who not only helps him to break into the music business but also to find love.

CAST

Elvis Presley	Vince Everett
Judy Tyler	Peggy Van Alden
Mickey Shaughnessy	Hunk Houghton
Peter Adams	Jack Lease
Vaughn Taylor	Mr. Shores
Dean Jones	Teddy Talbot
Jennifer Holden	Sherry Wilson
Percy Helton	Sam Brewster
Anne Neyland	Laury Jackson

CREW

Pandro S. Berman	Producer
Richard Thorpe	Director
Guy Trosper	Screenplay
Col. Tom Parker	Technical Advisor

SONGS

"Young and Beautiful" • "I Want to Be Free" • "Don't Leave Me Now" •
"Treat Me Nice" • "Jailhouse Rock" • "(You're So Square) Baby, I Don't Care"

THE <u>JAILHOUSE ROCK</u> DYNAMIC DUO: LEIBER AND STOLLER

Leiber and Stoller have been a songwriting dynamic duo since meeting in Los Angeles in 1950.

At that time, seventeen-year-old Jerry Leiber was writing lyrics to blues melodies written by a drummer friend at Fairfax High School. For Leiber, though, something was missing from the partnership. When the drummer told Lieber about a seventeen-year-old composer named Mike Stoller, Lieber discovered the collaborator of his dreams.

Baltimore-born Leiber and Long Island native Stoller both shared an affinity for rhythm and blues music. Within a year of meeting, one of their songs, "That's What The Good Book Says," was recorded by the Robins. By February 1952, the Leiber and Stoller composition "Hard Times," recorded by Charles Brown, became their first national rhythm and blues hit.

Of the six tunes Elvis sings in *Jailhouse Rock*, Leiber and Stoller contributed four. In fact, they wrote "(You're So Square) Baby, I Don't Care," "I Want to Be Free," "Jailhouse Rock," and "Treat Me Nice" in a mere four hours one afternoon. Mike Stoller also contributed a cameo appearance to the film. He can be seen as the piano player during Vince Everett's recording session.

Leiber and Stoller wrote twenty other compositions for Elvis, as well as numerous songs for other artists, including "Kansas City," "Yakety Yak," "Poison Ivy," and "On Broadway." Clearly, when it comes to songwriting, Leiber and Stoller are truly a dynamic duo.

"JAILHOUSE ROCK" ROCKS THE CHARTS

"Jailhouse Rock" was written for the production number in Elvis's third movie. Backed with "Treat Me Nice," the song entered *Billboard*'s Top 100 chart in October 1957 at number fifteen and climbed to number one three weeks later. There it stayed for seven weeks until "You Send Me" by Sam Cooke sent "Jailhouse Rock" packing. The song served a twenty-seven week sentence on the American chart. "Jailhouse Rock" was number one on the Country Best-Seller chart for one week and number one on the Rhythm & Blues chart for five weeks.

In England, "Jailhouse Rock" became the first single in history to debut in the number one spot, proving that the song was "Most Wanted" among British rock and rollers.

THE KING TO THE RESCUE

In *Jailhouse Rock*, Vince Everett (Elvis) becomes an actor, signing a nonexclusive movie contract with a Hollywood studio. However, his leading lady, played by Jennifer Holden, is less than thrilled with her new leading man. When the director calls for rehearsal of the love scene, the starlet balks.

"Do we have to do the love scene the very first shot?" she complains. "I wanted to sort of work myself up to it. Making love to that rube won't be easy."

Despite the initial reluctance of Holden's character, the two kiss on the couch and sparks soon fly. "I'm coming all unglued," is the leading lady's breathless reaction to the passionate smooches.

This three-minute love scene between Elvis and Jennifer took about four hours to capture on film. The scene was certainly steamy, but in real life, things became even hotter for Holden on the last day of filming.

A small heater in her dressing room caught fire. In the ensuing pandemonium, the prop man rushed in to quench the flames, while Elvis carried the brown-eyed, blonde damsel-in-distress to safety.

THE WOMAN ELVIS COULDN'T SAVE

The career of Elvis's costar Judy Tyler was launched when she won the title of Miss Stardust in a 1949 nationwide beauty pageant. Two years later, at the age of seventeen, she captured the part of Princess Summerfall Winterspring on the television series "Howdy Doody" (1947–1960).

After being with the show for three seasons, she next went to Broadway. There she had the romantic lead in the Rodgers and Hammerstein musical comedy *Pipe Dream.*

In 1957, she made her film debut in *Bop Girl Goes Calypso.* Tragically, her role of Peggy Van Alden in *Jailhouse Rock* would be her last film appearance.

On July 3, 1957, Tyler and her young husband of less than four months, actor Gregory Lafayette, were driving east from Hollywood. Near Billy the Kid, Wyoming, a car with a trailer suddenly pulled out onto U.S. Highway 30 and into the path of the newlyweds' car.

To avoid hitting the trailer, Lafayette swung his vehicle into the lane of oncoming traffic where he collided with a car heading west. The twenty-three-year-old driver of the westbound car and Judy Tyler were killed. Nineteen-year-old Lafayette died in a Cheyenne hospital the next morning after he was told that Tyler was dead.

Elvis reacted strongly to the death of his twenty-four-year-old costar. "Nothing has hurt me so bad in my life. All of us really loved that girl. I don't believe I can stand to see the movie we made together, now."

THE MAN WHO MOCKED THE KING

At the end of *Jailhouse Rock,* Vince Everett's former cellmate Hunk Houghton takes a swing at the King. The punch hits Vince in the throat, landing him in the hospital with damage to his voice. Ironically, the actor who played Hunk took pot shots at Elvis in real life, too.

Pug-faced comedian Mickey Shaughnessy performed a nightclub act which was described by *Variety* as "forty-five minutes of taking Elvis over the hurdles." The comic's caustic remarks about the King's music, singing style, even his hair, kept audiences howling with laughter. Presley fans were not amused.

ELVIS IS RUSHED TO THE HOSPITAL

During the "Jailhouse Rock" dance sequence, Elvis accidentally loosened a porcelain cap from one of his front teeth, and the cap went down his throat. He thought he was fine, but the next day he experienced chest pain.

An emergency visit to Cedars of Lebanon Hospital revealed that he hadn't swallowed the cap at all; he had inhaled it! The cap was removed from his lung, and Elvis was able to return to filming.

THE CRITICS WERE NOT KIND

When *Jailhouse Rock* opened nationally in fall 1957, the critics acted as judge, jury, and executioner in assessing Elvis's third film.

- *The New York Times*: "Presley fans may not like the idea of his being the churlish egotistical wonderboy of TV and screen for a good half of the picture."

- *Memphis Press–Scimitar*: "The new MGM film is the first which has to be carried solely by Presley . . . and he carries it easily. Whether it was worth carrying at all is open to question, however. Elvis' advisers might have thought twice before allowing the idol of teenagers to be cast as one who frequents bars, beats a man to death, and remains a pretty unsavory character until a few minutes before the fade-out."

- *Time*: "For moviegoers who may not care for that personality, Presley himself offers in the film a word of consolation: 'Don't worry,' he says, 'I'll grow on you.' If he does, it will be quite a depressing job to scrape him off."

Despite the scathing attacks of the critics, Elvis fans flocked to theaters. By December, *Jailhouse Rock* had earned four million dollars and had ranked number fourteen on *Variety*'s list of top-grossing films for 1957.

DID YOU KNOW THAT...

- Elvis walked out on a May 1, 1957, recording session for *Jailhouse Rock*? Studio officials were annoyed that Elvis was spending valuable time singing spirituals rather than rehearsing songs for the film. Elvis wasn't wasting time; he was using the time to warm up, something the officials didn't understand. When he learned about the studio's annoyance, Elvis walked, but he returned the following day.

- A former welterweight boxer was the technical advisor for the fight scenes? John Indrisano contributed his pugilistic expertise to *Jailhouse Rock*. The fighter later had minor roles in other Elvis movies, including *King Creole* (1958), *It Happened at the World's Fair* (1963), and *Fun in Acapulco* (1963).

- Actress Anne Neyland, who played Laury Jackson, dated Elvis during the filming of *Jailhouse Rock*? Elvis was drawn to the pretty actress, and they dated for a short time. Neyland's other films include *Hidden Fear* (1957), *Motorcycle Gang* (1957), and *Ocean's Eleven* (1960).

- Actor Dean Jones had a special coach for his disc jockey role? His mentor was none other than Dewey Phillips of Memphis who in 1954 had been the first DJ to play an Elvis song.

- Dean Jones is best known for the films he made for Walt Disney? Jones had roles in *That Darn Cat* (1965), *The Ugly Dachshund* (1966), *The Love Bug* (1969), *The Shaggy D.A.* (1976), and *Herbie Goes to Monte Carlo* (1977). He also had the starring role in the television series "Ensign O'Toole" a 1962–1963 military comedy set aboard the destroyer USS *Appleby* in the Pacific.

- *Jailhouse Rock* premiered in Memphis? The film opened there on October 17, 1957. The only star from the film who attended the premiere was Anne Neyland.

<u>JAILHOUSE ROCK</u> TRIVIA QUIZ

1. What was the number of the cellblock in which Vince Everett and Hunk Houghton were guests of the state?

2. How much time did Vince serve in prison?

3. What was the name of the live television show broadcast from the prison on which Vince sang "I Want to Be Free"?

4. Who was the fifteen-year-old girl from Riverport who wrote Vince a fan letter?

5. What was the name of the nightclub owned by Sam Brewster?

6. How much did Peggy Van Alden think it would cost to cut a demo record?

7. What was the name of the record company owned by Jack Lease?

8. Who was the singer who used Vince's style and arrangement on "Don't Leave Me Now"?

9. What was the name of the record label founded by Vince and Peggy?

10. What partnership percentage did Vince and Peggy offer to their attorney, Mr. Shores?

11. Disc jockey Teddy Talbot played "Treat Me Nice" during a commercial for what business?

12. What kind of car did Vince buy from World Motors?

13. How old was the bourbon Vince served to Hunk?

14. What Hollywood studio offered Vince a movie contract?

15. What number appeared on all the cell doors in the "Jailhouse Rock" dance number?

5.
KING CREOLE

(PARAMOUNT, 1958)

PLOT

*A*gainst his father's wishes, Elvis drops out of high school to pursue a career as a nightclub singer. He becomes involved with a mobster's girlfriend and a five-and-dime store clerk with tragic results.

CAST

Elvis Presley	Danny Fisher
Carolyn Jones	Ronnie
Walter Matthau	Maxie Fields
Dolores Hart	Nellie
Dean Jagger	Mr. Fisher
Vic Morrow	Shark
Brian Hutton	Sal
Jack Grinnage	Dummy
Paul Stewart	Charlie LeGrand
Jan Shepard.	Mimi Fisher
Liliane Montevecchi	Forty Nina

CREW

Hal B. Wallis	Producer
Michael Curtiz	Director
Herbert Baker and Michael Vincente Gazzo	Screenplay
Harold Robbins	Novel
Edith Head	Costumes
Charles O'Curran	Staging of Musical Numbers
Walter Scharf	Adapting and Scoring of Music

28

The Jordanaires .... Vocal Accompaniment
Norman Stuart .... Dialogue Coach
Col. Tom Parker .... Technical Advisor

SONGS
"Crawfish" • "Steadfast, Loyal and True" • "Lover Doll" • "Trouble" •
"Dixieland Rock" • "Young Dreams" • "New Orleans" • "Hard Headed Woman"
• "King Creole" • "Don't Ask Me Why" • "As Long as I Have You"

"HARD HEADED WOMAN" THWARTED BY COLORFUL SPACE ALIEN

"Hard Headed Woman," which was written by Claude DeMetrius, debuted at number fifteen on *Billboard's* Top 100 chart in June 1958. By the second week, the tenacious tune had leapt straight to number three. It hovered near the top spot but reached only number two because of Sheb Wooley's "The Purple People Eater," which held the number one position. "Hard Headed Woman" also claimed the number two spots on the Country Best-Seller and the Rhythm & Blues charts. The determined damsel was the first of Elvis's songs to receive the Gold Disc Award from the Recording Industry Association of America.

BE TRUE TO YOUR SCHOOL, DANNY FISHER

As Danny Fisher (Elvis) sweeps up at the Gilded Cage, he is pressed into singing by drunken friends of Maxie Fields.

"Sing your school song," Ronnie (Carolyn Jones) urges him. "You gotta have a school song . . . an alma mater. You know, the one with the words about 'loyal' and 'true'."

The song that Danny sings, "Steadfast, Loyal, and True," was composed by Jerry Leiber and Mike Stoller. The song was adopted as the official song of the International Elvis Presley Appreciation Society.

YOU'RE IN THE ARMY NOW BUT LATER WOULD BE OKAY, TOO

On January 4, 1957, Elvis had reported to the Kennedy Veterans Hospital in Memphis for his military preinduction physical. Not to worry, he was told. He probably wouldn't be called up for at least six months.

By October, the Memphis draft board chairman, Milton Bowers, indicated that the call from Uncle Sam would probably not be heard for at least a year. Yet on December 20, Bowers appeared in person at Graceland to deliver the order for Elvis to report for induction on January 20, 1958. Elvis felt it was his duty to serve and was willing to do so.

Elvis may have been willing to go, but Paramount Pictures was not willing to let him go. Elvis was scheduled to begin work on *King Creole* on January 20, and the studio would lose nearly $350,000 were Elvis to enter the army before March.

Studio production chief Frank Freeman immediately sent a letter to the Memphis draft board requesting an eight-week extension of Elvis's report date. The draft board insisted that Elvis make the deferment request, and Elvis wrote his letter on December 24.

The three-member board met in special session on December 27 to consider Elvis's request. They voted unanimously to grant a delay. The filming of *King Creole* could go on as planned because Elvis would not be inducted into the army until March 24.

A NOVEL APPROACH TO <u>KING CREOLE</u>

King Creole was based on the Harold Robbins novel *A Stone for Danny Fisher*. The book told the story of a boxer in New York City.

Producer Hal B. Wallis purchased the film rights to the novel in February 1955 for twenty-five thousand dollars. In writing the screenplay, Herbert Baker and Michael V. Gazzo transformed the hero, Danny Fisher, into a singer and transplanted the action to New Orleans. Two titles that were considered for the film were *Danny* and *Sing, You Sinners*.

THE UPS AND DOWNS OF STARDOM

While on location in New Orleans, Elvis enjoyed the hospitality of the Roosevelt Hotel near the French Quarter. The tenth floor was reserved exclusively for Elvis, and management gave strict orders that elevators were not to stop at that floor. But one elevator operator was a bit overzealous in carrying out the command.

Elvis and his entourage entered the elevator after a long day of filming and requested the tenth floor. The operator politely explained that he was unable to stop the car at that level because Elvis Presley was in residence there. Elvis identified himself, but the operator was not about to be dissuaded from duty. He let the King and his court off on the eleventh floor, and they walked down the stairs to the tenth.

THE WOMAN HAS "A PEEL"

Forty Nina, the stripper at the King Creole, had no idea just how Danny Fisher would impact on her act when he joined the Bourbon Street nightclub as a singer. Nina entertained male audiences with songs such as the expressive "Banana."

Then Danny debuted with the rollicking "Dixieland Rock" and was a smash. Nina soon discovered that she had lost her audience, all because of Danny. This gave actress Liliane Montevecchi the opportunity to infuse the foreboding *King Creole* with a light, humorous moment.

"He's ruining my performance. Ever since he started, there's nothing but women out there," she complained. "They don't want to see me. And tonight I heard one of them yell 'Leave it on.'"

DID YOU KNOW THAT...

- *King Creole* was Elvis's first on-location film? Spots in New Orleans where cameras rolled included the French Quarter, the Vieux Carré Saloon, Lake Pontchartrain, and a local high school.

- Michael Curtiz directed more than one hundred films during his career? He was nominated for Academy Awards for Best Director for *Angels with Dirty Faces* (1938), *Four Daughters* (1938), *Yankee Doodle Dandy* (1942), and *Casablanca* (1942). He took home an Oscar for the Humphrey Bogart–Ingrid Bergman classic, *Casablanca*.

- Actress Carolyn Jones, who played Ronnie, was best known for her role as the ghoulish yet glamorous Morticia in the television series "The Addams Family" (1964–1965)? Jones appeared in other television programs, including episodes of "Dragnet," "Playhouse 90," "Zane Grey Theater," and "The Dick Powell Show." Her film work included roles in *The Tender Trap* (1955), *The Seven Year Itch* (1955), *Marjorie Morningstar* (1958) and *A Hole in the Head* (1959). She received an Academy Award nomination as Best Supporting Actress for a six-minute appearance in *Bachelor Party* (1957) in which she played a Greenwich Village bohemian desperate to be loved. *Variety* called her performance in *King Creole* "a strong and bitter portrait of a good girl gone wrong, moving and pathetic."

- The real name of stage, screen, and television actor Walter Matthau, who played Maxie Fields, is Walter Matuschanskayasky? Matthau honed his acting skills on Broadway and is probably best known for his role as Oscar Madison in Neil Simon's acclaimed comedy *The Odd Couple*. Matthau reprised the Oscar Madison role for the 1968 film. His other film credits include *Slaughter on Tenth Avenue* (1957), *Ride a Crooked Trail* (1958), *Island of Love* (1961), *Charade* (1964), *Ensign Pulver* (1964), *Cactus Flower* (1969), *Plaza Suite* (1971), *The Front Page* (1974), *The Sunshine Boys* (1975), *The Bad News Bears* (1976), *House Calls* (1978), *Buddy Buddy* (1981), *Dennis the Menace* (1993), *Grumpy Old Men* (1993). Matthau won an Academy Award for Best Supporting Actor in 1966 for *The Fortune Cookie*.

- Actor Vic Morrow, who played Shark, made his film debut in 1955 in *The Blackboard Jungle*? He had roles in other films such as *Tribute to a Bad Man* (1956), *Men in War* (1957), *Portrait of a Mobster* (1961), and *The Bad News Bears* (1976) in which he was teamed up again with Walter Matthau. On the small screen, Morrow created the role of Sgt. Chip Saunders in the television series "Combat" (1962–1966). Ironically, Morrow was killed in a helicopter crash in 1982 during the filming of a Vietnam war scene for *The Twilight Zone—The Movie* (1983).

- Actor Dean Jagger, who played Mr. Fisher, began his career in vaudeville? Jagger has acted in Broadway productions, Hollywood films, and on television series. His films include *Brigham Young* (1940), *The Omaha Trail* (1942), *The Robe* (1953), and *White Christmas* (1954). He received an Academy Award for Best Supporting Actor for his performance as Major Stovall in *Twelve O'Clock High* in 1949. On television, he is best remembered for his role of Albert Vane, principal at Jefferson High School on "Mr. Novak" (1963–1965).

- The doorman in *King Creole*, Candy Candido, was well known for his voice? Candido lent his voice to the cartoon character Popeye in the 1930s.

- Filming of *King Creole* ended on March 10? That gave Elvis a bit of time to spend before his induction into the army on March 24.

KING CREOLE TRIVIA QUIZ

1. What was the name of Danny Fisher's high school?

2. What did Mr. Fisher bring home for Danny's graduation party?

3. Where did Mr. Fisher work as a pharmacist?

4. What was the address of the Fisher apartment?

5. Where was the five-and-dime located at which Nellie worked?

6. Who shoplifted while Danny sang at the five-and-dime?

7. At the hotel, what phony name did Danny give to Nellie?

8. How much did Charlie LeGrand pay Danny to sing at the King Creole?

9. How many shows a night did Danny perform?

10. What was the age difference between Charlie LeGrand and Mimi Fisher?

11. What contest had Ronnie won?

12. Who said "When you work for Maxie Fields, it's better than Blue Cross."?

13. Who did Nellie consult about her relationship with Danny?

14. What was the weapon of choice for Shark?

15. What is the significance of the song "As Long As I Have You" that Danny sings at the end of *King Creole*?

6.

GI BLUES

(PARAMOUNT, 1960)

PLOT

Elvis and three musician buddies have dreams of opening a nightclub after their discharge from the army, but they're short on cash. They see a way to make easy money by betting that Elvis can spend the night in the apartment of a beautiful nightclub dancer in Frankfurt, West Germany.

CAST

Elvis Presley	Tulsa McLean
Juliet Prowse	Lili
Robert Ivers	Cookey
Leticia Roman	Tina
James Douglas	Rick
Sigrid Maier	Marla
Arch Johnson	Sergeant McGraw
Jeremy Slate	Turk
Ken Becker	Mac
Ronald Starr	Harvey
Fred Essler	Papa Mueller
Edward Stroll	Sergeant "Dynamite" Bixby

CREW

Hal B. Wallis	Producer
Norman Taurog	Director
Edmund Beloin and Henry Garson	Screenplay
Edith Head	Costumes
Charles O'Curran	Staging and Choreographing of Musical Numbers

Joseph J. Lilley .... Scoring and Conducting of Music
The Jordanaires .... Vocal Accompaniment
Col. Tom Parker .... Technical Advisor
Capt. David S. Parkhurst .... Military Technical Advisor

SONGS
"What's She Really Like" • "GI Blues" • "Doin' the Best I Can" •
"Blue Suede Shoes" • "Frankfurt Special" • "Shoppin' Around" •
"Tonight Is So Right for Love" • "Wooden Heart" • "Pocketful of Rainbows"
"Big Boots" • "Didja Ever"

"BLUE SUEDE SHOES"–THE RIGHT-FOOT VERSION"

In *GI Blues*, a Rathskeller Club patron, annoyed by Tulsa McLean (Elvis) singing the ballad "Doin' the Best I Can," plunks coins into the jukebox and plays "Blue Suede Shoes." This interruption is like a kick in the teeth to Tulsa and his combo. A fight starts, and Tulsa and his buddies hot foot it out the back door.

The song that causes the commotion, "Blue Suede Shoes," was written by Carl Perkins in 1955. And just as any pair of footwear has a right foot and a left foot, so too does the story behind "Blue Suede Shoes" have two versions of how the song came to be written.

According to Perkins, he was playing at a high school dance in Jackson, Tennessee, in December 1955 when he caught sight of a beautiful girl dancing with a boy wearing blue suede shoes. Perkins heard the boy caution the girl "Uh-uh! Don't step on my blue suedes!" The incident stuck in Perkins's mind, and at three o'clock the next morning, he awoke inspired and wrote the lyrics to "Blue Suede Shoes" on a brown paper sack.

"BLUE SUEDE SHOES"– THE LEFT-FOOT VERSION

Johnny Cash remembers a different version of the inspiration for "Blue Suede Shoes." Cash, Perkins, and Elvis were performing in Amory, Mississippi, in 1955. One night, Cash shared with Perkins a story about his days in the Air Force. Then, Cash had had a black sergeant who frequently came into Cash's room, asked Cash how he looked, and then added, "Just don't step on my blue suede shoes!" Perkins liked the story, thought it might make a good song, and wrote "Blue Suede Shoes" while Elvis was singing on stage.

THE BEAT OF "WOODEN HEART"

At the German puppet show, Tulsa sings "Wooden Heart," a song adapted by Bert Kaempfert, Kay Twomey, Fred Wise, and Ben Weisman from the German folk song, "Muss I Denn Zum Stadtele Hinaus." "Wooden Heart" was released as a single in the United Kingdom and beat its way to the top of the foreign chart where it remained for one week.

Singer Joe Dowell recorded "Wooden Heart" in the summer of 1961 for Smash Records and had a similar experience in the United States. His version throbbed its way to the number one spot on *Billboard's* Hot 100 chart for one week.

RCA twice released Elvis's "Wooden Heart" as a single in the United States. Both in 1964 and in 1965, the record landed with a thud on the Bubbling Under

34

list but failed to chart. However, the song was far from a dud. Worldwide, the record was a million seller, and especially in West Germany.

THE KING HOSTS MEMBERS OF ROYALTY

While Elvis filmed *GI Blues* on the Paramount lot, a number of special visitors to the studio were given the royal treatment. The king and queen of Nepal, the king and queen of Thailand as well as princesses from Sweden, Norway, and Denmark received specially guided tours, plus they met and spoke with the King of Rock and Roll.

GI "BRUISE"

Patrons at the Americas Theatre in Mexico City were enjoying a screening of *GI Blues*. Spirits were high, and an electric feeling crackled through the audience. Suddenly the exuberance of having a good time turned into a riot. Fists flew, seats were destroyed, and windows broken. Did the larger-than-life, on-screen Elvis provoke rage in an jealous boyfriend? Was an overreacting mother unsuccessful in dragging her young daughter away from the Presley presence? Did an Elvis hater shout out an caustic comment? No one really knows, but when dust finally settled, and the damage to the theater was assessed, the Mexican government placed a ban on all Elvis films.

DID YOU KNOW THAT...

- Three sets of twin boys played Rick and Marla's baby in the film? California law prevented a child from working more than four hours per day or more than two hours in front of the camera. Paramount held a talent search that recruited the three sets of twins: Kerry Charles Ray and Terry Earl Ray, David Paul Rankin and Donald James Rankin, and Donald Clark Wise and David Clark Wise. Each day of work earned each child the grand sum of $22.05.

- All of Elvis's scenes were shot in Hollywood? In August 1959, when Paramount announced that Elvis's next film would be *GI Blues*, a camera crew was dispatched to West Germany to shoot location footage in and around Frankfurt. At this time, Elvis was in Germany serving in the army, but producer Hal Wallis fearful of criticism and misunderstanding, balked at using Elvis for the location footage. However, the army provided tanks and tank crews from the Third Armored Division—character Tulsa McLean's outfit—for the location shooting. Following Elvis's discharge, he went into production for *GI Blues* and completed his work on the Paramount lot.

- Edith Head was the chief costume designer at Paramount for nearly thirty years? She worked on one thousand films, was nominated for thirty-five Academy Awards and received a record eight Oscars. Some of the films to which she contributed her talents include: *The Heiress* (1949), *Samson and Delilah* (1949), *All About Eve* (1950), *A Place in the Sun* (1951), *The Greatest Show on Earth* (1952), *Roman Holiday* (1953), *Sabrina* (1954), *Rear Window* (1954), *High Society* (1956), *Butch Cassidy and the Sundance Kid* (1969), and *The Sting* (1973).

- *GI Blues* was the first Elvis movie directed by Norman Taurog? He directed eight other Elvis films: *Blue Hawaii* (1961), *Girls! Girls! Girls!* (1962), *It Happened at the World's Fair* (1963), *Tickle Me* (1965), *Spinout* (1966), *Double Trouble* (1967), *Speedway* (1968) and *Live a Little, Love a Little* (1968).

- *GI Blues* was Elvis's costar Juliet Prowse's third film? Born in Bombay, India, and raised in South Africa, the dancer-actress made her film debut in *Gentlemen Marry Brunettes* (1955) then was featured in *Can-Can* (1960). She starred in the series "Mona McCluskey" (1965–1966).

- A special showing of *GI Blues* was held at the Fox Wilshire Theatre in Los Angeles on November 15, 1960? The screening was a benefit for the Hemophilia Foundation. Among the stars in attendance were Ronald Reagan, Cesar Romero, and Juliet Prowse.

- *GI Blues* opened nationally on November 23, 1960? By the end of the year, the film had earned $4.3 million and ranked number fourteen on *Variety*'s list of top-grossing films.

GI BLUES TRIVIA QUIZ

1. What was the name of Tulsa McLean's trio?

2. How much money did Tulsa, Rick, and Cookey owe to Sergeant McGraw?

3. What was the former name of the business that Tulsa, Rick, and Cookey wanted to turn into a nightclub?

4. Who was the proprietor of the Rathskeller?

5. Where did Tulsa work before he joined the Army?

6. Whom did Turk describe as "steam heat outside, iceberg inside"?

7. To what remote location was Sergeant "Dynamite" Bixby sent?

8. Where was Lili employed?

9. According to Tulsa, who taught him to play the guitar?

10. Where was Tina from?

11. What was the number of the cable car Tulsa and Lili took to the top of the mountain?

12. Where were Rick and Marla married?

13. By what nickname did Tulsa and Lili refer to Rick and Marla's baby?

14. What time did Tulsa go into Lili's apartment?

15. Who spent the night in the restaurant across from Lili's apartment, waiting for Tulsa to leave?

FLAMING STAR

(Twentieth Century–Fox, 1960)

PLOT

*A*s the son of a white father and a Native American mother, Elvis finds he must choose sides when his mother's people declare war on the encroaching white settlers.

CAST

Elvis Presley	Pacer Burton
Steve Forrest	Clint Burton
Barbara Eden	Roslyn Pierce
Dolores Del Rio	Neddy Burton
John McIntire	Sam Burton
Rudolph Acosta	Buffalo Horn
Karl Swenson	Dred Pierce
Ford Rainey	Doc Phillips
Richard Jaeckel	Angus Pierce
Anne Benton	Dorothy Howard
L. Q. Jones	Tom Howard
Douglas Dick	Will Howard
Tom Reese	Jute

CREW

David Weisbart	Producer
Don Siegel	Director
Clair Huffaker and Nunnally Johnson	Screenplay
Clair Huffaker	Novel
Col. Tom Parker	Technical Advisor
The Jordanaires	Vocal Accompaniment

THE PRE-PRODUCTION SAGA OF <u>FLAMING STAR</u>

It almost seemed as if Elvis's sixth film would never get to the screen.

The saga began in April 1958 when Simon & Schuster announced the upcoming publication of a novel, *The Brothers of Broken Lance* by Clair Huffaker, and the purchase of movie rights to that book by Twentieth Century-Fox. In May 1958, Simon & Schuster announced a title change for the book, to *Brothers of Flaming Arrow*, and indicated that this title would mirror the eventual title of the film.

Later that month, Twentieth Century–Fox announced that two stars—Marlon Brando and Frank Sinatra—had accepted roles as the two Burton brothers. The date set for the start of filming was June 16, 1958, but the studio failed to reach agreement with the actors during contract negotiations. The only agreement seemed to be on a new title for both the book and the projected film—*Flaming Lance*. The book was published in 1958, but the movie was put on hold.

The idea for the film *Flaming Lance* was taken out of mothballs two years later, and on June 12, 1960, the studio announced that Elvis had been signed for the lead. Selecting an actress for the role of Roslyn Pierce was more problematic.

The part was originally offered to Barbara Eden. She turned the role down because she was working on another film. A British actress, Barbara Steele, accepted the part, but her accent proved too troublesome. She was released from her contract, and the studio again approached Barbara Eden. At the time, she was between pictures, so she accepted the role.

FLAMING STAR IN PRODUCTION

Filming began in August 1960, but even before director Don Siegel called "Action" the movie had another title change—to *Flaming Heart*. No sooner was it called *Flaming Heart* than it was changed to *Black Star*. Another change made it *Black Heart*. The final change in title was made in September 1960, when the picture was christened *Flaming Star*.

Before filming ended in October 1960, cast and crew had shot interior footage on Stage 14 at the Twentieth Century–Fox studio and had gone out on location. The location work was done on three ranches in the San Fernando Valley.

While on location, Red West, who had a minor role in the film, injured his arm during a fight scene with Elvis. Elvis himself had a bit of trouble, too. He was thrown from a horse that suddenly bolted, but was not hurt in the fall.

PLAYING AROUND WITH THE SCREENPLAY

For several years, author Clair Huffaker had mentally kicked around the story line for a novel about the conflict between two brothers. When he finally settled down to write the book, he pounded out the prose in ten days.

After Twentieth Century–Fox had purchased the movie rights, Huffaker wanted to take a crack at writing the script. However, he was new to script writing; in fact, the screenplay for *Flaming Star* was his first. He followed that success by writing the scripts for *The Comancheros* (1961), *The War Wagon* (1967), *Flap* (1970), *The Deserter* (1971) and others.

The studio decided to team neophyte Huffaker with a screen-writing pro who had been turning out scripts since the 1920s, Nunnally Johnson. Johnson had written screenplays for *Bulldog Drummond Strikes Again* (1934), *Moulin Rouge* (1934), *The Grapes of Wrath* (1940), *Tobacco Road* (1941), *How to Marry a Millionaire* (1953), *The World of Henry Orient* (1964), and *The Dirty Dozen* (1967). He also produced and directed a number of films during his career.

The two writers set to work. It took them much longer to write the screenplay than they had thought it would. While Huffaker had written his novel in ten days, the team of Huffaker and Johnson spent thirty weeks writing the screenplay for Elvis's sixth film.

"FLAMING STAR"

Sid Wayne and Sherman Edwards wrote the theme song for the film. Elvis recorded "Flaming Star" in August 1960, and the song appeared as the first track on side one of the EP *Elvis by Request*. "Flaming Star" shone brightly on *Billboard*'s Hot 100 chart for seven weeks, hitting a high of number fourteen.

Elvis by Request was an unusual extended-play album in that it was the size of a 45 RPM record but had a small spindle hole. The EP played at 33 1/3 RPM—the only EP released by RCA that did. The second track on side one was "Summer Kisses, Winter Tears." Side two contained "Are You Lonesome Tonight" and "It's Now or Never." The EP was a million seller for Elvis.

SNEAK PEEKS AND THE PREMIERE OF FLAMING STAR

The audience at the Loyola Theatre in Westchester, California, enjoyed a sneak peek of *Flaming Star* on November 23, 1960. The version those patrons enjoyed contained only two songs, "Flaming Star" and "A Cane and a High Starched Collar."

On November 25, the audience at the Academy Theatre in Inglewood, California, also had a preview of *Flaming Star*, but the version seen that night featured four songs. Two additional Elvis songs—"Britches" and "Summer Kisses, Winter Tears"—were included in the film. Audience reaction was tested at both sneak peeks, and moviegoers seemed to prefer the two-song print over the four-song print.

The studio decided to go with the two-song version of *Flaming Star*, which premiered in Los Angeles on December 20, 1960. The film went into national release the next day.

DID YOU KNOW THAT...

- Elvis almost wore brown contact lenses for *Flaming Star*? That had been the plan, but when tests were made, it was decided that his beautiful baby blues would be just fine without the addition of colored contacts.

- Director Don Siegel produced and directed the modern-day action film *Dirty Harry* (1971)? Siegel's distinguished Hollywood film credits include art director of *Casablanca* (1942), director of *The Duel at Silver Creek* (1952), *Riot in Cell Block 11* (1954), *Invasion of the Body Snatchers* (1956), and producing and directing *Charley Varrick* (1973) and *Escape from Alcatraz* (1979).

- Actress Barbara Eden, who played Roslyn Pierce, the girl who was sweet on Clint Burton, is best known for playing a genie sweet on an American astronaut? Eden starred as Jeannie with costar Larry Hagman, who played Major Tony Nelson, the object of her affections, in the television series "I Dream of Jeannie" (1965–1970). Her other television series have included "How to Marry a Millionaire" (1958–1960), "Harper Valley PTA" (1981), and "Harper Valley" (1981–1982). In addition to her role in *Flaming Star*, Eden has had parts in *The Wayward Girl* (1957), *Voyage to the Bottom of the Sea* (1961), *The Brass Bottle* (1964), *Harper Valley PTA* (1978), and *Chattanooga Choo Choo* (1984). In 1958, she wed Michael Ansara, who appeared with Elvis in *Harum Scarum* (1965), but the marriage lasted only until 1973.

- Actor Steve Forrest, who played Clint Burton, the half-brother of Pacer Burton, was reunited with actress Barbara Eden three years after filming *Flaming Star*? The pair costarred in *The Yellow Canary* (1963). Forrest's other films include *The Bad and the Beautiful* (1952), *Phantom of the Rue Morgue* (1954), *Five Branded Women* (1960), *The Wild Country* (1971), *North Dallas Forty* (1979), *Mommie Dearest* (1981), and *Sahara* (1984). On television, Forrest starred as a police officer, Lt. Dan "Hondo" Harrelson, on the series "S.W.A.T." (1975–1977).

- Actress Dolores Del Rio, who played Neddy Burton, Pacer's mother, was known as the "First Lady of the Mexican Cinema"? She was discovered in Mexico City and invited to Hollywood for a role in the 1925 silent film *Joanna*. She made a number of American films, such as *Evangeline* (1929), *Bird of Paradise* (1932), *Flying Down to Rio* (1933), before returning to Mexico in 1943 to pursue her career in her homeland. In the 1960s, she ventured back to Hollywood occasionally to accept character parts, such as in *Flaming Star*.

- *Flaming Star* was the second film in which actor Richard Jaeckel, who played Dred Pierce's son Angus, costarred with actor L. Q. Jones? They acted together in *The Naked and the Dead* (1958) and would costar in a third film in 1973, *Pat Garrett and Billy The Kid*. Jaeckel's other film credits include *3:10 to Yuma* (1957), *Sands of Iwo Jima* (1949), *Come Back, Little Sheba* (1952), *Apache Ambush* (1955), *The Dirty Dozen* (1967), and *Starman* (1984).

- *Flaming Star* marked the second appearance in an Elvis movie for actor L. Q. Jones, who played Tom Howard, neighbor to the Burton family? Jones appeared in *Love Me Tender* (1956) as Pardee Fleming and would portray Bronc Hoverty in *Stay Away, Joe* (1968). His other films include *Cimarron* (1960),

Apache Rifles (1964), *Major Dundee* (1965), and *Hang 'em High* (1968). He was also known for the roles he played in television Westerns such as Pee Jay, a cattle drover, on "Rawhide" (1959–1966), Belden, a ranch hand, on "The Virginian" (1962–1970), and Wild Bill Hickok on the two-part miniseries "Wild Times" (1980).

- Actress Virginia Christine, who played Mrs. Phillips, the doctor's wife, is best known for her work on television? For twenty years she was Mrs. Olson in the commercials for Folgers Coffee.

- Elvis received instructions on handling a pistol from a *Flaming Star* stuntman? Rodd Redwing was the expert who worked with Elvis. Redwing counted among his former students television's Lone Ranger (Clayton Moore) and Annie Oakley (Gail Davis).

- *Flaming Star* was banned in South Africa? Because the film portrayed the character of Pacer Burton as the son of a white father and a Native American mother, *Flaming Star* went up against South Africa's strict laws of racial separation. Therefore, the government did not permit the film to be shown in the country.

FLAMING STAR TRIVIA QUIZ

1. What present did Roslyn Pierce give to Clint Burton for his birthday?

2. To whom was Dorothy Howard engaged to be married?

3. Who was the only member of the Howard family to survive the attack by the Kiowas?

4. What was the Crossing?

5. What was Neddy Burton's relationship to Lame Crow?

6. What was the meaning of the name the Kiowas had for Neddy?

7. How long had Sam and Neddy Burton been married?

8. What had Sam given to Neddy's father for her?

9. What was the name of Pacer Burton's Kiowa friend?

10. Who was the leader of the band of white settlers who demanded to know on which side the Burtons would fight?

11. Who molested Neddy in the cabin?

12. What was the significance of the flaming star seen by Neddy?

13. What was the name of Doc Phillips's daughter whom Pacer held hostage?

14. What two wounds did Clint sustain in the attack on the trail?

15. Who said: "Don't try to help me. I've been killed already. Stubborn about dying."

WILD IN THE COUNTRY

(TWENTIETH CENTURY–FOX, 1961)

PLOT

*A*s a hot-headed country boy, Elvis is branded a juvenile delinquent because of his rebellious attitude. With the help of a court-appointed counselor, he overcomes his hostility and learns to believe in his potential to become a writer.

CAST

Elvis Presley	Glenn Tyler
Hope Lange	Irene Sperry
Tuesday Weld	Noreen
Millie Perkins	Betty Lee Parsons
Rafer Johnson	Davis
John Ireland	Phil Macy
Gary Lockwood	Cliff Macy
William Mims	Rolfe Braxton
Christina Crawford	Monica George
Ruby Goodwin	Sarah
Will Cory	Willie Dace
Alan Napier	Professor Larson
Harry Shannon	Sam Tyler
Red West	Hank Tyler
Pat Buttram	Mr. Longstreet

CREW

Jerry Wald	Producer
Philip Dunne	Director
Clifford Odets	Screenplay
J. R. Salamanca	Novel

Kenyon Hopkins .... Music
Edward B. Powell .... Orchestration
Col. Tom Parker .... Technical Advisor

SONGS
"Wild in the Country" • "I Slipped, I Stumbled, I Fell" • "In My Way" •
"Husky Dusky Day"

WILD ABOUT "WILD IN THE COUNTRY"

Hugo Peretti, Luigi Creatore, and George Weiss wrote "Wild in the Country" which was the title song for Elvis's 1961 film. Elvis sang the song over the movie's opening credits. The single release was on *Billboard*'s Hot 100 chart for five weeks, during which time the song peaked at number twenty-six.

PROFILE OF THE PROLIFIC WEISMAN AND WISE

"In My Way" and "I Slipped, I Stumbled, I Fell" were two compositions from *Wild in the Country* written by the prolific team of Ben Weisman and Fred Wise. "Forget Me Never," a third song written by the pair, was cut from the film.

Ben Weisman, who was born in Providence, Rhode Island, cowrote with others more than fifty songs for Elvis. Fred Wise, born in New York City, cowrote with others more than thirty songs for Elvis. Together the songwriting team of Weisman and Wise wrote more than fifteen songs for the King of Rock and Roll, including "Almost Always True," "Follow That Dream," and "This Is Living."

A NOVEL APPROACH TO WILD IN THE COUNTRY

Writer Clifford Odets based his screenplay of *Wild in the Country* on J. R. Salamanca's first novel, *The Lost Country*. In the novel, Glenn Tyler was an artist, and Irene Sperry was a teacher. In the screenplay, Glenn was a writer, and Irene was a psychologist. The title for the film came from a line in Walt Whitman's *Leaves of Grass*.

At first *Wild in the Country* was scheduled to be filmed without Elvis songs. That decision was quickly reversed. Six songs were added, but two—"Lonely Man" and "Forget Me Never" were cut from the final print.

Filming began in early November 1960 on location at the Victorian Ink House in St. Helena, California. Cameras also captured footage in and around Napa Valley and at the University of California at Los Angeles. For the college scenes, the studio hired UCLA students as extras. Interior shots were done on the Twentieth Century–Fox lot. Two weeks overdue, filming wrapped up in mid-January 1961.

Director Philip Dunne had filmed two different endings for *Wild in the Country*. In one, Irene Sperry dies, and in the other, she lives. Audiences who at-

44

tended sneak peeks of the film voted to see Irene survive her suicide attempt, and that ending was selected by Dunne for the general release of the movie.

DID YOU KNOW THAT...

- During the filming of *Wild in the Country*, Elvis received a special gift from RCA? The recording company presented to Elvis a platinum watch to commemorate his having sold seventy-five million records.

- Actress Hope Lange, who played counselor Irene Sperry, made her film debut in *Bus Stop* (1956)? That film also heralded the screen debut of actor Don Murray, whom Lange later married. The pair were divorced during the production of *Wild in the Country*. Lange is best known to television audiences as Carolyn Muir in the series "The Ghost and Mrs. Muir" (1968–1970).

- The real name of actress Tuesday Weld is Susan Ker Weld? She debuted in the film *Rock, Rock, Rock* (1956) and mentioned Elvis in a line of the movie's dialogue. During the 1959–1960 television season, Weld played Thalia Menninger in "The Many Loves of Dobie Gillis" (1959–1963). While filming *Wild in the Country*, Weld was also acting in the movie *Return to Peyton Place* (1961).

- Actress Millie Perkins, who played Glenn Tyler's girlfriend, Betty Lee Parsons, played Elvis's mother in a television series? Perkins was a regular cast member on the television series "Elvis" (1990). In addition to *Wild in the Country*, Perkins appeared in other films, including *Ensign Pulver* (1964), *Wild in the Streets* (1968), *Cockfighter* (1974), *Table for Five* (1983), *Wall Street* (1987), and *Two Moon Junction* (1988).

- Actor John Ireland, who played Phil Macy, received an Academy Award nomination for Best Supporting Actor for his work in *All the King's Men* (1949)? His other film credits include *A Walk in the Sun* (1945), *I Shot Jesse James* (1949), *The Good Die Young* (1954), *Gunfight at the OK Corral* (1957), *Spartacus* (1960), *The Fall of the Roman Empire* (1964), and *The Incubus* (1981).

- Actor Gary Lockwood, who played Cliff Macy, began his career as a movie stuntman? That work led to leads and supporting roles in films such as *Tall Story* (1960), *Splendor in the Grass* (1961), and *2001: A Space Odyssey* (1968). He costarred as Elvis's pilot sidekick in *It Happened at the World's Fair* (1963).

- Elvis's close friend Red West enjoyed his first speaking part in *Wild in the Country*? West played Glenn's brother, Hank Tyler. In the film, he propositions Irene Sperry as she is on her way into the coroner's inquest. West had bit parts in a number of other Elvis films.

- *Wild in the Country* was Rafer Johnson's second film? The Olympic decathalon champion turned actor, played Davis, an assistant in Phil Macy's legal firm. Johnson had his first acting role in *The Fiercest Heart* (1961).

- Christina Crawford, who played Cliff Macy's date, Monica George, is the adopted daughter of movie queen Joan Crawford? Christina is more well known for writing the 1978 blockbuster autobiographical book *Mommie Dearest*.

- Writer J. R. Salamanca received rave reviews for *The Lost Country*, the novel upon which *Wild in the Country* was based? *Time* magazine called the book "a torrential first novel." *The Lost Country* was published in 1958, and in 1961 an abridged version was published in paperback under the title *Wild in the Country*. Salamanca is also known for the novels *Lilith* (1961), *A Sea Change* (1969), *Embarkation* (1973), and *Southern Light* (1986).

- Screenwriter Clifford Odets had a reputation as the most talented of the American social-protest playwrights of the 1930s? He wrote screenplays for *Waiting for Lefty* (1935), *Awake and Sing* (1935), *Golden Boy* (1937), *Clash by Night* (1942), and *The Country Girl* (1950).

- Elvis and Tuesday Weld won the Damp Raincoat Award for Most Disappointing Performers of 1961? The dubious honors were bestowed upon them by the readers of *Teen* magazine.

WILD IN THE COUNTRY TRIVIA QUIZ

1. What materials did Irene Sperry think Glenn Tyler read?

2. How old was Glenn when his mother died?

3. What was the name of the elixir sold by Rolfe Braxton?

4. What was Glenn's weekly salary while working for Uncle Rolfe?

5. What was the name of the establishment to which Glenn took Betty Lee Parsons for their date?

6. What was the occupation of the father of Noreen's baby?

7. What was the name of Irene Sperry's Irish setter?

8. What medical problem plagued Cliff Macy?

9. What birthday present did Noreen receive from her father?

10. What was the name of Irene Sperry's deceased husband?

11. Who arranged the job at the garage for Glenn?

12. Who asked Glenn to think about the following: "For man to discover fire was nothing. To learn to use and control it was everything."?

13. What flavor of soda did Glenn and Irene enjoy at Spangler's Rest Motel?

14. What was the usual room rate at the motel?

15. How did Irene attempt suicide?

9.

BLUE HAWAII

(PARAMOUNT, 1961)

PLOT

*E*lvis returns home from the army and enters into a skirmish with his parents, who want him to become employed in the pineapple business. Instead, he becomes a guide with a Hawaiian tourist agency. When he escorts a group of high school girls and their chaperon on a tour of the islands, complications develop.

CAST

Elvis Presley	Chad Gates
Joan Blackman	Maile Duval
Angela Lansbury	Sarah Lee Gates
Nancy Walters	Abigail Prentice
Roland Winters	Fred Gates
John Archer	Jack Kelman
Howard McNear	Mr. Chapman
Steve Brodie	Tucker Garvey
Iris Adrian	Enid Garvey
Hilo Hattie	Waihila
Jennie Maxwell	Ellie Corbett
Pamela Kirk	Selena Emerson
Darlene Tompkins	Patsy Simon
Christian Kay	Beverly Martin
Guy Lee	Ping Pong
Gregory Gay	Paul Duval
Flora K. Hayes	Mrs. Maneka

CREW

Hal B. Wallis .... Producer
Norman Taurog .... Director
Hal Kanter .... Screenplay
Edith Head .... Costumes
The Jordanaires .... Vocal Accompaniment
Charles O'Curran .... Staging of Musical Numbers
Col. Tom Parker .... Technical Advisor

SONGS

"Blue Hawaii" • "Almost Always True" • "Aloha Oe" • "No More"
• "Can't Help Falling in Love" • "Rock-a-Hula Baby" • "Moonlight Swim" •
"Ku-u-i-Po" • "Ito Eats" • "Slicin' Sand" • "Hawaiian Sunset" •
"Beach Boy Blues" • "Island of Love (Kauai) • "Hawaiian Wedding Song"

COME WITH ELVIS TO "BLUE HAWAII"

Elvis was not the first to sing about the heavenly night, the moon on the sea, and dreams coming true in "Blue Hawaii."

Written in 1937 by Leo Robin and Ralph Rainger, the song was introduced by Bing Crosby in the 1937 film *Waikiki Wedding*. Crosby recorded the song for Decca, and in 1959 Billy Vaughn recorded a release for Dot. Vaughn's version reached number thirty-seven on the Hot 100 chart.

"Blue Hawaii" was one of fourteen songs included on the soundtrack album of Elvis's 1961 movie. The LP took a leisurely eight weeks to hit the top of *Billboard*'s Top LPs chart, and once the album arrived, it was in no hurry to leave. *Blue Hawaii* basked in the sun as number one for twenty consecutive weeks and set a record that remained unchallenged until 1977 brought the phenomenal success of Fleetwood Mac's LP *Rumors*. Total time for *Blue Hawaii* on the Top LPs chart was seventy-nine weeks, and the album was chosen by disc jockeys as their second most favorite LP of 1961 in a poll by *Billboard* magazine.

"ALOHA OE"

"Aloha Oe," which means "Farewell to Thee," was written in 1878 by Liliuokalani, the last reigning queen of the Hawaiian Islands. The song was recorded by Bing Crosby in 1936 and by Harry Owens in 1938. In *Blue Hawaii*, Elvis sang "Aloha Oe" while in a canoe. Although not released as a single, the song does appear on the *Blue Hawaii* album.

CAN'T HELP FALLING IN LOVE WITH "CAN'T HELP FALLING IN LOVE"

In *Blue Hawaii*, Chad Gates (Elvis) presents as a birthday gift to Maile's grandmother, Mrs. Maneka (Flora K. Hayes), an Austrian music box that plays "Can't Help Falling in Love."

Composers George Weiss, Hugo Peretti, and Luigi Creatore were inspired to write "Can't Help Falling in Love" by Giovanni Martini's classical French com-

position, "Plaisir d'Amour."

Elvis's single release had a four-teen-week love affair with *Billboard*'s Hot 100 chart, going all the way to number two. "Can't Help Falling in Love" couldn't help staying at the top spot on the Easy-Listening chart for six weeks. On the English chart, the song was number one for four weeks.

In the 1970s, Elvis closed his concerts with "Can't Help Falling in Love" which became his signature song. And fans couldn't help falling in love all over again with this beautiful ballad.

A MELEE OVER MAILE

In 1960, Juliet Prowse had ener-gized the role of Lili in *GI Blues*, so producer Hal B. Wallis naturally thought of Prowse for the part of Maile Duval in *Blue Hawaii*. The actress would comple-ment Elvis's portrayal of Chad Gates. Prowse was on loan to Paramount from her home studio, Twentieth Century–Fox, and in February 1961, she was signed to do the role. But one month later, troubled waters surrounded *Blue Hawaii*, and Prowse was at the eye of the storm.

She had demanded that her makeup man from Fox be loaned out for work on the film and wanted her secretary to accompany her to Hawaii, with all travel expenses paid by Paramount. The actress also wanted the billing clause in her contract altered. Unless the conditions were met, Prowse had no intention of reporting for work.

Heated negotiations followed, and just a week after having received her demands, Hal Wallis told Prowse she was off the picture. Then Twentieth Century–Fox joined in the fray and put Prowse on suspension. Within forty-eight hours, Wallis announced that Elvis's new costar would be Joan Blackman.

CHAD'S FOLKS

After Chad is released from jail, he returns home to his mother, Sarah Lee. "My baby's home from the Big House," she cries.

"Oh, Sarah Lee, will you forget those old movies," Mr. Gates exclaims.

The two film veterans who played Mr. and Mrs. Gates—Angela Lansbury and Roland Winters—were well known in Hollywood for the many classic mov-ies in which they had roles.

London-born Lansbury debuted as a maid in *Gaslight* (1944), and this per-formance earned an Academy Award nomination as Best Supporting Actress. She was honored with other nominations in that category for her work in *The Picture of Dorian Gray* (1945) and *The Manchurian Candidate* (1962). Her other films include *National Velvet* (1944), *The Three Musketeers* (1948), and *Samson and Delilah* (1949).

After *Blue Hawaii*, Lansbury had roles in *The World of Henry Orient* (1964),

The Greatest Story Ever Told (1965), *Bedknobs and Broomsticks* (1971), *Death on the Nile* (1978), and *The Pirates of Penzance* (1983). On television, she is best known as Jessica Fletcher in the series "Murder, She Wrote."

Roland Winters was the third actor to portray the Chinese detective Charlie Chan. His debut film as the wily detective was *The Chinese Ring* (1947), and he went on to make five other Charlie Chan films for Monogram Pictures: *Docks of New Orleans* (1948), *The Shanghai Chest* (1948), *The Golden Eye* (1948), *The Feathered Serpent* (1948), and *Sky Dragon* (1949). His other film credits include *Cry of the City* (1948) which featured Elvis's first costar, Debra Paget, *Bigger Than Life* (1956), and *Cash McCall* (1959). Winters played Judge Wardman in Elvis's next film, *Follow That Dream* (1962).

BLUE HAWAII'S PRESLEY PERPLEXERS

Here and there in Elvis's films are instances that cause the keen-eyed fan to do a double take: minor mistakes resulting from errors in continuity, slips in the editing process, or goofs that are simply unexplainable. Did you catch or miss either of these Presley Perplexers in *Blue Hawaii*?

- The sign on the door to Mr. Chapman's office indicates that the name of the company is Hawaiian Island Tours. Yet when introducing herself to Abigail Prentice, Maile says she is an associate of Hawaiian Tourist Guide Service.

- In the pineapple field, everyone except for Ellie Corbett scrambles out of the car and heads to the pineapple stand. In their haste, they leave the door on the driver's side of the car open. Yet when Chad brings a plate of pineapple to Ellie, the door is closed.

DID YOU KNOW THAT...

- The original title of the film was *Hawaii Beach Boy*? The title was changed to *Blue Hawaii* in January 1961.

- The plot for *Blue Hawaii* came from a former Los Angeles newspaperman? The story line was the brainchild of Allan Weiss—the first of his to be the basis for a film—and his book *Beach Boy* provided the inspiration. Later, Weiss was involved with the story ideas or screenplays of *Girls! Girls! Girls!* (1962), *Fun in Acapulco* (1963), *Roustabout* (1964), *Paradise, Hawaiian Style* (1966), and *Easy Come, Easy Go* (1967).

- Prior to beginning work on the film, Elvis presented a live concert in Hawaii? On March 25, 1961, Elvis performed at a concert at the Bloch Arena at Pearl Harbor to benefit the USS *Arizona* Memorial Fund.

- Location filming took place on

the islands of Oahu and Kauai? Cameras rolled at spots such as Waikiki Beach, Honolulu International Airport, Ala Moana Park, Kauai Airport, Coco Palms Resort Hotel, and Lydgate Park.

- Three Elvis songs were cut from *Blue Hawaii*? "Steppin' Out of Line," "La Paloma," and "Playing with Fire" were axed from the final print.

- Ku-u-i-po means "Hawaiian sweetheart"? Chad sings "Ku-u-i-po" at the luau. The song was written by George Weiss, Hugo Peretti, and Luigi Creatore.

- Actress Joan Blackman played another love interest of Elvis's? She played Rose Grogan in *Kid Galahad* (1962). Blackman's other films include *Good Day for a Hanging* (1958), *Career* (1959), *Visit to a Small Planet* (1960), and *The Great Imposter* (1960).

- Actor Howard McNear, who played Mr. Chapman, the owner of the tourist agency, played another scatterbrained character on a long-running television series? McNear played Floyd Lawson, the barber on "The Andy Griffith Show" (1960–1968).

- A former Hawaii Territorial Representative to the United States Congress had a role in *Blue Hawaii*? She was Flora K. Hayes, who played Maile's grandmother, Mrs. Maneka.

- Mexico's Office of Public Entertainment banned *Blue Hawaii*? Officials remembered the unruly behavior of audience members at the screening of *GI Blues* (1960) and canceled the showing of *Blue Hawaii* at the Mexico Theatre.

BLUE HAWAII TRIVIA QUIZ

1. Who was the motorcycle officer who stopped Maile Duval for speeding?

2. On what airline did Chad Gates fly?

3. Why was Maile angry with Chad at the airport?

4. How long had Chad been in the army?

5. What was the bogus Hawaiian holiday concocted by Chad?

6. What was the name of Chad's dog?

7. What was Chad's complete first name?

8. At which firm was Mr. Gates employed?

9. What was the nickname Mrs. Gates had for her husband?

10. Where had Chad been born?

11. How long had Chad lived in Hawaii?

12. How old was Ellie Corbett?

13. What items did Ellie take from her roommates?

14. What was the cocktail that Jack Kelman called a "tummy warmer"?

15. What was the name of the travel agency Chad and Maile wanted to start?

10.

FOLLOW THAT DREAM

(UNITED ARTISTS, 1962)

PLOT

*E*lvis is part of a family that decides to homestead on an unopened stretch of Florida highway. In the course of setting up and running a fishing business, Elvis is pursued by the family's nineteen-year-old babysitter, a lusty social worker, and two gangsters operating a floating gambling trailer.

CAST

Elvis Presley	Toby Kwimper
Arthur O'Connell	Pop Kwimper
Anne Helm	Holly Jones
Joanna Moore	Alicia Claypoole
Alan Hewitt	H. Arthur King
Herbert Rudley	Mr. Endicott
Simon Oakland	Nick
Jack Kruschen	Carmine
Robin Koon	Teddy Bascombe
Gavin Koon	Eddy Bascombe
Pam Ogles	Ariadne Pennington
Howard McNear	George Binkley
Roland Winters	Judge Wardman
Robert Carricart	Al
John Duke	Blackie
Harry Holcombe	Governor
Red West	Bank Guard

CREW

David Weisbart	Producer
Gordon Douglas	Director

Charles Lederer .... Screenplay
Col. Tom Parker .... Technical Advisor

SONGS
"What a Wonderful Life" • "I'm Not the Marrying Kind" • "Sound Advice" •
"On Top of Old Smokey" • "Follow That Dream" • "Angel"

KEEPING ON TOP OF MUSICAL HISTORY

During the word-association test that Alicia Claypoole (Joanna Moore) administers to Toby Kwimper (Elvis) at the beach, one of the words she offers is "girl." Toby's response is "Dad" which Alicia asks him to explain. "That's the song they play," he says and then sings "On top of Old Smokey / Where things get real hot / Where girls are a problem / Which Dad knows I got."

"On Top of Old Smokey" is an American southern highlands folk song that has been recorded by a number of artists, including the Weavers, Vaughn Monroe, and Burl Ives. In 1963, there was even a parody of the song called "On Top of Spaghetti" recorded by John Glazer and the Do-Re-Mi Children's Chorus.

The ten seconds of the song that Elvis sang in *Follow That Dream* were recorded on the set rather than in a recording studio. Because the rendition was so short, RCA chose not to release the song.

MR. LIVINGSTON, I PRESUME

Pennsylvania-born Jay Livingston coauthored "What a Wonderful Life," which Elvis sings over the opening credits of *Follow That Dream*. His collaborator was New York–born Sid Wayne.

Livingston composed the theme songs for television series, including "Mr. Lucky" and "Mr. Ed." With collaborator Ray Evans, Livingston wrote songs such as "To Each His Own," "Tammy," "Mona Lisa," and "Silver Bells."

"Silver Bells" was written for the Bob Hope–Marilyn Maxwell film *The Lemon Drop Kid* (1951). Elvis recorded the Christmas classic for his LPs *Elvis Sings the Wonderful World of Christmas* and *Memories of Christmas*.

A NOVEL IDEA FOR FOLLOW THAT DREAM

Richard Powell's 1957 novel *Pioneer, Go Home* was the basis for Elvis's 1962 movie. In fact, the title of the book was the original title for the film. However, the song composers found the word "Pioneer" too difficult to rhyme, so the title went back to the drawingboard. *It's a Beautiful Life*, *Here Come the Kwimpers* and *What a Wonderful Life* were other titles suggested before *Follow That Dream* was chosen.

YOU CAN ALWAYS GET WHAT YOU NEED EVEN IN A PINCH

The props required for *Follow That Dream* included dice tables plus other gambling equipment. And that was a problem for the crew. In 1961, gambling

was illegal in Florida, the location of filming. Where would they get the items?

They didn't have to wonder for long. After a few contacts were made, the needed equipment was delivered to the location site by a local Chamber of Commerce member and several representatives of organized crime.

DID YOU KNOW THAT...

- Elvis traveled to location filming in Florida by bus? Along with his toothbrush, he brought a twenty-one-foot speedboat and two automobiles. Filming in Florida took place in Crystal River, Tampa, Ocala, Yankeetown, Inverness, and Bird Creek.

- During his career, Gordon Douglas directed both Elvis and Frank Sinatra? Douglas directed Sinatra in *Young at Heart* (1954) and in *Tony Rome* (1967), a film which featured *Follow That Dream* alumnus Simon Oakland. In the 1930s, Douglas directed several *Our Gang* shorts and many Hal Roach features.

- Actress Joanna Moore, who played social worker Alicia Claypoole, pursued a medical career in a popular television series? Moore played Peggy McMillan, the town nurse in Mayberry, on "The Andy Griffith Show" (1960–1968). In addition to *Follow That Dream*, Moore's other movie credits include *Slim Carter* (1957), *Ride a Crooked Trail* (1958), *The Last Angry Man* (1959), *Walk on the Wild Side* (1962), *Son of Flubber* (1963), and *The Hindenburg* (1975).

- Actor Arthur O'Connell who played Pop Kwimper was a vaudeville and theater actor before entering the motion picture industry? He was known for roles in which he played gentle, slightly befuddled country characters. He received Academy Award nominations for Best Supporting Actor for his work in *Picnic* (1956) and *Anatomy of a Murder* (1959). His other films include *Freshman Year* (1938), *The Man in the Gray Flannel Suit* (1956), *Bus Stop* (1956), *Fantastic Voyage* (1966), *Ben* (1972), and *The Hiding Place* (1975).

- Eight-year-old identical twins played Teddy and Eddy Bascombe? Toby described Teddy and Eddy as "some sort of fourth cousins or something" to the Kwimpers, and the parts were played by Robin and Gavin Koon. *Follow That Dream* was their film debut. Their father, Charles Koon, was the art director on "The Lawrence Welk Show" (1955–1971).

- Actor Simon Oakland, who played Nick the gangster, began his entertainment career as a violinist? When he switched to film work, he found roles in *The Brothers Karamazov* (1958), *Psycho* (1960), *The Satan Bug* (1965), *The Plainsman* (1966), *The Sand Pebbles* (1967), *Emperor of the North* (1973) and *Evening in Byzantium* (1978). He had television roles in "Toma" (1973–1974), "Kolchak: The Night Stalker" (1974–1975), "Baa Baa Black Sheep" (1976–1978), and "David Cassidy—Man Undercover" (1978–1979).

54 • Actor Jack Kruschen, who played Carmine the gangster, received an Academy Award nomination for Best Supporting Actor for his role in *The Apartment?* Kruschen played the character Dr. Dreyfuss in the 1960 film that starred Jack Lemmon and Shirley MacLaine. Unfortunately, Kruschen lost the Oscar to Peter Ustinov for his work in *Spartacus.* Kruschen's other films include *Red, Hot and Blue* (1949), *Tropical Heat Wave* (1952), *Abbott and Costello Go to Mars* (1953), *Soldier of Fortune* (1955), *Seven Ways From Sundown* (1960), *Cape Fear* (1962), *The Unsinkable Molly Brown* (1964), *Freebie and the Bean* (1974), and *Under the Rainbow* (1981).

FOLLOW THAT DREAM TRIVIA QUIZ

1. What reward did the twins Teddy and Eddy Bascombe receive for good behavior?

2. How had Toby Kwimper injured his back?

3. What was the amount of Toby's monthly disability check?

4. At the beach, what did Toby use to dig for water?

5. How long did the Kwimpers have to live on the property in order to claim it?

6. What did Toby use for a fishing hook?

7. What two items did Pop Kwimper buy at the junkyard?

8. How much did Toby and Holly earn on the first day of their fishing business?

9. How old was Holly?

10. How much did Toby and Holly borrow from the bank?

11. How did Toby divert his mind when a woman "bothered" him?

12. Who described the Kwimper property as "the hideosity with the dock"?

13. What was Alicia Claypoole's job title?

14. Who were the "muscle" who worked for Carmine and Nick?

15. What was the scheduled time for the court hearing that determined the guardianship of the children?

KID GALAHAD

(UNITED ARTISTS, 1962)

PLOT

*E*lvis takes a job as a sparring partner at a training camp for boxers and knocks out a professional fighter. The unscrupulous owner of the camp, who owes gambling debts to gangsters, transforms Elvis into a money-making, championship boxer. Elvis wins one last fight so that he can go into business with a local garage owner and marry the sister of the camp's owner.

CAST

Elvis Presley	Walter Gulick
Gig Young	Willy Grogan
Lola Albright	Dolly Fletcher
Joan Blackman	Rose Grogan
Charles Bronson	Lew Nyack
Ned Glass	Mr. Lieberman
David Lewis	Otto Danzig
Michael Dante	Joie Shakes
Richard Devon	Marvin
Liam Redmond	Father Higgins
Ralph Moody	Peter J. Prohosko
Orlando de la Fuente	Ramon "Sugarboy" Romero
Ed Asner	Frank Gerson
Robert Emhardt	Mr. Maynard

CREW

David Weisbart	Producer
Phil Karlson	Director
William Fay	Screenplay
Col. Tom Parker	Technical Advisor
Mushy Callahan	Boxing Advisor

SONGS
"King of the Whole Wide World" • "This Is Living" • "Riding the Rainbow" •
"Home Is Where the Heart Is" • "I Got Lucky" • "A Whistling Tune"

ELVIS IS "KING OF THE WHOLE WIDE WORLD"

Elvis sings "King of the Whole Wide World" over the opening credits of *Kid Galahad*. The song, which was written by Ruth Batchelor and Bob Roberts, was not released as a single by RCA. But did that stop the King of Rock and Roll from hitting the singles chart? No way.

Because of the song's appearance on the successful EP *Kid Galahad*, "King of the Whole Wide World" ascended *Billboard*'s Hot 100 chart for a seven-week reign. During that time, the tune reached as high as number thirty.

EDWARDS AND DAVID DON'T "KID" AROUND

Composer and arranger Sherman Edwards and Academy Award winning lyricist Hal David composed both "Home Is Where the Heart Is" and "A Whistling Tune." Both were used in *Kid Galahad*, although "A Whistling Tune" had been originally recorded for *Follow That Dream*.

New York City-born Edwards collaborated with Sid Wayne on other Elvis songs, including "Frankfurt Special," "Big Boots," "Didja Ever," "Britches," and "Flaming Star."

Hal David, who also hails from The Big Apple, is best known as the partner of Burt Bacharach. Together they have composed dozens of hits for artists, including many songs for Dionne Warwick.

KID GALAHAD—THE ROUND BEGINS

The story upon which *Kid Galahad* was based was written by Francis Wallace and appeared in the 1930s within the pages of *The Saturday Evening Post*. That was round one.

In 1937, Warner Bros. transformed the story into the film, which was directed by Michael Curtiz, a director with whom Elvis had worked in *King Creole* (1958). This round two incarnation of *Kid Galahad* starred Edward G. Robinson as the promoter, Wayne Morris as the naive boxer, and Bette Davis as the love interest.

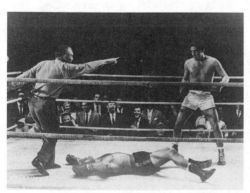

Kid Galahad was remade by Warner Bros. in 1941. For round three, the setting was a circus. Humphrey Bogart starred as the circus master, Eddie Albert was the country boy turned lion tamer, and Sylvia Sidney was the star of the Big Top.

Round four occurred in 1962, when the 1937 *Kid Galahad* was brought to television. The film was retitled *Battling Bellhop* to avoid confusion with Elvis's version of *Kid Galahad*. The King's version, round five, won the hearts of fans with a knock-out punch.

ELVIS PUTS UP HIS DUKES

To look convincing in his fight scenes, Elvis needed expert training. Who better to serve as coach than Mushy Callahan? From 1926 to 1930, Callahan had been world junior welterweight boxing champion. Assisting Callahan was Al Silvani, who worked as trainer and cornerman for fighters such as Floyd Patterson, Jake LaMotta, Rocky Graziano, and Carmen Basilio. With a powerhouse team behind him, Elvis was more than ready to put up his dukes for the *Kid Galahad* cameras.

DID YOU KNOW THAT...

- Location filming for *Kid Galahad* took place in a popular resort town? The place was Idylwild, California, situated about ninety miles east of Los Angeles.

- A well-known voice announced two fights in *Kid Galahad*? Jimmy Lennon, fight announcer at the Olympic Auditorium in Los Angeles, did the film honors.

- The actor who played Sugarboy Romero made his film debut in *Kid Galahad*? Eighteen-year-old Orlando de la Fuente brought realism to the role because he was an undefeated welterweight boxer.

- Actor Gig Young, who played Willy Grogan, was born Byron Elsworth Barr? He took his professional name from the character Gig Young that he played in *The Gay Sisters* (1942). He was nominated for an Academy Award for Best Supporting Actor for *Come Fill the Cup* (1951) and *Teacher's Pet* (1958). He captured the Academy Award for his supporting role as the master of ceremonies for the marathon dance contest in *They Shoot Horses, Don't They?* (1969).

- Actress Joan Blackman, who played Rose Grogan, had a role in a previous Elvis film? She played the role of Maile Duval in *Blue Hawaii* (1961). Television viewers may remember Blackman as Marian Fowler, the wife of District Attorney John Fowler, which she played on "Peyton Place" from 1965 to 1966.

- Actress Lola Albright, who played Dolly Fletcher, was a model before making her movie debut? Her first film was *The Pirate* (1948). Her other films include *Champion* (1949), *The Tender Trap* (1955), *A Cold Wind in August* (1961), *Lord Love a Duck* (1966), and *The Impossible Years* (1968). Her television credits include playing Edie Hart, the featured singer at a jazz nightclub and the girl-friend of Peter Gunn, on the television series "Peter Gunn" (1958–1961).

58

- Actor Charles Bronson, who played Lew Nyack, had a role in *House of Wax* (1953) which required no lines? In that 3D film, Bronson, who was billed under his real name, Charles Buchinsky, played a mute who was Vincent Price's assistant. His other films include *The Magnificent Seven* (1960), *The Great Escape* (1963), and *The Dirty Dozen* (1967). Stardom came to Bronson with *Death Wish* (1974).

- Actor Ed Asner, who played Frank Gerson, made his acting debut in *Kid Galahad*? He is better known for his television work, including the role of cantankerous WJM–TV news producer Lou Grant on "The Mary Tyler Moore Show" (1970–1977) and the irascible city editor of the *Los Angeles Tribune* on "Lou Grant" (1977–1982). He won an Emmy for his work in the television drama "Roots" (1977).

- Seven songs were planned for *Kid Galahad*? Six were featured, but "Love Is for Lovers," written by Ruth Batchelor and Sharon Silbert, was cut from the film.

- *Kid Galahad* grossed $1.75 million in 1962? The film was ranked number thirty-seven on *Variety*'s list of top-grossing films for the year.

KID GALAHAD TRIVIA QUIZ

1. What was the company name of the truck on which Walter Gulick rode into town?

2. In what mountain area was Cream Valley located?

3. Although born in Cream Valley, where was Walter raised?

4. While serving with the army in Okinawa, where was Walter assigned to work?

5. How much did Willy Grogan owe to the company that financed his convertible?

6. How much did Willy agree to pay to Walter for sparring with Joie Shakes?

7. Who gave Walter the nickname Galahad?

8. Where did Walter refurbish the Model T?

9. In what city was Kid Galahad's fight with Ezzard Bailey scheduled?

10. What color trunks did Kid Galahad wear?

11. Who gave this advice to Kid Galahad: "Now cover up your head once in awhile. Like I told you, it's not a disgrace to block a punch."?

12. Where was Cream Valley's Independence Day picnic held?

13. To what eatery did Walter and Rose go after the picnic?

14. How much did Willy bet on Kid Galahad in his bout with Sugarboy Romero?

15. At which church did Walter and Rose plan to be married?

12.
GIRLS!
GIRLS! GIRLS!

(PARAMOUNT, 1962)

PLOT

*E*lvis is a poor charter boat pilot with a dream of buying his late father's sailboat. To earn money, he works by day as a tuna fisherman for an unscrupulous boat owner and sings by night at a local club. At every turn he is pursued by a bevy of lovely ladies.

CAST

Elvis Presley	Ross Carpenter
Stella Stevens	Robin Gantner
Jeremy Slate	Wesley Johnson
Laurel Goodwin	Laurel Dodge
Benson Fong	Kin Yung
Robert Strauss	Sam
Guy Lee	Chen Yung
Frank Puglia	Papa Stavros
Lili Valenty	Mama Stavros
Beulah Quo	Madam Yung
Ginny Tiu	Mai Ling
Elizabeth Tiu	Tai Ling

CREW

Hal B. Wallis	Producer
Norman Taurog	Director
Edward Anhalt and Allan Weiss	Screenplay
Edith Head	Costumes
Charles O'Curran	Staging of Musical Numbers
Joseph J. Lilley	Scoring and Conducting of Music
The Jordanaires	Vocal Accompaniment
Col. Tom Parker	Technical Advisor

SONGS

"Girls! Girls! Girls!" • "I Don't Wanna Be Tied" • "We'll Be Together" •
"A Boy Like Me, a Girl Like You" • "Earth Boy" • "Return to Sender" •
"Because of Love" • "Thanks to the Rolling Sea" • "Song of the Shrimp" •
"The Walls Have Ears" • "We're Coming in Loaded" •
"Dainty Little Moonbeams" • "Girls! Girls! Girls!" (second version)

"GIRLS!" TIMES THREE

Jerry Leiber and Mike Stoller wrote "Girls! Girls! Girls!" not for Elvis's 1962 film but for the Coasters, who took the song to number ninety-six on *Billboard*'s Hot 100 chart in 1960.

Elvis sings "Girls! Girls! Girls!" at the opening and at the closing of *Girls! Girls! Girls!*. But the end title version has different lyrics. The version selected for use on LPs was the one heard at the film's opening.

"EARTH BOY" FINDS <u>TWO</u> ANGELS

Sid Tepper and Roy C. Bennett wrote the song "Earth Boy" for *Girls! Girls! Girls!* The version heard in the film is different from the one heard on the LP. In the film, Mai Ling (Ginny Tiu) and Tai Ling (Elizabeth Tiu) share the vocals with Ross Carpenter (Elvis). In parts of the song, Ross translates the girls' Chinese lyrics into English, and in other parts, he sings the lyrics in Chinese.

A DATE GOES TO THE DEAD-LETTER OFFICE

Ross Carpenter applies for a singing job at the Pirates Den, and Sam (Robert Strauss) asks him to go on that night. One of the songs Ross sings is the Otis Blackwell–Winfield Scott composition "Return to Sender."

Elvis's single of the song zipped to number two on *Billboard*'s Hot 100 chart, where it stayed for five consecutive weeks. "Return to Sender" spent a total of sixteen weeks on the chart. This first-class song hit the Rhythm & Blues chart as well. There "Return to Sender" posted a twelve-week stay, peaking at number five. The song even put its stamp on the chart in England. "Return to Sender" became the first number one single to feature a saxophone (played expertly by Boots Randolph) and stayed at the top for three weeks.

In *Girls! Girls! Girls!*, after Ross sings "Return to Sender," the audience begs

for more. Ross extends his set although he has a date with Laurel Dodge (Laurel Goodwin). When the lady arrives and she finds Ross with Robin Gantner (Stella Stevens), Laurel is furious. Laurel and Ross have a confrontation, and the date they had looked forward to is sent to the dead-letter office.

SHARING THE MUSICAL SPOTLIGHT

In *Girls! Girls! Girls!*, Elvis shares the musical spotlight with Stella Stevens and the Four Amigos.

At the anniversary party for Mama and Papa Stavros, the Four Amigos sing "Mama." Elvis had recorded this song, written by Charles O'Curran and Dudley Brooks, for the film, but his version was cut.

Girls! Girls! Girls! marked the first time that Stella Stevens sang in a film, and she was a hit with a couple of standards, "Never Let Me Go" and "The Nearness of You."

Written by Jay Livingston and Ray Evans, "Never Let Me Go" was introduced by Nat King Cole in Paramount's 1956 film *The Scarlet Hour.* Gladys Swarthout introduced "The Nearness of You" in Paramount's 1938 film *Romance in the Dark.* The ballad was written by Ned Washington and Hoagy Carmichael.

DID YOU KNOW THAT...

- *Girls! Girls! Girls!* was not the original title for Elvis's 1962 film? *A Girl in Every Port* and *Welcome Aboard* were batted around as possible titles until *Gumbo Yu-Yu* was chosen a few months before filming began. That was dropped in favor of *Girls! Girls! Girls!* a month before filming started.

- Location filming was done in Hawaii? Cast and crew were in the Aloha State for most of April 1962. Interior shots were completed at the Paramount studio.

- Elvis's arrival in Hawaii caused pandemonium? Thousands of fans mobbed him, and he was lucky enough to lose only his diamond ring, a tie clip, and a watch.

- Elvis danced the Twist in *Girls! Girls! Girls!?* He added the hip motion to his performances of "I Don't Wanna Be Tied" and "Return to Sender."

- Elvis and Laurel Goodwin danced the flamenco in *Girls! Girls! Girls!?* Their vigorous, rhythmic dance took place during "The Walls Have Ears" number. After *Girls! Girls! Girls!* which marked Goodwin's film debut, she had roles in *Papa's Delicate Condition* (1963), *Stage to Thunder Rock* (1964), and *The Glory Guys* (1965).

- Actress Stella Stevens, who played Robin Gantner, was *Playboy*'s Playmate of the Month for January 1960? She played a vamp, Apassionata von Climax, in the film version of *Li'l Abner* (1959). Her other films include *The Courtship of Eddie's Father* (1963), *The Nutty Professor* (1963), *Synanon* (1965), *The Mad Room* (1969), *The Ballad of Cable Hogue* (1970), *The Poseidon Adventure* (1972), *Arnold* (1973), *Nickelodeon* (1976), and *The Manitou* (1978).

- Actor Robert Strauss, who played Sam, the nightclub owner, worked with Stella Stevens in *Li'l Abner* (1959)? Strauss was featured as Romeo Scragg in the Gene DePaul–Johnny Mercer musical, which was based on the Broadway version of Al Capp's comic strip. Another memorable performance for Strauss was the role of Animal in the Broadway production of *Stalag 17*. He re-created the role for the 1953 film version and was nominated for an Academy Award for Best Supporting Actor. His other films include *The Bridges at Toko-Ri* (1954), *The Seven Year Itch* (1955), *The Man with the Golden Arm* (1955), *Wake Me When It's Over* (1960), *The Thrill of It All* (1963), and *Fort Utah* (1968).

- Actor Benson Fong, who played Kin Yung, owner of Paradise Cove, played Tommy Chan, son of famous detective Charlie Chan, in a number of films in the series? Fong was featured in *Charlie Chan in the Secret Service* (1944), *The Chinese Cat* (1944), *The Scarlet Clue* (1945), *The Red Dragon* (1945), *The Shanghai Cobra* (1945), and *Dark Alibi* (1946).

- The song "I Don't Want To" was cut from the final print of *Girls! Girls! Girls!?* Although the Janice Torre–Fred Spielman composition was eliminated, "I Don't Want To" was heard in the trailer for the film. The other songs given the boot were "Plantation Rock," "Potpourri," and "Twist Me Loose."

- *Girls! Girls! Girls!* had its world premiere in Honolulu? The premiere was held on October 31, and the film opened nationally on November 21, 1962.

- Despite its late-in-the-year release, *Girls! Girls! Girls!* earned $2.6 million in 1962? *Variety* ranked the film number thirty-one for the year.

GIRLS! GIRLS! GIRLS! TRIVIA QUIZ

1. What was the name of Ross Carpenter's charter fishing boat?

2. What was the name of the sailboat built by Ross and his father?

3. Where were Laurel and Ross supposed to have lunch?

4. At what time did Laurel and Ross agree to meet for the Stavros anniversary party?

5. Where did Kin and Madam Yung live?

6. What tasks did Madam Yung assign to Laurel and Ross?

7. Who said: "I like you. You remind me of me."?

8. Where was Laurel from?

9. Where did Laurel find a job?

10. What was Laurel's address?

11. With what did Ross put out the oven fire in Laurel's apartment?

12. What was Wesley Johnson's nickname for Ross?

13. How much tuna did Ross and his crew bring in during their first run?

14. What was the price Wesley Johnson wanted for the sailboat?

15. What special quality did Kin Yung's cat, Kapoo, possess?

IT HAPPENED AT THE WORLD'S FAIR

(METRO–GOLDWYN–MAYER, 1963)

PLOT

*W*hen their airplane is confiscated by the sheriff because of bad debts, Elvis and his copilot hitchhike to Seattle to seek money-making opportunities. There Elvis becomes responsible for the niece of a Chinese farmer and involved with an attractive nurse. A suspected double cross, a runaway child, and a smuggling deal turned sour play themselves out against the background of the 1962 World's Fair.

CAST

Elvis Presley	Mike Edwards
Joan O'Brien	Diane Warren
Gary Lockwood	Danny Burke
Vicky Tiu	Sue-Lin
H. M. Wynant	Vince Bradley
Edith Atwater	Head Nurse
Guy Raymond	Barney Thatcher
Dorothy Green	Miss Ettinger
Kam Tong	Walter Ling
Yvonne Craig	Dorothy Johnson
Russell Thorson	Sheriff Garland
Olan Soule	Henry Johnson
Jacqueline Dewitt	Emma Johnson

CREW

Ted Richmond	Producer
Norman Taurog	Director

Si Rose and Seaman Jacobs	Screenplay
Col. Tom Parker	Technical Advisor
The Jordanaires and the Mello Men	Vocal Backgrounds
Jack Baker	Staging of Musical Numbers

SONGS
"Beyond the Bend" • "Relax" • "Take Me to the Fair" •
"They Remind Me Too Much of You" • "One Broken Heart for Sale" •
"I'm Falling in Love Tonight" • "Cotton Candy Land" • "A World of Our Own" •
"How Would You Like to Be" • "Happy Ending"

"ONE BROKEN HEART FOR SALE" PLUS AN EXTRA VERSE

Otis Blackwell and Winfield Scott composed "One Broken Heart for Sale" for *It Happened at the World's Fair*. In the film, Mike Edwards (Elvis) sings the song at the trailer park. Movie audiences received a bonus because the film version of "One Broken Heart for Sale" contains one extra verse.

The single release, which kept its beat on *Billboard*'s Hot 100 chart for nine weeks, eventually reached number eleven. On the Rhythm & Blues chart, "One Broken Heart for Sale" was hardly a cardiac closeout—the song hit number twenty-one.

A SOUVENIR FROM IT HAPPENED AT THE WORLD'S FAIR

Fans could buy a souvenir of Elvis's adventures at the 1962 World's Fair: the RCA LP *It Happened at the World's Fair*.

This soundtrack album, which contained all ten songs, glided as swiftly as a monorail onto *Billboard*'s Top LPs chart. There it stayed for twenty-six weeks, reaching number four. The stereo version of the LP stayed for seventeen weeks on the Stereo LPs chart and peaked at number fifteen.

PROTECTING THE KING

Although filming for *It Happened at the World's Fair* began in August 1962 at MGM's studio in Culver City, cameras moved to Seattle in early September for the fair sequences. And, of course, Elvis went with them.

The probability of fair goers mingling with and mauling the King was too harrowing a thought for MGM executives. So the studio arranged for a contingent of Pinkerton plainclothes detectives to accompany Elvis during every off-camera moment. That kept the King safe from the adoring multitudes.

When Elvis returned to MGM from location shooting, he acquired a dressing room that was fit for a king. Elvis moved his belongings into Clark Gable's old dressing room. Gable, known as the King of Hollywood, had used the dressing room during his twenty-four-year association with MGM.

ONE GIRL IN ELVIS'S LITTLE BLACK BOOK

"You spend all your dough on dolls and duds," Danny Burke (Gary Lockwood) complains to Mike Edwards. Indeed, after Danny and Mike complete their crop dusting job, Mike heads to town not in search of duds but in search of dolls. He fingers his little black book and decides to visit Dorothy Johnson (Yvonne Craig).

In the Johnson living room, Dorothy fends off Mike's romantic overtures by offering to make iced tea, answering the telephone, trying to eat an apple, and attempting to light a cigarette. Mike rebuffs those attempts while singing "Relax." Once they are in each other's arms, Dorothy's parents return home suddenly. Mr. Johnson (Olan Soule) runs for his gun, and Mike runs for his life.

In real life, during production of *It Happened at the World's Fair*, Elvis dated Yvonne Craig. Their dates were more sedate and usually included dinner and just watching television, proving that life does not always imitate art.

DID YOU KNOW THAT...

- Several working titles were proposed for *It Happened at the World's Fair*? Early titles considered were *Mister, Will You Marry Me; Take Me Out to the Fair;* and *Take Me to the Fair.*

- *It Happened at the World's Fair* featured a number of actual World's Fair attractions? These included the Monorail Ride, Skyride, Dream Car Exhibit, Bell Telephone Exhibit, Floating City of Tomorrow, Theme Building, Science Exhibit, Filipino Building, Space Needle, and the restaurant in the Space Needle.

- The price tag for Elvis's *It Happened at the World's Fair* wardrobe was ninety-three hundred dollars? That chunk of change purchased ten suits, four sports jackets, thirty shirts, fifteen pairs of slacks, two cashmere coats, and fifty-five ties.

- The real name of actor Gary Lockwood is John Yusolfsky? While the actor was working on his debut film, *Tall Story* (1960), Director Josh Logan suggested that he adopt the surname Lockwood, which was Logan's middle name. Lockwood had the role of Cliff Macy in Elvis's seventh film, *Wild in the Country* (1961). In the 1963–1964 television season, Lockwood starred as marine corps lieutenant William (Bill) Rice in "The Lieutenant."

- Vicky Tiu, who played Sue-Lin, made her film debut in *It Happened at the World's Fair*? In fact, Elvis's film was the only motion picture in which she had a role.

66 • Actress Yvonne Craig had a role in a later Elvis movie? Craig played the role of Azalea Tatum in *Kissin' Cousins* (1964). One of Craig's television roles was that of Linda Sue Faversham, friend of Dobie Gillis, on *The Many Loves of Dobie Gillis* (1959–1963). From 1967 to 1968, Craig appeared on "Batman" as Commissioner Gordon's daughter, Barbara. She was a young librarian who fought crime as Batgirl.

• Actor Kurt Russell, the boy who kicks Elvis, began his career playing cute, blond kids? His film debut was in *The Absent-Minded Professor* (1961), and his other films include *Charley and the Angel* (1973) and *Superdad* (1974). As an adult, Russell played Elvis in the 1979 television movie *Elvis*. *Elvis* was an ABC-TV broadcast on February 11, 1979, which aired opposite two mega movies, *Gone With the Wind* (starring Clark Gable, Vivien Leigh, Leslie Howard, and Olivia de Havilland) on CBS and *One Flew Over the Cuckoo's Nest* (starring Jack Nicholson and Louise Fletcher) on NBC. In the Nielsen ratings, *Elvis* had a 27.3 rating, *Gone With the Wind* had a 24.3 rating, and *One Flew Over the Cuckoo's Nest* had a 22.5 rating. Kurt Russell was later nominated for an Emmy Award for his portrayal of the King of Rock and Roll in *Elvis*.

• *It Happened at the World's Fair* debuted in Los Angeles? The film opened there on April 3, 1963, and opened nationally on April 10. The film earned $2.25 million in 1963.

IT HAPPENED AT THE WORLD'S FAIR TRIVIA QUIZ

1. What was the name of the plane owned by Mike Edwards and Danny Burke?

2. How much did Mike and Danny earn from their crop-dusting job?

3. What was Dorothy Johnson's street address?

4. How much did Danny lose at gambling?

5. What gift did Sue-Lin tell Mike she had received for her birthday?

6. What name did Sue-Lin give to the large stuffed dog she won at the fair?

7. How much was a seven-course Chinese dinner at the fair?

8. Why did Mike and Sue-Lin visit the dispensary?

9. Who did Danny characterize as "the worst gin rummy player in the world"?

10. What was the name of the trailer park at which Mike and Danny stayed?

11. How much did Mike pay the boy to kick him in the shin?

12. In what government program had Diane Warren applied for a job?

13. How much did Vince Bradley advance to Danny?

14. Where did Mike find Sue-Lin?

15. What did Vince Bradley want Mike and Danny to smuggle into Canada?

FUN IN ACAPULCO

(Paramount, 1963)

PLOT

While working as a nightclub singer and relief lifeguard in Acapulco, Elvis tries to overcome a fear of heights that developed after a tragic trapeze accident. He is aided in his career aspirations by a shoe-shine boy and is entangled in romantic escapades with a lady bullfighter and the assistant social director of a hotel.

CAST

Elvis Presley	Mike Windgren
Ursula Andress	Margarita Dauphin
Elsa Cardenas	Dolores Gomez
Paul Lukas	Maximillian Dauphin
Larry Domasin	Raoul Almeido
Alejandro Rey	Moreno
Robert Carricart	Jose Garcia
Teri Hope	Janie Harkins
Mariachi Los Vaqueros	Themselves
Mariachi Aguila	Themselves
Howard McNear	Dr. John Stevers
Mary Treen	Mrs. Stevers
Alberto Morin	Mr. Ramirez, Manager of the Hilton
Salvador Baguez	Mr. Perez, Manager of La Perla
Edward Colmans	Mr. Delgado, Manager of the Ambassador
Martin Garralaga	Manager of the Tropicana Hotel
Charles Evans	Mr. Harkins

CREW

Hal B. Wallis .... Producer
Richard Thorpe .... Director
Allan Weiss .... Screenplay
Edith Head .... Costumes
Charles O'Curran .... Staging of Musical Numbers
Joseph J. Lilley .... Scoring and Conducting of Music
The Jordanaires
and the Four Amigos .... Vocal Accompaniment
Col. Tom Parker .... Technical Advisor

SONGS

"Fun in Acapulco" • "Vino, Dinero y Amor" • "I Think I'm Gonna Like It Here" •
"Mexico" • "El Toro" • "Marguerita" • "The Bullfighter Was a Lady" •
"(There's) No Room to Rhumba in a Sports Car" • "Bossa Nova Baby" •
"You Can't Say No in Acapulco" • "Guadalajara"

ELVIS IS BOSS WITH "BOSSA NOVA BABY"

Tippy and the Clovers recorded "Bossa Nova Baby" in 1962 on the Tiger label. Their recording of the Jerry Leiber–Mike Stoller song went nowhere, baby.

When Elvis's single of "Bossa Nova Baby" was released, the song bounced onto *Billboard*'s Hot 100 chart, where it sambaed for ten weeks, peaking at number eight. The song peaked at number twenty on the Rhythm & Blues chart.

Only one other bossa nova record ever charted. That was "Blame It on the Bossa Nova" by Eydie Gorme. Her 1963 song hit number seven on the Hot 100 chart.

AND FOR AN ENCORE, "GUADALAJARA"

After making his spectacular dive at La Perla, Mike Windgren (Elvis) sings "Guadalajara." The song was written by Pepe Guizar but not for Elvis's 1963 film. "Guadalajara" was written much earlier and became popular because of the recording Xavier Cugat made in 1944 for Columbia Records.

FUN IN THE LP FUN IN ACAPULCO

The eleven songs featured in Elvis's film *Fun in Acapulco* were included on the LP of the same name. However, fans were treated to two additional songs as a bonus. "Love Me Tonight" and "Slowly but Surely" were the extras included on the album, and they appear as the last two tracks on side two. "Slowly but Surely" was heard in the film *Tickle Me*. The LP reached number three on *Billboard*'s Top LPs chart, and the album had a total chart run of twenty-four weeks.

DID YOU KNOW THAT...

- Elvis did not travel to Acapulco to film *Fun in Acapulco*? All of Elvis's scenes were filmed at Paramount studios in Hollywood.

- Actress Elsa Cardenas, who played the bullfighter Dolores Gomez, debuted in a film that had a bullfighting theme? *The Brave One* (1956) told the story of a peasant boy and his love for a bull that was destined for the arena. Cardenas's other film credits include *Giant* (1956), *For the Love of Mike* (1960), *Taggart* (1964), and *The Wild Bunch* (1969).

- Actress Ursula Andress made her American film debut playing Margarita Dauphin in *Fun in Acapulco*? Other films made by the Swiss-born actress include *Dr. No* (1962), *Four for Texas* (1963), *She* (1964), *What's New Pussycat?* (1965), *The Blue Max* (1966), and *Casino Royale* (1967).

- Actor Paul Lukas, who played Maximillian Dauphin, was born on a train while his mother was traveling to Budapest, Hungary? His film career began in Europe. Then Lukas was brought to Hollywood to appear in *Loves of an Actress* (1928) which launched a distinguished American career. His films include *Little Women* (1933), *The Three Musketeers* (1935), *Dodsworth* (1936), *The Lady Vanishes* (1938), *20,000 Leagues Under the Sea* (1954), *Tender Is the Night* (1962), and *Lord Jim* (1965). Lukas won an Academy Award for Best Actor for his role in *Watch on the Rhine* (1943).

- Actor Alejandro Rey, who played Elvis's nemesis Moreno, was known for portraying a handsome playboy on television? He played the role of Carlos Ramirez, rich owner of a disco, patron of the Convent San Tanco, and admirer of Sister Bertrille (Sally Fields) on the series, "The Flying Nun" (1967–1970). His films include *The Wild Pack* (1971), *Mr. Majestyk* (1974), *Breakout* (1975), and *Moscow on the Hudson* (1984).

- Paramount had a unique promotional gimmick for *Fun in Acapulco*? The studio created passports to use during their promotion of the film and even showed a passport on movie posters for the film.

FUN IN ACAPULCO TRIVIA QUIZ

1. Who was the family for which Mike Windgren worked as a sailor on their boat?

2. What were the first names of the Four Amigos?

3. At what nightclub did Mike meet Dolores Gomez?

4. What was the price of a dance at the nightclub?

5. What beverages did Mike order for the Four Amigos?

6. Where did Mike and Raoul Almeido agree to meet the next day?

7. What singer did Mike replace at the Acapulco Hilton?

8. What was the name of the cabaret at the Acapulco Hilton at which Mike appeared?

9. How much did it cost Mike to send a telegram to his parents?

10. Where was Mike's hometown?

11. How high were the La Perla cliffs?

12. What percentage did Raoul want as Mike's manager?

13. What was Mike's nickname for Margarita?

14. What was Moreno's nickname for Mike?

15. What was the name of the trapeze act of which Mike was a part?

KISSIN' COUSINS

(METRO–GOLDWYN–MAYER, 1964)

PLOT

*E*lvis is an air force officer charged with persuading a hillbilly family to lease their land to the government for use as a missile site. He tangles with his look-alike cousin and a passel of beautiful mountain ladies.

CAST

Elvis Presley	Josh Morgan
Elvis Presley	Jodie Tatum
Arthur O'Connell	Pappy Tatum
Glenda Farrell	Ma Tatum
Jack Albertson	Capt. Robert Salbo
Pam Austin	Selena Tatum
Yvonne Craig	Azalea Tatum
Cynthia Pepper	Pfc. Midge Riley
Donald Woods	Gen. Alvin Donford
Tommy Farrell	M. Sgt. George Bailey
Hortense Petra	Dixie Cate
Robert Carson	Gen. Sam Kruger
Maureen Reagan	Lorraine, Leader of the Kittyhawks

CREW

Sam Katzman	Producer
Gene Nelson	Director
Gerald Drayson Adams and Gene Nelson	Screenplay
Col. Tom Parker	Technical Advisor

SONGS
"Kissin' Cousins" • "Smokey Mountain Boy" • "There's Gold in the Mountains"
• "One Boy, Two Little Girls" • "Catchin' on Fast" • "Tender Feeling" •
"Barefoot Ballad" • "Once Is Enough" • "Kissin' Cousins (No. 2)"

A DOUBLE SMACK OF "KISSIN' COUSINS"

The title tune, "Kissin' Cousins," was written by Fred Wise and Randy Starr. The song endeared itself to fans, who kept the single on *Billboard*'s Hot 100 chart for nine weeks, topping out at number twelve.

The song featured at the end of the film, "Kissin' Cousins (No. 2)," was written by Bill Giant, Bernie Baum, and Florence Kaye. This was a completely different song from the title tune. Both songs were featured on the *Kissin' Cousins* LP. The album stayed on *Billboard*'s Top LPs chart for thirty weeks, peaking at number six.

SONGWRITING TRIPLE THREAT: GIANT, BAUM, AND KAYE

For *Kissin' Cousins*, the songwriting team of Bill Giant, Bernie Baum, and Florence Kaye composed five of the nine songs: "There's Gold in the Mountains", "One Boy, Two Little Girls," "Catchin' on Fast," "Tender Feeling", and "Kissin' Cousins (No. 2)."

This trio is something of a songwriting triple threat because they composed a total of forty-one songs that Elvis recorded, many of which were featured in his films. Among their songs are "(You're the) Devil in Disguise," "Roustabout," and "Paradise, Hawaiian Style."

ANOTHER KING ON THE SET: SAM KATZMAN

Elvis was not the only "King" on the set of *Kissin' Cousins*. Hollywood called producer Sam Katzman the "King of the Quickies" because he made low-budget films in record time.

Prior to producing *Kissin' Cousins*, Katzman had completed *Hootenanny Hoot* (1963) in eight and a half days. He finished the film biography of Hank Williams, *Your Cheatin' Heart* (1964), in fifteen days. *Kissin' Cousins* took less than two and a half weeks to shoot in October 1963.

Kissin' Cousins was budgeted at $800,000. When it was released nationally in April 1964, the film grossed $1,750,000 in its first six weeks. By the end of the year, *Kissin' Cousins* had earned $2.8 million.

Katzman's other films include *Spooks Run Wild* (1941), *Jungle Jim* (1948), *Rock Around the Clock* (1956), and Elvis's nineteenth film, *Harum Scarum* (1965).

KISSES FOR KISSIN' COUSINS

As gimmicks to promote *Kissin' Cousins*, some theaters offered kisses of the chocolate variety to their patrons at showings of the film. Other theaters featured kisses of the charitable kind. Those theaters set up booths in their lobbies with volunteers selling "Kisses for Charity." Either way, Elvis moviegoers could indulge in lip-smacking delight.

INCOMING KITTYHAWKS

When Josh Morgan (Elvis), Captain Salbo (Jack Albertson), and the platoon of soldiers arrive at the Tatum house, there's soon a hoopin' and a hollerin' as the Kittyhawks descend upon the scene and attack the menfolk. Pappy Tatum fires his shotgun and chases the girls off.

"Those are awful pretty girls, Pappy," Josh says. "Why are they so much trouble?"

"Them and their kind have been runnin' around this here mountain for years, stirring up the game, looking for men to marry who'll give them boy babies, that's why," Pappy says.

"There ain't been nothin' but gals born in Kittyhawk Valley in twenty years," Ma Tatum says.

Metro–Goldwyn–Mayer hired thirteen actresses to play this band of lust-seeking mountain maidens. The actress selected to play Lorraine, the leader of the Kittyhawks, was Maureen Reagan. Her film debut was in *It's a Great Feeling* (1949), a film that spoofed Hollywood and featured cameo appearances by many Warner Bros. stars, including Maureen's parents, Ronald Reagan and Jane Wyman.

KISSIN' COUSINS'S PRESLEY PERPLEXERS

Here and there in Elvis's films are instances that cause the keen-eyed fan to do a double take: minor mistakes resulting from errors in continuity, slips in the editing process, or goofs that are simply unexplainable. Did you catch or miss any of these Presley Perplexers in *Kissin' Cousins*?

- Lance Le Gault played Elvis's on-screen double in *Kissin' Cousins*. When both characters were in a scene—for instance, Elvis in the blond wig, Lance in the black wig — Le Gault kept his back to the camera. Yet in the fight scene between the cousins, Le Gault was filmed facing the camera. Producer Sam Katzman left the footage in because he didn't think anyone would notice. Oops! Was he wrong!

- While on the telephone at the newspaper office, reporter Dixie Cate thanks Mr. Billingsley for his tip about the military buying a large order of bikinis. Later, when she confronts Josh Morgan, she indicates that the tip came from Mr. Billings.

- Josh Morgan drives to Big Smokey Mountain in a jeep with the serial number 11A-3142491. Yet later, when General Donford arrives at Big Smokey Mountain, he's using the same jeep.

DID YOU KNOW THAT...

- Location filming was done at Big Bear Lake in California? For interior shots, cast and crew used MGM's studios in Culver City.

- There were originally ten songs planned for *Kissin' Cousins*? Elvis recorded "Anyone (Could Fall in Love with You)," but the song was eliminated from the final print.

- Actress Pam Austin, who played Selena Tatum, was the "Dodge Girl" in the automobile maker's print advertisements and television commercials? In addition to that work, Austin had roles in movies such as *Hootenanny Hoot* (1963), *The Perils of Pauline* (1967), and *The Phynx* (1970). She was also in the pilot for "Rowan and Martin's Laugh-In" (1967).

- Actress Glenda Farrell, who played Ma Tatum, was the wisecracking, mystery-solving reporter in the Torchy Blane film series? Farrell made six Torchy Blane films for Warner Bros. Her other film work includes roles in *Lucky Boy* (1929), *Little Caesar* (1930), *I Am a Fugitive from a Chain Gang* (1932), *Gold Diggers of 1935* (1935), and *Tiger by the Tail* (1968).

- Glenda Farrell sang a duet in *Kissin' Cousins*? She shared the vocal honors on "Pappy, Won't You Please Come Home" with the Tatum's hound dog.

- Actor Arthur O'Connell, who played Pappy Tatum, had a similar paternal role in an earlier Elvis film? O'Connell played Pop Kwimper in *Follow That Dream*. He took his paternal persona to television commercials for Crest toothpaste and was known as the friendly druggist, Mr. Goodwin.

- Actor Jack Albertson, who played Captain Salbo, was a military man in a television series? He played Lt. Comdr. Virgil Stoner, executive officer of the destroyer USS *Appleby* on the series "Ensign O'Toole" (1962–1963).

- Actor Tommy Farrell, who played M. Sgt. George Bailey, is the son of Glenda Farrell? Tommy Farrell had a role in another Elvis film, *Girl Happy* (1965).

- *Kissin' Cousins* had a sneak preview? A sneak peek was offered to patrons of the Crest Theatre in North Long Beach, California, in February 1964. The film premiered in Phoenix, Arizona, in March 1964.

KISSIN' COUSINS TRIVIA QUIZ

1. What was the name of the Pentagon plan to lease the property owned by the Tatum family?

2. What type of jet did Josh Morgan fly?

3. What air force aerobatic team was Josh a member of?

4. Where was Josh born?

5. How many days was Josh given to obtain the lease?

6. What was the name of Josh's great-great aunt who had married Jubal Tatum?

7. What was tied to the aerial of the walkie-talkie that Josh carried as a cease-fire sign?

8. What was the name of the Tatum clan's hound dog?

9. Where did the army establish its camp?

10. According to WAC stenographer Midge Riley, what were her measurements?

11. What was the code name of the search party led by Josh that was looking for Pappy?

12. What was the name of the gorge in which Pappy was found stuck in a tree?

13. Over what game did Josh try to convince Pappy to lease the land?

14. What was the name of Ma Tatum's moonshine?

15. How much money did the government agree to pay per month to lease the Tatum land?

16.

VIVA LAS VEGAS

(METRO–GOLDWYN–MAYER, 1964)

PLOT

*O*n the road to winning the Grand Prix racing car competition in Las Vegas, Elvis becomes temporarily detoured by engine problems, an Italian racing rival, and a beautiful swimming instructor.

CAST

Elvis Presley	Lucky Jackson
Ann-Margret	Rusty Martin
Cesare Danova	Count Elmo Mancini
William Demarest	Mr. Martin
Nicky Blair	Shorty Farnsworth
Jack Carter	Himself
The Forte Four	Themselves

CREW

Jack Cummings and George Sidney	Producers
George Sidney	Director
Sally Benson	Screenplay
George Stoll	Music
Col. Tom Parker	Technical Advisor

SONGS

"Viva Las Vegas" • "The Yellow Rose of Texas"/"The Eyes of Texas" •
"The Lady Loves Me" • "C'mon Everybody" • "Today, Tomorrow and Forever" •
"What'd I Say" • "Santa Lucia" • "If You Think I Don't Love You" •
"I Need Somebody to Lean On"

VIVA POMUS AND SHUMAN

"Viva Las Vegas," the title song to Elvis's 1964 movie, was written by one of the great songwriting teams of the rock and roll era, Jerome "Doc" Pomus and Mort Shuman.

Brooklyn-born "Doc" Pomus began his career as a blues singer. Although he recorded steadily in the early 1950s, he turned more toward writing songs for other artists. He composed "Boogie Woogie Country Girl" for Joe Turner and "Lonely Avenue" for Ray Charles.

After meeting New York City-born Mort Shuman, Pomus recognized musical talent in the younger man and encouraged Shuman to study songwriting. The pair scored their first hit with "A Teenager in Love," which Dion and the Belmonts took to number five in 1959. One year later, they really celebrated as their song "Save the Last Dance for Me," recorded by the Drifters, hit the number one spot.

The Pomus-Shuman partnership lasted seven years. During that time, their collaboration produced phenomenal hits for various artists. For the Drifters, Pomus and Shuman wrote "This Magic Moment," "Sweets for My Sweet," and "I Count the Tears." They composed "Seven Day Weekend" for Gary "U.S." Bonds and "Spanish Lace" for Gene McDaniels. For Elvis, they wrote "Doin' the Best I Can," "Double Trouble," "Gonna Get Back Home Somehow," "(Marie's the Name) His Latest Flame," "I Need Somebody to Lean On," "Kiss Me Quick," "Little Sister," "(It's a) Long Lonely Highway," "A Mess of Blues," "Never Say Yes," "Night Rider," "Surrender," "Suspicion," and "What Every Woman Lives For."

The pair hit the jackpot with "Viva Las Vegas," which Elvis sings three times in the movie: over the opening credits, in the hotel's talent contest, and at the end of the film. With "What'd I Say" on the flip side, "Viva Las Vegas" rolled like a hot pair of dice onto *Billboard*'s Hot 100 chart. During its seven-week stay, the song peaked at number twenty-nine.

Pomus cowrote Elvis hits with other writers. He wrote "Girl Happy" with Norman Meade, "I Feel That I've Known You Forever" with Alan Jeffries, and "She's Not You" with Jerry Leiber and Mike Stoller. Mort Shuman scored a solo Elvis hit with "You'll Think of Me."

When you think of one of the great songwriting teams in the history of rock and roll, you'll think of Pomus and Shuman.

FLIP SIDE: "WHAT'D I SAY"

The flip side of "Viva Las Vegas" is the Ray Charles composition "What'd I Say." Charles recorded the song for Atlantic in 1959, and "What'd I Say" became his first million seller. Other artists have had success with the song, including Jerry Lee Lewis on the Sun label in 1961, Bobby Darin on the Atco label in 1962, and Rare Earth on the Rare Earth label in 1972.

Elvis's version of the song was released in 1964. "What'd I Say" stayed on *Billboard*'s Hot 100 chart for six weeks and peaked at number twenty-one. The song was a concert favorite.

MUSICAL NOTES

- Lucky Jackson (Elvis) sings "The Yellow Rose of Texas" and "The Eyes of Texas" to clear the rowdy Texans from the Swingers Casino. "The Yellow Rose of Texas" was a march written in 1853, and the song gained popularity during the Civil War. A version of the song was a million seller for Mitch Miller in 1955. "The Eyes of Texas" was written in 1903, and its melody was based on the song "I've Been Working on the Railroad." "The Eyes of Texas" is the fight song of the University of Texas Longhorns.

- "The Lady Loves Me" is a duet between Elvis and Ann-Margret. Although the song, written by Sid Tepper and Roy C. Bennett, was deliciously sassy, RCA chose not to release "The Lady Loves Me" for twenty years. The song appears as the first track on side two of the 1983 LP *Elvis—A Legendary Performer, Volume 4.*

- "Today, Tomorrow and Forever" was written by Bill Giant, Bernie Baum, and Florence Kaye. They based their composition on "Liebestraume" written by Franz Liszt in 1850.

- "Santa Lucia" was written in 1850 by Italian songwriter Teodoro Cottrau. Thomas Oliphant wrote the English lyrics.

- "If You Think I Don't Need You" was written by Red West and Joe Cooper.

- The Forte Four perform "The Climb" in *Viva Las Vegas*. This Jerry Leiber–Mike Stoller composition was recorded by the Coasters in 1962.

- Ann-Margret performs two solo songs in the film: "Appreciation" and "My Rival."

- Elvis recorded three additional songs for *Viva Las Vegas,* but they were not used: "You're the Boss," "Do the Vega," and "Night Life."

VIVA LAS VEGAS BANNED

Viva Las Vegas was released in Europe under the title *Love in Las Vegas.* And the Roman Catholic authorities on the island of Gozo in the Mediterranean Sea were not pleased, no matter what the film was called.

The Gozo College of Parish Priests called the film indecent. Priests condemned the movie from the pulpit. Catholics were urged to abstain from seeing the film. As a result of the protests, the Aurora Theatre on Gozo canceled all the showings of Elvis's latest picture. Only on the nearby island of Malta were fans able to enjoy a full run of *Viva Las Vegas.*

VIVA LAS VEGAS PRESLEY PERPLEXERS

Here and there in Elvis's films are instances that cause the keen-eyed fan to do a double take: minor mistakes resulting from errors in continuity, slips in the editing process, or goofs that are simply unexplainable. Did you catch or miss any of these Presley Perplexers in *Viva Las Vegas*?

• When Count Elmo Mancini (Cesare Danova) notices Lucky Jackson (Elvis) entering the garage, His Grace is smoking a cigarette. Lucky answers questions about his car from the other drivers and pays the garage owner for the use of the facility. A moment later, Mancini approaches Lucky, the two discuss racing, and then the Count allows Lucky to inspect the racing car.

As the two slide underneath the vehicle, Lucky says "Well, you have made some changes, haven't you?" Amazingly, the Count replies clearly, "I got my little secrets" while holding the smoldering cigarette firmly between his lips, leading some viewers to believe that Mancini is a ventriloquist as well as a race car driver.

Then when Rusty Martin (Ann-Margret) asks for help with her auto, Mancini and Lucky emerge from beneath the car to offer assistance. By this time, Mancini should be ready to tamp out a mere stub of a cigarette, yet the cigarette he throws on the floor appears to be the same length as it was when the scene started.

• After a day of fun-filled activities, Lucky brings Rusty home.

"I never had a better day," Lucky says, gazing lovingly into Rusty's eyes.

"Me, too."

"Let's don't let it end," Lucky suggests.

"I'll go change."

Rusty leaves, then reappears a mere thirty-five seconds later in a new outfit, with her makeup perfect, and her hair beautifully coiffed. Her quick change was probably due to the fact that Lucky had just begun singing "Today, Tomorrow and Forever" and what girl would want to miss out on that?

• While discussing Lucky's racing, Rusty shares a dream she has: "When I get married, I want a little white house with a tree in the front yard. A real kind of tree with green leaves."

The conversation leads to an argument, and the scene ends as Rusty walks out on Lucky. In the very next scene, an angry Rusty arrives home. Seconds later, a deliveryman appears at the door with a tree, making this perhaps the fastest floral delivery in the history of motion pictures.

• Working as a waiter, Lucky carries a tray loaded with luncheon dishes through the garden of the hotel. He spots his partner and mechanic, Shorty, casually dressed, lounging in a chaise, and smoking a cigar. Lucky asks why Shorty isn't in his waiter's uniform.

"I'm not a waiter anymore and neither are you," Shorty tells him. "The Italian just couldn't stand us race drivers being waiters so he paid off our debt to this joint. From now on, we're free."

Their freedom is apparently short-lived. In the next scene, Shorty is back in the kitchen and Lucky is serving dinner to Rusty and Mancini in the Count's suite. Their sudden re-employment is never explained.

DID YOU KNOW THAT...

- *Viva Las Vegas* was not the original title for the film? The original title was *Only Girl in Town.*

- The Old Vegas Amusement Park in Henderson, Nevada, was the setting for the western shootout scene? Other locations used in *Viva Las Vegas* included the drag strip in Henderson, Nevada, the skeet-shooting range at the Tropicana Hotel, the University of Nevada–Las Vegas gymnasium, and the swimming pool at the Flamingo Hotel.

- Actress Ann-Margret was born in Valsjobyn, Sweden? Her family moved to the United States when Ann-Margret was five years old. Later, while singing and dancing in a nightclub, she was discovered by comedian George Burns, who helped her break into films. Ann-Margret's film credits include *Pocketful of Miracles* (1961), *State Fair* (1962), *Bye Bye Birdie* (1962), *Bus Riley's Back in Town* (1965), *Stagecoach* (1966), *Carnal Knowledge* (1971), *Tommy* (1975), *The Cheap Detective* (1978), *52 Pickup* (1986) and *Grumpy Old Men* (1993). She had a role in the television miniseries *The Two Mrs. Grenvilles* (1987). During the filming of *Viva Las Vegas,* there were reports of a romance between Ann-Margret and Elvis.

- Actor William Demarest, who played Rusty Martin's father, played fatherly roles on two television series? Demarest is familiar to audiences as Uncle Charley O'Casey in the television series "My Three Sons" (1960–1972). He also played Mr. Daly, Kathy Williams's father, on "Make Room for Daddy" (1953–1957) and "The Danny Thomas Show" (1957–1964). Demarest began in vaudeville, worked as a carnival and stock performer and was even a professional boxer before he made his screen debut in 1927. He received an Academy Award nomination for his role in *The Jolson Story* (1946). His film credits include *Fingerprints* (1927), *The Jazz Singer* (1927), *Broadway Melody* (1929), *Rebecca of Sunnybrook Farm* (1938), *Mr. Smith Goes to Washington* (1939), *Son of Flubber* (1963), *It's a Mad, Mad, Mad, Mad World* (1963), *That Darn Cat* (1965), and *Won Ton, the Dog Who Saved Hollywood* (1976). In addition to his work in "My Three Sons," Demarest also had roles in "Tales of Wells Fargo" (1957–1962) and "Love and Marriage" (1959–1960).

- Actor Cesare Danova, who played racing rival Count Elmo Mancini, is best known for playing suave Italian leading men? His film credits include *The Three Corsairs* (1952), *Crossed Swords* (1954), *Don Juan* (1955), *The Man Who Understood Women* (1959), *Cleopatra* (1963), *Gidget Goes to Rome* (1963), *Chamber of Horrors* (1966), *Che* (1969), and *National Lampoon's Animal House* (1978).

- Comedian Jack Carter, who played himself in *Viva Las Vegas,* was not only a nightclub and television performer but also an actor? His film roles include *The Horizontal Lieutenant* (1962), *The Extraordinary Seaman* (1969), *Won Ton, The Dog Who Saved Hollywood* (1976), *History of the World, Part 1* (1981), and *Hambone and Hillie* (1984).

- Actor Nicky Blair, who played Shorty Farnsworth, Lucky's friend and mechanic, had roles in three other films that featured Las Vegas? Blair was in *Crashing Las Vegas* (1956), *Ocean's Eleven* (1960), and *Diamonds Are Forever* (1971).

- The spectacular race sequence was spliced together from a series of special-effects shots? In fact, forty-three special-effects shots were used in the editing process. Racing sounds were added, and a seamless race sequence resulted.

- MGM initially released *Viva Las Vegas* abroad rather than in the United States? The film did boffo box office in Tokyo and Manila and other Far Eastern cities. In the United States, *Viva Las Vegas* premiered in New York City in April 1964 and opened nationally two months later.

- *Viva Las Vegas* grossed $4.6 million dollars for 1964? *Variety* rated the film as the fourteenth highest grosser of the year.

VIVA LAS VEGAS TRIVIA QUIZ

1. What was the name of the machine shop owner who had the engine Lucky Jackson wanted to buy?

2. What was the name of the Las Vegas garage where Lucky met Rusty Martin?

3. What was the number on Lucky's race car?

4. What was the number on Count Elmo Mancini's car?

5. What was the name of the rowdy group at the Swingers Casino?

6. Where did Rusty Martin work as a swimming instructor?

7. Why had Rusty's family moved to Las Vegas?

8. What was Rusty's dream concerning her father?

9. Who was the race car driver who crashed and was killed during a race?

10. What appetizer did Lucky serve in a silver bowl to Rusty and Count Mancini?

11. What type of coin did host Jack Carter use in the toss to decide the winner of the talent contest?

12. What did Rusty call in the coin toss?

13. What first prize did Lucky win in the talent contest?

14. What second prize did Rusty win in the talent contest?

15. How was Count Mancini eliminated from the race?

17.

ROUSTABOUT

(PARAMOUNT, 1964)

PLOT

*E*lvis joins a carnival as a handyman, rescues the business from fore-closure by creditors, and finds true love on the midway.

CAST

Elvis Presley	Charlie Rogers
Barbara Stanwyck	Maggie Morgan
Joan Freeman	Cathy Lean
Leif Erickson	Joe Lean
Sue Ane Langdon	Madame Mijanou
Pat Buttram	Harry Carver
Joan Staley	Marge
Dabbs Greer	Arthur Nielsen
Steve Brodie	Freddie
Norman Grabowski	Sam, a College Student
Jack Albertson	Lou
Jane Dulo	Hazel
Wilda Taylor	Little Egypt
Billy Barty	Billy
Richard Kiel	Strong Man

CREW

Hal B. Wallis	Producer
John Rich	Director
Anthony Lawrence and Allan Weiss	Screenplay
Edith Head	Costumes
The Jordanaires	Vocal Accompaniment
Col. Tom Parker	Technical Advisor

SONGS

"Roustabout" • "Poison Ivy League" • "Wheels on My Heels" •
"It's a Wonderful World" • "It's Carnival Time" • "Carny Town" •
"One Track Heart" • "Hard Knocks" • "Little Egypt" • "Big Love, Big Heartache"
• "There's a Brand New Day on the Horizon"

IT'S A WONDERFUL THING FOR "IT'S A WONDERFUL WORLD"

As he and Cathy Lean (Joan Freeman) enjoy the ride on the ferris wheel, Charlie Rogers (Elvis) sings "It's a Wonderful World." The composers of the song— Sid Tepper and Roy C. Bennett—were on top of the world when "It's a Wonderful World" was considered for an Academy Award nomination for Best Song. Unfortunately, the song was not nominated. However, it stands in the record books as the only Elvis song ever to be in contention for an Oscar nomination.

"ROUSTABOUT" REDUX

To promote *Roustabout*, Paramount Pictures distributed to selected theaters copies of a special single of the title song. Theater managers were to play side one before the film's release. Side one featured Elvis singing "Roustabout" and, at the end of the song, an announcer saying that *Roustabout* was coming soon to the theater.

Managers were to play the flip side once the film arrived at the theater. Side two featured the same take of "Roustabout" and, at the end of the song, an announcer saying that *Roustabout* was now playing. This "Roustabout" redux inspired ticket sales in much the same way as Charlie Rogers's singing efforts encouraged folks to buy tickets to the carnival.

"LITTLE EGYPT" CREATES A BIG PROBLEM

Jerry Leiber and Mike Stoller wrote "Little Egypt," which was recorded by the Coasters in 1961. The song shimmied its way to number twenty-three on *Billboard*'s Hot 100 chart. In 1964, Elvis recorded "Little Egypt" for use in *Roustabout*.

Three months after the national release of the film, professional dancer Little Egypt sued Paramount Pictures, RCA Victor, and Elvis Presley Music, Inc., for $2.5 million in damages. Her suit, filed in New York Supreme Court, also sought an injunction against showing *Roustabout* and selling the *Roustabout* LP.

Little Egypt contended that she did not authorize the use of the song "Little Egypt" nor the use of the name Little Egypt in the film. As a result, she claimed to have been irreparably harmed and held up to public ridicule. Her legal arguments did not sway the court, and Little Egypt lost her case.

EL'S ANGELS

Although Charlie Rogers rode a Honda in *Roustabout*, Elvis preferred a Harley–Davidson in real life. He would hop on his Harley and, with his buddies astride Triumphs, would ride around the hills of Bel Air, California. News reporters referred to the bikers as "El's Angels."

ROUSTABOUT'S SET-'EM-UP-AND-BREAK-'EM-DOWN PRODUCTION NOTES

The plan to film *Roustabout* was announced in May 1961, but production was delayed until March 1964, with some changes made along the way:

- *Right This Way Folks* was the original title for the film.

- Mae West was the actress chosen originally to portray Maggie Morgan. She subsequently changed her mind about playing the role.

DID YOU KNOW THAT...

- Producer Hal Wallis employed a large traveling carnival for the exterior shots? The carnival erected tents and built a midway on land near Thousand Oaks, California, to lend an air of authenticity to filming.

- Three stages were used for the interior shots? The doors to stages twelve, fourteen, and fifteen on the Paramount lot were opened, and the combined area accommodated the sets for the interior big-tent scenes. This was the first time in the history of the studio that the three stages were used together for one film.

- Actress Barbara Stanwyck was born Ruby Stevens? Stanwyck was known for playing tough, aggressive women, and she continued that tradition by playing the role of Maggie Morgan in *Roustabout*. She was nominated for Best Actress four times but failed to win Oscars for her performances in *Stella Dallas* (1937), *Ball of Fire* (1941), *Double Indemnity* (1944), and *Sorry, Wrong Number* (1948). She won a Special Academy Award in 1981 "for superlative creativity and unique contribution to the art of screen acting." When her career moved to television, she captured Emmy Awards for "The Barbara Stanwyck Show" (1960–1961), "The Big Valley" (1965–1969), and "The Thorn Birds" (1983).

- *Roustabout* was a reunion for actor Leif Erickson and actress Barbara Stanwyck? Both had had roles in *Sorry, Wrong Number* (1948). Erickson's film career included *Show Boat* (1951), *On the Waterfront* (1951), *Tea and Sympathy* (1957), and *The Carpetbaggers* (1964). On television he portrayed John Cannon, owner of the High Chapparal Ranch, in the 1967–1971 series "High Chapparal."

- Actress Raquel Welch made her movie debut in *Roustabout*? She played one of the two college girls who accompany their boyfriends to Mother's Tea House. Her memorable first line is: "Uh, how come they call this place a tea house, dear?"

- Actor Jack Albertson, who played Lou, the owner of Mother's Tea House, began his long film career with *Miracle on 34th Street* (1947)? He won an Academy Award for Best Supporting Actor in *The Subject Was Roses* (1968) and an

Emmy Award for the lead in the television series "Chico and the Man."

- *Roustabout* featured both the tallest and shortest of actors? Actor Richard Kiel, 7' 2", played the Strong Man, and actor Billy Barty, 3' 9", played Billy the Midget. Kiel is best known as the steel-toothed villain Jaws in the James Bond films *The Spy Who Loved Me* (1977) and *Moonraker* (1979). Barty is best remembered as the irascible dwarf in the cockfight episode of *The Day of the Locust* (1975).

Photofest

- Actor Pat Buttram, who played carnival owner Harry Carver, is best known for playing a wily character on television? Buttram played Eustace Haney on the television series "Green Acres" (1965–1971) and was constantly taking advantage of Oliver Wendell Douglas played by Eddie Arnold.

ROUSTABOUT TRIVIA QUIZ

1. Who introduced Charlie Rogers as "a young man who would undoubtedly be playing in one of the larger cities like Chicago or San Francisco if the authorities there didn't misunderstand him."

2. How much money did Charlie have when he was released from jail?

3. Where was Charlie heading before he was run off the road?

4. In carnival language, what is a "mitt camp"?

5. What was the real first name of Madame Mijanou?

6. What did Madame Mijanou's boyfriend do in the carnival?

7. How old was Billy the Midget?

8. Where was the bank located that held the mortgage on the carnival?

9. How much was general admission to Morgan's shows?

10. Why was Harry Carver nicknamed "Harry the Undertaker"?

11. What was the name of Harry Carver's carnival?

12. What weekly salary did Carver offer to Charlie?

13. What was the name of the ball team for which Freddie the baseball thrower played?

14. What speed did motorcycles in the "Wall of Death" have to attain?

15. How much did Charlie give to Arthur Nielsen as a partial payment on Maggie Morgan's overdue loan payment?

18.

GIRL HAPPY

(METRO–GOLDWYN–MAYER, 1965)

PLOT

*E*lvis and his musical combo are hired by a Chicago nightclub owner to keep an eye on his daughter vacationing in Fort Lauderdale during spring break.

CAST

Elvis Presley	Rusty Wells
Shelley Fabares	Valerie Frank
Harold J. Stone	Mr. Frank
Gary Crosby	Andy
Joby Baker	Wilbur
Jimmy Hawkins	Doc
Mary Ann Mobley	Deena Shepherd
Fabrizio Mioni	Romano
Jackie Coogan	Sergeant Benson
Peter Brooks	Brentwood Von Durgenfeld
John Fiedler	Mr. Penchill
Chris Noel	Betsy
Lyn Edgington	Laurie
Nita Talbot	Sunny Daze
Norman Grabowski	Wolf Call O'Brien

CREW

Joe Pasternak	Producer
Boris Sagal	Director
Harvey Bullock and R. S. Allen	Screenplay

George Stoll .... Music
The Jordanaires .... Vocal Accompaniment
Col. Tom Parker .... Technical Advisor

SONGS
"Girl Happy" • "Spring Fever" • "Fort Lauderdale Chamber of Commerce" •
"Startin' Tonight" • "Wolf Call" • "Do Not Disturb" •
"Cross My Heart and Hope to Die" • "The Meanest Girl in Town" •
"Do the Clam" • "Puppet on a String" • "I've Got to Find My Baby"

FANS DIDN'T "DO THE CLAM"

Sid Wayne, Ben Weisman, and Dolores Fuller composed the song "Do the Clam," which Rusty Wells (Elvis) sings at the nighttime beach party in *Girl Happy*. While Rusty sings, the partygoers do a new dance called the Clam, which was created for the film by choreographer David Winters.

Released in February 1965, the single of "Do the Clam" spent eight weeks on *Billboard*'s Hot 100 chart, peaking at number twenty-one. RCA hoped that the bouncy number would start a new dance craze across the country. But fans failed to "Do the Clam," and the song was washed away on the tide of more popular records.

FANS ARE HAPPY WITH GIRL HAPPY

The soundtrack album *Girl Happy* featured the eleven songs from Elvis's 1965 film plus a bonus song, "You'll Be Gone," which Elvis had previously recorded in 1962. The LP spent a leisurely thirty-one week vacation on *Billboard*'s Top LPs chart, peaking at number eight. The fourth track on side two of the album, "Puppet on a String," was released as a single and hung around *Billboard*'s Hot 100 chart for ten weeks, reaching number fourteen.

ELVIS'S FAVORITE CO-STAR: SHELLEY FABARES

When asked once, Elvis said that his favorite costar was Shelley Fabares, and *Girl Happy* was the first

of three films in which the two were paired. In *Girl Happy*, Fabares played Valerie Frank, the sun-loving college student on spring break in Fort Lauderdale. She also played Cynthia Foxhugh, the spoiled daughter of a millionaire in *Spinout* (1966), and in *Clambake* (1967) she played Dianne Carter, a woman out to snare a rich husband.

THE ACTOR WHO INFLUENCED THE LAW: JACKIE COOGAN

"And just who's the lamebrain that's been making arrests on the group plan?" the police captain asks as he bursts into the jailhouse. "Everyone's been calling—the mayor, the Chamber of Commerce, the newspapers. Sounds like one of your bright ideas, Benson."

Sergeant Benson, played by Jackie Coogan, was responsible for the arrests at the nightclub, and this long arm of the law in Fort Lauderdale has a funny scene with Elvis at the jailhouse. In real life, Coogan had a connection to the law in the state of California.

At the tender age of seven, Coogan appeared opposite comedian Charlie Chaplin in *The Kid* (1921). The role of the street-smart orphan made Coogan the first major child star in the history of American film as well as one of the highest-paid actors in Hollywood. Coogan earned millions with that role and with parts in *Peck's Bad Boy* (1921), *Oliver Twist* (1922), *A Boy of Flanders* (1924), *Tom Sawyer* (1930), and *Huckleberry Finn* (1931). As his guardians, his parents controlled his earnings and gave him a weekly allowance of $6.25.

Shortly before Coogan's twenty-first birthday, his father was killed in an automobile accident. His mother, Lillian, married the family's lawyer, Arthur Bernstein, and when Coogan turned twenty-one, his stepfather announced that the pair would not release any of Coogan's money to him. The scandal rocked Hollywood, and Coogan was forced to file a lawsuit to recover the money.

The shock waves of the scandal were felt all the way to the California State Legislature. Forty-eight hours after Coogan's suit was filed, the legislature rushed a new bill into law, requiring that the earnings of child actors be deposited into court-administered trust funds.

Coogan's lawsuit dragged on for eighteen months before it was settled; unfortunately, Coogan was able to recover only thirty-five thousand dollars. But Coogan was comforted by the knowledge that the Child Actors Law—also known as the Coogan Act—would protect other child actors from what had happened to him.

DID YOU KNOW THAT...

- Location filming of *Girl Happy* took place in Fort Lauderdale, Florida? For the interior shots, cameras rolled on the sound stages of MGM's studios in Culver City.

- Hungarian-born producer Joe Pasternak began his career as a busboy and waiter at Paramount studios? He rose from food service to service as second assistant director in 1923. Three years later, he left Paramount for Universal and was appointed manager of the studio's operations in Berlin. While in Europe, Pasternak produced a string of hit musical films before returning to Hollywood in 1935 to bring the magic of musicals to American theaters.

- Actress Shelley Fabares took her talents to television in a number of series? From 1958 to 1963, she played Mary Stone on "The Donna Reed Show" (1958–1966); she played Dr. Anne Jamison on "The Brian Keith Show" (1972–1974); she played Jenny Bedford on "The Practice" (1976–1977); and she captured the role of Christine Armstrong on "Coach," which debuted in 1989.

- Actor Jimmy Hawkins, who played combo member Doc, shared the television screen with Shelley Fabares? Hawkins had the role of kid brother Tagg Oakley on "Annie Oakley" (1953–1956), a show on which Fabares made guest appearances. He also played the role of Scotty Simpson, Shelley's boyfriend in later episodes of "The Donna Reed Show" (1958–1966).

- Actor Gary Crosby, who played combo member Andy, made his film debut at the age of eight? He had a role in *Star-Spangled Rhythm* (1942) along with his father, Bing Crosby, and Bob Hope, Veronica Lake, Dorothy Lamour, and other Paramount stars. In addition to his work in movies, Crosby had roles in the television series "The Bill Dana Show" (1963–1965), "Adam-12" (1968–1975), "Chase" (1973–1974), "Mobile One" (1975), and "Hunter" (1984–1985).

- Actress Mary Ann Mobley, who played Deena Shepherd, was the original Girl from U.N.C.L.E.? Mobley, the former Miss America of 1959, was selected for the role of April Dancer and appeared in the pilot episode entitled "The Moonglow Affair." The pilot received high ratings, and the series "The Girl from U.N.C.L.E." was scheduled for NBC's fall 1966 lineup. But Mobley was not asked to continue in the role. Instead, the part of April Dancer went to Stefanie Powers.

- Actress Nita Talbot, who played Sunny Daze, portrayed a nightclub performer on a television series? Talbot played the role of singer Lusti Weather on "Bourbon Street Beat" (1959–1960). She has played wry characters in films such as *Bundle of Joy* (1956), *A Very Special Favor* (1965), *Buck and the Preacher* (1971), *The Day of the Locust* (1975), and *Night Shift* (1982).

- Advertisements for *Girl Happy* carried provocative lines? They were "What Happens during Easter Vacation at the Beach?" and "See How Youth Reacts When the Gates Are Opened."

- *Girl Happy* earned $3.1 million? The film was number twenty-five on *Variety's* list of top-grossing movies for 1965.

GIRL HAPPY TRIVIA QUIZ

1. What was the name of the Chicago nightclub where Rusty Wells and his combo performed?

2. What was the name of the Fort Lauderdale motel where Valerie Frank was registered?

3. What was Valerie's room number?

4. What were the names of Valerie's two girlfriends?

5. What was Valerie studying in college?

6. Who said: "No pets or animals, no toys in the pool, no cooking, no noisy parties, no loud radios, and no boys in the room. Remember, we want you to have a good time."?

7. What was Romano doing in Valerie's room?

8. What was the name of one of the colleges mentioned in "Startin' Tonight"?

9. What was the nickname of Brentwood Von Durgenfeld?

10. Where did Brentwood attend college?

11. Where was Romano's boat anchored?

12. At what nightclub did Sunny Daze perform?

13. What was the message Deena left for Rusty on his motel room mirror?

14. What did Deena use to write her message?

15. What did Deena order for herself and Rusty from room service?

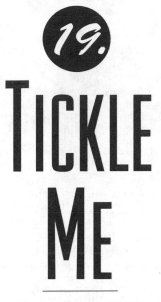

19.

TICKLE ME

(ALLIED ARTISTS, 1965)

PLOT

*E*lvis accepts a job at an all-girl's dude ranch, falls in love with a beautiful staff member, and helps find her grandfather's fortune hidden in an Old West ghost town.

CAST

Elvis Presley	Lonnie Beale
Julie Adams	Vera Radford
Jocelyn Lane	Pam Merritt
Jack Mullaney	Stanley Potter
Merry Anders	Estelle Penfield
Bill Williams	Deputy Sheriff John Sturdivant
Edward Faulkner	Brad Bentley
John Dennis	Adolph, the Chef
Robert Hoy	Henry, the Gardener
Grady Sutton	Mr. Dabney
Dorothy Conrad	Mrs. Dabney

CREW

Ben Schwalb	Producer
Norman Taurog	Director
Elwood Ullman and Edward Bernds	Screenplay
Walter Scharf	Scoring and Conducting of Music
The Jordanaires	Vocal Accompaniment
Col. Tom Parker	Technical Advisor

NO QUESTION ABOUT "(SUCH AN) EASY QUESTION"

Songwriters Otis Blackwell and Winfield Scott composed, and Elvis recorded, "(Such an) Easy Question" in 1962. The tune was stockpiled, but when it was included in *Tickle Me*, RCA released the song as a single in May 1965. And there was no question about the success of "(Such an) Easy Question" on the charts.

The song landed on *Billboard*'s Hot 100 chart and peaked at number eleven during its eight-week tenure. "(Such an) Easy Question" enjoyed a seven-week stay on the Easy Listening chart. There in July 1965, Horst Jankowski's "A Walk in the Black Forest" stumbled out of the top spot to make way for "(Such an) Easy Question." The song reigned at number one for two weeks.

THE SIMILAR SAGA OF "I'M YOURS"

Composers Don Robertson and Hal Blair wrote "I'm Yours," which Elvis recorded in 1961. That song, too, spent time on RCA's back burner. In fact, it was not until August 1965 that the company released the single to capitalize on the tune's appearance in *Tickle Me*.

Just as "(Such an) Easy Question" had done, "I'm Yours" also topped out at number eleven on *Billboard*'s Hot 100 chart. "I'm Yours" stayed on the chart for eleven weeks.

Fans of easy-listening music forgot about We Five's "You Were on My Mind" in October 1965. That song slipped from number one on the Easy Listening chart, and "I'm Yours" was enthroned for a three-week stay.

OTIS BLACKWELL: SONG WRITER EXTRAORDINAIRE

Brooklyn-born songwriter Otis Blackwell has left his distinctive mark on rhythm and blues music since the early 1950s. Although he never met the King, Blackwell was one of Elvis's best songwriters.

With Eddie Cooley, Blackwell wrote "Don't Be Cruel," "All Shook Up," "Make Me Know It," "Fever," and "Paralyzed." With Winfield Scott, Blackwell wrote "Return to Sender," "One Broken Heart for Sale," "Please Don't Drag That String Around," and "We're Coming in Loaded."

Blackwell also cut demo records of his own songs and the songs of other writers for Elvis because both Blackwell and Elvis have similar styles. These similarities were evident in the album Blackwell recorded in 1977. *These Are My Songs* included "Fever," "All Shook Up," "Return to Sender," and "Don't Be Cruel."

ROBERTSON AND BLAIR: HITTING ALL THE RIGHT NOTES

Singer, musician, and composer Don Robertson has been rocking and rolling since rock and roll began. He wrote, recorded, and even did the whistling on

"The Happy Whistler," which was a million seller for him in 1956.

A joke told to him by his son that Robertson repeated to Sheb Wooley was the inspiration for Wooley's 1958 number-one smash, "The Purple People Eater."

Robertson penned Lorne Greene's 1964 million seller "Ringo" as well as "I Really Don't Want to Know" (cowritten with Howard Barnes), "Please Help Me, I'm Falling", and "I Love You More and More Every Day."

For Elvis, Robertson wrote "Anything That's Part of You," "I'm Counting on You," "I'm Falling in Love Tonight," "Love Me Tonight," "Marguerita," "Starting Today," and "There's Always Me."

Robertson found a good songwriting partner in Hal Blair, a member of the Jazz String Quartet and the Rhythm Rangers western band. In addition to "I'm Yours," Robertson and Blair composed for Elvis "I Met Her Today", "I Think I'm Gonna Like It Here", "No More", and "What Now, What Next, Where To."

ELVIS RESCUES ALLIED ARTISTS FROM BANKRUPTCY

Plans to make a movie about hijinks at an all-female dude ranch and the search for a lost fortune were first discussed in 1958. Six years later, with the titled changed from *Rodeo* to *Tickle Me*, Allied Artists announced the start of production.

Elvis was signed for the role of Lonnie Beale. The financially strapped Hollywood studio guaranteed Elvis's $750,000 salary plus promised him fifty percent of the film's profits.

For the part of Pam Merritt, producer Ben Schwalb selected Jocelyn Lane. Lane had been one of five women featured in a *Life* magazine layout called the "Great Girl Drought." When Schwalb saw the lovely Lane, he lassoed her for an audition, and she won the role.

Cameras began rolling on the studio lot in October 1964, and in May 1965 *Tickle Me* previewed in Hollywood, then premiered in Atlanta, Georgia. In anticipation of tremendous fan support, Allied Artists had ordered more than five hundred prints of the film. How the critics would react was another question.

The critics bashed *Tickle Me*. The reviewer for *The New York Times* wrote, "This is the silliest, feeblest and dullest vehicle for the Memphis Wonder in a long time."

Despite such poor reviews, *Tickle Me* tickled fans. In fact, the film corraled so much money for Allied Artists that *Tickle Me* was declared the third highest grossing film in the history of the studio. Elvis had single-handedly rescued Allied Artists from the very brink of bankruptcy.

DID YOU KNOW THAT...

- An historic downtown Los Angeles landmark was used as a model for *Tickle Me*'s ghost-town sequence? The crew reproduced on the studio lot the Presidential Suite of the old Pico House. Pio Pico was the last Mexican governor of California.

- The budget for *Tickle Me* was nearly $1.5 million? It was $4,000 under the original estimate.

- Actress Merry Anders, who played dude-ranch guest Estelle Penfield, began her film career with *Les Miserables* (1952)? While acting in a series of B films in the fifties and sixties, Anders also ventured into television. She played Joyce Erwin in "The Stu Erwin Show" (1954–1955), Val Marlowe in "It's Always Jan" (1955–1956), and "Mike" McCall in "How to Marry a Millionaire" (1957–1959).

- Actor Grady Sutton, who played Mr. Dabney, one of the financial backers of the dude ranch, was better known as the foil of W. C. Fields? Sutton played slow-witted characters in two classic Fields films: *You Can't Cheat an Honest Man* (1939) and *The Bank Dick* (1940). Sutton appeared in other films, including *Alice Adams* (1935), *My Man Godfrey* (1936), *Since You Went Away* (1944), *Anchors Aweigh* (1945), *White Christmas* (1954), *My Fair Lady* (1964), and *Support Your Local Gunfighter* (1971).

- Allied Artists did not distribute *Tickle Me*? In the United States, distribution was handled by Warner–Pathé.

- "(It's a) Long Lonely Highway" was the flip side of "I'm Yours"? Elvis sang "(It's a) Long Lonely Highway" over the film's opening credits.

- "It Feels So Right" was the flip side of "(Such an) Easy Question"? "It Feels So Right," which was sung in the Corral Bar, had a six-week layover on *Billboard*'s Hot 100 chart. The song peaked at number fifty-five.

- *Tickle Me* premiered on network television in 1967? The film was shown on "CBS Friday Night at the Movies" on December 8, 1967.

TICKLE ME TRIVIA QUIZ

1. What was the name of the town in *Tickle Me*?

2. What was the name of the bar at which Lonnie Beale was supposed to meet Pete Bowman?

3. What was the name of the ranch owned by Vera Radford?

4. What was the nickname given to the Radford ranch by Stanley Potter?

5. What was Brad Bentley's occupation at the ranch?

6. How much did guests pay to stay at the ranch?

7. What was the name of the ghost town?

8. What was the name of the gold mine owned by Pam Merritt's grandfather?

9. Of what was the hidden fortune comprised?

10. What beverage did the Panhandle Kid drink?

11. What was the theme of the party for Mr. and Mrs. Dabney?

12. What was the name of the bull that threw Lonnie at the Phoenix rodeo?

13. What was the name of the bucking bronco that threw Lonnie at the Phoenix rodeo?

14. What was the name of Pam's grandfather?

15. Where was the hidden treasure found?

HARUM SCARUM

(Metro–Goldwyn–Mayer, 1965)

PLOT

*O*n an official tour of the Middle East, movie and recording star Elvis is kidnapped by political terrorists who involve him in a plot to murder the king of Lunarkand. Elvis finds romance with the king's daughter and adventure with a gang of pickpockets who help him save the king from assassination.

CAST

Elvis Presley	Johnny Tyronne
Mary Ann Mobley	Princess Shalimar
Fran Jeffries	Aishah
Michael Ansara	Prince Dragna of Lunarkand
Jay Novello	Zacha
Philip Reed	King Toranshah, Ruler of Lunarkand
Theo Marcuse	Sinan, Lord of the Assassins
Billy Barty	Baba
Dirk Harvey	Mokar
Jack Costanza	Julna
Larry Chance	Captain Herat
Barbara Werle	Leilah, Aide to Princess Shalimar
Brenda Benet	Emerald
Gail Gilmore	Sapphire
Wilda Taylor	Amethyst
Vicki Malkin	Sari
Ryck Rydon	Mustapha
Joey Russo	Yussef

CREW

Sam Katzman .... Producer
Gene Nelson .... Director
Gerald Drayson Adams .... Screenplay
Fred Karger .... Supervising and Conducting
                                                          of Music
The Jordanaires .... Vocal Accompaniment
Col. Tom Parker .... Technical Advisor

SONGS
"Harem Holiday" • "My Desert Serenade" • "Go East, Young Man" • "Mirage" •
"Kismet" • "Shake That Tambourine" • "Hey, Little Girl" • "Golden Coins" •
"So Close, Yet So Far (from Paradise)"

BONUSES WITH <u>HARUM SCARUM</u> LP

Fans who purchased the soundtrack LP of Elvis's film *Harum Scarum* received three bonuses. In addition to the nine songs from the film, RCA included the two songs that were cut: "Animal Instinct" and "Wisdom of the Ages." The third bonus was a twelve-inch by twelve-inch color still from the movie. The LP was popular with fans. It spent a twenty-three-week harem holiday on *Billboard*'s Top LPs chart, peaking at number eight.

PRESLEY PERPLEXER: <u>HARUM SCARUM</u>'S MOVIE-WITHIN-A-MOVIE

When *Harum Scarum* begins, Johnny Tyronne, United States Ambassador McCord, and an audience of Middle Eastern dignitaries are watching the thrilling conclusion to Tyronne's latest film, *Sands of the Desert*. Tyronne's character in the film uses karate to battle desert desperadoes and a wild leopard in order to free an Arabian heroine.

Here's a Presley Perplexer concerning this movie-within-a-movie: as Tyronne's character faces the anger of the animal, the leopard strains at the collar around its neck, and extends its chain to the fullest length. Yet the animal manages to leap forward to attack the character played by Tyronne. Then when the leopard is unconscious on the sands of the desert, the collar and chain have suddenly vanished.

ELVIS'S TALENTED HANDS

When Sinan, Lord of the Assassins (Theo Marcuse), brings Johnny Tyronne into his lair, the kidnapped singer soon learns the reason for the dubious invitation.

"If what Aishah tells me is true, I have

need of your talented hands to eliminate a person of great importance," Sinan says.

"Look, you don't understand. The skill is used for self-defense not for killing off people you don't like," Johnny says.

Sinan was referring to Johnny's skill at karate. In real life, Elvis was a martial-arts practitioner who first became interested in karate while in the army in Germany. He received his black belt in 1960 and advanced to the second degree in 1963. He eventually earned an eighth-degree black belt.

Elvis displayed his martial-arts expertise not only in *Harum Scarum* but in several other films, including *GI Blues* (1960), *Wild in the Country* (1961), *Blue Hawaii* (1961), *Follow That Dream* (1962), *Kid Galahad* (1962), and *Roustabout* (1964).

HARUM SCARUM PRODUCTION NOTES

• The temple set used in *Harum Scarum* was an artifact from the Cecil B. deMille silent film *King of Kings* (1927). At the time, the cost for constructing the set was thirty-eight hundred dollars. When MGM brought the set out of mothballs for use in *Harum Scarum*, the studio spent more than forty thousand dollars remodeling the temple for Elvis's film.

• One hundred extras in the film wore costumes that were originally used both in the 1944 film *Kismet* and in the 1955 remake.

• The dagger that Elvis carried in *Harum Scarum* saw service in the Hedy Lamarr–Robert Taylor film *Lady of the Tropics* (1939).

• Col. Tom Parker suggested that a talking camel be added to the film, but his suggestion was politely ignored.

• Producer Sam Katzman needed twelve chickens for the marketplace scene. When a Hollywood animal-rental agency quoted a price Katzman considered outrageous, the plucky producer obtained the chickens himself.

• *Harum Scarum* was shot in eighteen days.

DID YOU KNOW THAT...

• The dictionary defines the word "harum-scarum" as meaning "reckless, irresponsible"? The word "harem" refers to the secluded house or part of a house designated for the women of a Muslim household. Before *Harum Scarum* was selected, other titles were considered for Elvis's 1965 film, including *In My Harem*, *Harem Holiday*, and *Harem Scarum*.

• *Harum Scarum* was the second Elvis movie in which actress Mary Ann Mobley had a role? Mobley had played Deena Shepherd in *Girl Happy* (1965). She had made her motion-picture debut in 1964's *Get Yourself a College Girl*. During that year, she was named Hollywood's Lady Ambassador of Goodwill and served as a representative of the community at nationwide civic and social functions. The following year, Mobley was named Deb Star, the newest motion picture star with the brightest future.

- Actor Michael Ansara, who played villain Prince Dragna, had the role of an evil Middle Eastern genie on a popular television series? Ansara played the Blue Djin on "I Dream of Jeannie" (1965–1970). When Jeannie (Barbara Eden) refused the marriage proposal of the Blue Djin, he turned her into a genie and placed her into a bottle, which he abandoned on a deserted island. Jeannie's bottle was later found by Capt. Tony Nelson (Larry Hagman). In real life, Michael Ansara and Barbara Eden were once married to each other. Ansara's other television roles included Cochise on "Broken Arrow" (1956–1958) and Deputy U.S. Marshal Sam Buckhard, an Apache Indian lawman, on "Law of the Plainsman" (1959–1960 and during the 1962 television season).

- Actor Billy Barty, who played Baba, did not have any dialogue in *Harum Scarum*? The character of Baba was a mute. In real life, the actor, who stands 3 feet 9 inches, championed the cause of physically challenged people. The Billy Barty Foundation in Burbank, California, provides medical, educational, vocational, social, and psychological support for people less than 4 feet, 10 inches tall. The organization also promotes the Billy Barty Collection of furniture, which is designed for use by people of small stature.

- *Harum Scarum* was the last film for actor Philip Reed, who played King Toranshah? His long film career included roles in *Female* (1933), *The Case of the Curious Bride* (1935), *The Girl from Tenth Avenue* (1935), *Klondike Annie* (1936), *Merrily We Live* (1938), *A Gentleman After Dark* (1942), *Song of the Thin Man* (1947), *Bodyguard* (1948), *The Girl in the Red Velvet Swing* (1955), and *The Tattered Dress* (1957).

- Actor Jack Costanza, who played the musician Julna, was called "Mr. Bongo"? He provided the bongo beat for the musical numbers in *Harum Scarum*. His interest in the instrument was piqued during a trip to Africa where he was able to study the instrument. In the early 1950s, he was the first bongo player to play with a jazz band.

- *Harum Scarum* premiered in Los Angeles on November 24, 1965? For the Thanksgiving holiday, MGM had more than 550 prints of the film in theaters across the country.

HARUM SCARUM TRIVIA QUIZ

1. Where was Johnny Tyronne scheduled to visit next on his tour?

2. What was the capital of Lunarkand?

3. What mountain range kept Lunarkand isolated from the rest of the world for two thousand years?

4. By what phrase did Zacha first refer to Johnny?

5. What was the guild to which Zacha belonged?

6. How much money did Johnny offer Zacha to help him escape from Lunarkand?

7. Where had Princess Shalimar taken refuge for her safety?

100

8. Upon meeting Johnny, Shalimar told him she was a slave girl. What name did she give?

9. Whose palace had Sinan and his assassins taken over?

10. What kind of horses did Shalimar provide to Johnny?

11. Where did Zacha and his pickpockets live?

12. What was the name of the company that wanted to drill for oil in Lunarkand?

13. How many gold dinars did Prince Dragna offer Sinan to kill the king?

14. Who were the orphans held hostage by Sinan?

15. Who was called "the root of all evil"?

21.

FRANKIE
AND JOHNNY

(United Artists, 1966)

PLOT

*E*lvis is a riverboat singer and a gambler with a losing streak. Believing a gypsy prediction that his luck will change when a redhead enters his life, he gets involved with the carrot-topped former girlfriend of the riverboat's owner. Both the riverboat owner and Elvis's singing partner/paramour become jealous, and this leads to an unexpected finale to the riverboat's grand production number.

CAST

Elvis Presley .... Johnny
Donna Douglas .... Frankie
Harry Morgan .... Cully
Sue Ane Langdon .... Mitzi
Nancy Kovack .... Nellie Bly
Audrey Christie .... Peg
Robert Strauss .... Blackie
Anthony Eisley .... Clint Braden
Joyce Jameson .... Abigail
Jerome Cowan .... Joe Wilbur
James Milhollin .... Proprietor of the Costume Shop
Naomi Stevens .... Princess Zolita
Henry Corden .... Gypsy
Dave Willock .... Pete the Bartender

CREW

Edward Small .... Producer
Frederick de Cordova .... Director
Alex Gottlieb .... Screenplay
The Jordanaires .... Vocal Accompaniment
Col. Tom Parker .... Technical Advisor

SONGS
"Come Along" • "Petunia, the Gardener's Daughter" • "Chesay" •
"What Every Woman Lives For" • "Frankie and Johnny" •
"Look Out, Broadway" • "Beginner's Luck" •
"Down by the Riverside"/"When the Saints Go Marching In" •
"Shout It Out" • "Hard Luck" • "Please Don't Stop Loving Me" •
"Everybody Come Aboard"

"FRANKIE AND JOHNNY"

Hughie Cannon is credited with having the first published version of the song that memorializes the legend of Frankie and Johnny. Cannon's song, "He Done Me Wrong," was published in 1904.

Since then, a number of artists have recorded "Frankie and Johnny," including Ted Lewis in 1927, Gene Autry in 1929, Brook Benton in 1961, and Sam Cooke in 1963. Johnny Cash recorded the song in 1959, but the title was "Frankie's Man, Johnny."

Mae West sang the traditional version of "Frankie and Johnny" in her 1933 film *She Done Him Wrong* in which she played a Gay Nineties Bowery belle being pursued by Cary Grant.

To the traditional "Frankie and Johnny," composers Alex Gottlieb, Fred Karger, and Ben Weisman added new words and a new arrangement to create the version that Elvis recorded in 1965. When the song was released, it shot up *Billboard*'s Hot 100 chart where it stayed for eight weeks, hitting number twenty-five.

FRANKIE AND JOHNNY: THE FIRST TIME AROUND

The story of Frankie and Johnny was first brought to the silver screen in 1936 by Republic Pictures. The film had been completed in 1934, but the studio ran into censorship problems with the Hays Office, which delayed release of the picture for two years.

Torch singer Helen Morgan played Frankie, a singer in a St. Louis casino. Chester Morris, who was later to star in the Boston Blackie series of films, played gambler Johnny. The third side of the triangle, Nellie Bly, was played by Lilyan Tashman. Other cast members included Florence Reed, Walter Kingsford, William Harrigan, John Larkin, and Cora Witherspoon. Songs included "Give Me a Heart to Sing To," "Get Rhythm In Your Feet," "If You Want My Heart," and "Frankie and Johnny."

ELVIS ON PARADE

In the New Orleans parade, Johnny (Elvis) sings a medley of the standard "Down by the Riverside" and the New Orleans funeral hymn "When the Saints Go Marching In." In the latter tune, Johnny actually sings the line as "when the saints *come* marching in."

"Down by the Riverside" and "When the Saints Go Marching In" were not released as singles, but they do appear on the LPs *Elvis Sings Hits From His Movies, Volume 1*, and *Frankie and Johnny*. Elvis sang both songs during the legendary Million Dollar Quartet session with Carl Perkins, Johnny Cash, and Jerry Lee Lewis on December 4, 1956.

FRANKIE AND JOHNNY: THE LP

This soundtrack album presented all the songs from Elvis's 1966 film. Additionally, fans who bought an original issue of the LP found inside a twelve-inch by twelve-inch color portrait of Elvis. *Frankie and Johnny* cruised on *Billboard*'s Top LPs chart for nineteen weeks, peaking at number twenty.

THE REAL NELLIE BLY

Johnny believes the gypsy fortune teller's prediction that a redhead will come into his life and change his luck. The redhead who shashays onto the riverboat is singer Nellie Bly (Nancy Kovack).

History's real Nellie Bly was a newspaper reporter. She was born Elizabeth Cochrane in Cochran's Mills, Pennsylvania, in 1867. When she was eighteen, she took a job as a feature writer for *The Pittsburgh Dispatch*. At the suggestion of her managing editor, she adopted the pen name Nellie Bly, which was the title of an 1849 Stephen Foster song. Bly wrote articles about divorce, slum life, and conditions in Mexico.

In 1887, she joined the staff of the New York *World* where she became known as a writer of exposés on tenement conditions, crime, and political scandals. To report on the conditions of an asylum on Blackwell's Island, Bly feigned insanity to gain admittance to the facility. Her articles presented an insider's view of the horrendous conditions and treatment of the mentally ill and were the catalyst for needed reform.

Two years later, Bly set out to beat the record set by Phileas Fogg, the character in the Jules Verne romance *Around the World in Eighty Days*. She sailed from New York amidst great fanfare that was generated by daily articles in the *World* and a contest to guess her time in circling the globe. First prize was a trip to Europe. The newspaper was flooded with nearly one million entries.

Brass bands and fireworks greeted Bly's arrivals at stopover points as she traveled around the world by ship, train, ricksha, sampan, horse, and burro. For the last leg of her journey, the *World* sent a special train to San Francisco to whisk her back to New York. She completed her journey in seventy-two days, six hours, eleven minutes, and fourteen seconds.

FRANKIE AND JOHNNY AS CELEBRATED BY THOMAS HART BENTON

Although *Frankie and Johnny* was released by United Artists, filming took place at the Culver City studios of Metro–Goldwyn–Mayer. To maintain the proper tone for filming, MGM reproduced and displayed on the lot the mural of the legendary Frankie and Johnny that had been painted by the best-known American muralist of the 1930s and 1940s.

In 1934, native son Thomas Hart Benton was commissioned by the Missouri legislature to create a mural for the state capitol in Jefferson City. The mural that Benton created, "Social History of the State of Missouri," depicted the life and mythology of Missouri plus what Benton called "our great, but somewhat disreputable, heroes." The heroes he included were Jesse James, Huck Finn, and Frankie and Johnny.

When Benton completed the work in December 1936, storm clouds of criticism greeted its unveiling and its artist. As Benton wrote in his book *An American in Art*, the criticism came "from good old hidebound, middle-class Missouri conservatives who saw its 'common life' representations as an insult to the State."

However, Benton reported that through the years the mural gained respectability and that school children from all over the state regularly visit the mural.

DID YOU KNOW THAT...

- Director Frederick de Cordova is best known for having directed "The Tonight Show Starring Johnny Carson" (1962–1992)? In fact, de Cordova won Emmys for his work on the show in 1976, 1977, 1978, and 1979. He directed episodes of other television shows, including "The George Burns and Gracie Allen Show" (1950-1958), "The Jack Benny Program" (1950–1965), "The Donna Reed Show" (1958–1966), "My Three Sons" (1960–1972), and "The Doris Day Show" (1968–1973). De Cordova made his film directorial debut with *Too Young to Know* (1945) and went on to direct *Bedtime for Bonzo* (1951) starring Ronald Reagan, and *Bonzo Goes to College* (1952).

- Actress Donna Douglas, who played Frankie, is best known for her role on a popular television series? Douglas played Elly May Clampett on "The Beverly Hillbillies" (1962–1971).

- Donna Douglas did not really sing in *Frankie and Johnny*? Her singing was dubbed in by Eileen Wilson.

- Actress Nancy Kovack, who played Nellie Bly, married famous conductor Zubin Mehta in 1969? Kovack's film credits that predate her marriage include *Cry for Happy* (1961), *Jason and the Argonauts* (1963), *Sylvia* (1965), *The Great Sioux Uprising* (1965), *The Silencers* (1966), *Enter Laughing* (1967), and *Marooned* (1969).

- Actor Harry Morgan, who played songwriter and sidekick Cully, had roles in four successful television series? He played sardonic next-door neighbor Pete Porter on *December Bride* (1954–1961). He played the same character in the spin-off *Pete and Gladys* (1960–1962). From 1967 to 1970 he played Officer Bill Gannon on *Dragnet* (1952–1970), and from 1975 to 1983 he played Col. Sherman Potter on *M*A*S*H* (1972–1983).

- Actor Anthony Eisley, who played handsome, swinging riverboat owner Clint Braden, played a handsome, swinging character on a popular television series? From 1959 to 1962, he played detective Tracy Steele on "Hawaiian Eye"

(1959–1963). His film credits include *Portrait of a Mobster* (1961), *The Naked Kiss* (1964), *One Way Wahini* (1965), *The Navy vs. The Night Monsters* (1966), *Journey to the Center of Time* (1967), *The Blood of Frankenstein* (1970), and *The Doll Squad* (1973).

• Actress Audrey Christie, who played Cully's wife, Peg, made her New York stage debut in 1928 in a dancing act? Christie had roles in a number of Broadway shows, including *Good News*, *Sweet and Low*, *Of Thee I Sing*, *Shady Lady*, *No, No, Nanette*, *A Connecticut Yankee*, and *Mame*. Her films include *Carousel* (1956), *Splendor in the Grass* (1961), *The Unsinkable Molly Brown* (1964), *The Ballad of Josie* (1967), and *Mame* (1974).

• The premiere of *Frankie and Johnny* was held in Louisiana? The Gordon Theatre in Baton Rouge was the site for the March 31, 1966, premiere, which was attended by Elvis's costars Donna Douglas, Sue Ane Langdon, and Nancy Kovack. Elvis did not attend.

FRANKIE AND JOHNNY TRIVIA QUIZ

1. What was the name of the riverboat on which Frankie and Johnny were performers?

2. What did Johnny lose at the gambling tables along with his cash?

3. What did Johnny do before going on stage, to bring him good luck?

4. How many weeks salary did Johnny owe to Braden?

5. According to the film, what is the Gypsy word for good luck?

6. What was Nellie Bly's billing on the Broadway stage?

7. What was Nellie's favorite number?

8. What winning number did Abigail suggest that Johnny play on the roulette wheel?

9. How much money did music publisher Joe Wilbur pay Cully for the song "Frankie and Johnny"?

10. What identical costumes did Frankie, Nellie, and Mitzi rent for the Mardi Gras costume party?

11. What was the name of the New Orleans hotel at which the riverboat performers stayed?

12. Who was dressed as Father Time?

13. What consecutive numbers won Johnny ten thousand dollars on the roulette wheel?

14. Who placed the real bullet into Frankie's gun?

15. What insect was on the medallion that saved Johnny's life?

22.

PARADISE HAWAIIAN STYLE

(PARAMOUNT, 1966)

PLOT

*A*fter being fired from his job as a commercial pilot, Elvis becomes co-owner of a helicopter charter service. This provides time for romancing the local lovelies while drumming up business. When his partner is in serious trouble, Elvis rescues him despite the danger of permanently losing his license to fly.

CAST

Elvis Presley	Rick Richards
Suzanna Leigh	Judy Hudson
James Shigeta	Danny Kohana
Donna Butterworth	Jan Kohana
Marianna Hill	Lani Kaimana
Irene Tsu	Pua
Linda Wong	Lehua Kawena
Julie Parrish	Joanna
Jan Shepard	Betty Kohana
John Doucette	Donald Belden
Grady Sutton	Mr. Cubberson
Doris Packer	Daisy Barrington
Mary Treen	Mrs. Belden

CREW

Hal B. Wallis	Producer
Michael Moore	Director
Allan Weiss and Anthony Lawrence	Screenplay

Edith Head	Costumes
Joseph J. Lilley	Scoring and Conducting of Music
The Jordanaires	Vocal Accompaniment
Col. Tom Parker	Technical Advisor

SONGS

"Paradise, Hawaiian Style" • "Queenie Wahine's Papaya" •
"Scratch My Back (Then I'll Scratch Yours)" • "Drums of the Islands" •
"A Dog's Life" • "Datin'" • "House of Sand" • "Stop Where You Are" •
"This Is My Heaven"

PARADISE, HAWAIIAN STYLE: THE LP

The soundtrack album to *Paradise, Hawaiian Style* included all nine songs from the film plus "Sand Castles," which had been cut. The songs "Paradise, Hawaiian Style," "Queenie Wahine's Papaya," "Scratch My Back (Then I'll Scratch Yours)," "House of Sand," "Stop Where You Are," and "This Is My Heaven" were written by Bill Giant, Bernie Baum, and Florence Kaye. The album flew up *Billboard*'s Top LPs chart for a nineteen-week vacation, where it peaked at number fifteen.

HAL WALLIS'S HAWAIIAN HEADACHE

According to the script, Rick Richards (Elvis) sings "Drums of the Islands" while gliding with Pua (Irene Tsu) in a canoe through the Hawaiian village. Written by Sid Tepper and Roy C. Bennett, the song was based on "Bula Lai," an old Tongan chant by Iserati Recula. Problems erupted over the use of the song and the canoe.

Producer Hal Wallis wanted a war canoe for the production number, but the only one his crew could locate was a Samoan canoe. Because Tongan rowers and a Tongan-based song were used in the scene with a Samoan canoe, Samoans on the set were offended. The rival factions clashed, and several fights ensued, giving Hal Wallis a gigantic Hawaiian headache.

PARADISE, HAWAIIAN STYLE PRODUCTION NOTES

- The first scene that Elvis filmed was the helicopter rescue of James Shigeta and Donna Butterworth.

- Many of the scenes were filmed at the Polynesian Cultural Center on Oahu. Other locations included Honolulu, Kauai, Maui, and the Kona Coast.

- Elvis's dressing room at the Polynesian Cultural Center was a replica of a Hawaiian royal palace.

- The musical numbers were staged by Jack Regas, who was the choreographer at the Polynesian Cultural Center.

ALOHA, MARY TREEN

While transporting a client's canines to the dog show at Kauai, Rick's helicopter goes out of control over a pineapple field and a highway, causing the car driven by Donald Belden (John Doucette) to go into an irrigation ditch. Screaming as the car goes off the road is Mrs. Belden (Mary Treen). Keen-eyed Elvis fans probably noted that this was Mary Treen's third appearance in an Elvis film.

Her first appearance was in *Girls! Girls! Girls!* (1962) in which she played Mrs. Figgett, the troublesome customer attended to by Laurel Dodge (Laurel Goodwin) in the hat shop.

Treen's second appearance was as Mrs. Stevers in *Fun in Acapulco* (1963). Along with her husband Dr. Stevers (Howard McNear), Mrs. Stevers is introduced to bullfighter Dolores Gomez (Elsa Cardenas) in the nightclub so that Mike Windgren (Elvis) can slip away with Margarita Dauphin (Ursula Andress).

Treen has had a successful career as a character actress supporting major stars. Her films include *Happiness Ahead* (1934), *Kitty Foyle* (1940), *They All Kissed the Bride* (1942), *It's a Wonderful Life* (1946), *Room for One More* (1952), *All in a Night's Work* (1961), and *The Strongest Man in the World* (1975). On television, Treen played Millie, secretary to Carl Stevenson of Stevenson Aircraft and Associates, the employer of Chester A. Riley (Jackie Gleason) on "The Life of Riley" (1949–1950). She also played Rose, Andy Taylor's original housekeeper on "The Andy Griffith Show" (1960–1968) and Hilda, a nurse, on "The Joey Bishop Show" (1962–1965).

Although Mary Treen has a small role in *Paradise, Hawaiian Style*, the part of Mrs. Belden is pivotal nevertheless. At the climax of the film, Rick flies with a suspended pilot's license in order to rescue his partner, Danny Kohana (James Shigeta). This action results in Rick's being permanently grounded by Mr. Belden, one of the regional directors of the Island Aviation Bureau. At the Polynesian

Welcoming Festival, Rick hopes to square things, so he introduces himself to Mr. Belden.

"Rick Richards! Oh you're the one responsible for my wife's not being here. She threw her back out when you ran us off the road."

Rick then explains that he is in big trouble if he doesn't get the license reinstated. His partner, Danny, could lose everything he has invested in the business. Danny can't work because of his broken leg. Belden cuts him off, indicating that he knows about Rick's rescue of Danny.

"We're not trying to run you out of business, and we're not unfairly rigid in our interpretation of the law," Belden says. "We realize that occasionally there are mitigating circumstances."

"Then I'll get my license back?" Rick asks.

"Well, the board meets next week. I'll make the recommendation," Belden says. "If a man risks his entire future to save a friend, he can't be all bad. Besides this is the first time I've been able to get out without my wife in years. I think I like it."

Thanks and aloha, Mary Treen!

DID YOU KNOW THAT...

- *Paradise, Hawaiian Style* was not the original title for Elvis's twenty-first film? Other titles considered were *Polynesian Paradise*, *Hawaiian Paradise*, and *Polynesian Holiday*.

- Actress Suzanna Leigh, who played Judy Hudson, and actress Julie Parrish, who played Joanna, were reunited in *Paradise, Hawaiian Style*? Both had had roles in *Boeing Boeing* (1965). Leigh's other films include *The Deadly Bees* (1967), *The Lost Continent* (1968), and *Son of Dracula* (1974). Parrish's other films include *It's Only Money* (1962), *The Nutty Professor* (1963), and *Fireball 500* (1966). Parrish turned to television in 1967 and had roles on "Good Morning World" (1967–1968) and "Return to Peyton Place" (1972–1974).

- Actor James Shigeta, who played business partner Danny Kohana, was born in Hawaii? Shigeta has enjoyed acting roles in both films and television. His films include *The Crimson Kimona* (1959), *Walk Like a Dragon* (1960), *Cry for Happy* (1961), *Bridge to the Sun* (1961), *Flower Drum Song* (1961), *Nobody's Perfect* (1968), *Lost Horizon* (1973), *Midway* (1976), *Enola Gay—the Men, the Mission, the Atomic Bomb* (1980), and *Die Hard* (1988). On television, Shigeta portrayed Wizard Wong on the four-part miniseries "The Moneychangers" (1976) and played Lin Tsu-Han on the nine-hour miniseries "Once An Eagle" (1976–1977).

- Actress Irene Tsu, who played Pua, was reunited with actor James Shigeta in *Paradise, Hawaiian Style*? Both had had roles in *Flower Drum Song* (1961). Tsu began her career as a child actress in *China* (1943). Her other films include *Cleopatra* (1963), *How To Stuff a Wild Bikini* (1965), *Caprice* (1967), *The Green Berets* (1968), and *Hot Potato* (1976).

- A 16-mm short film was shot about the making of *Paradise, Hawaiian Style*? This short feature showcased the beautiful scenery of Hawaii and a musical production number. Released in May 1966 as a promotional tool for the film, the short feature was made available to schools, church groups, television stations, and travel agencies.

- *Paradise, Hawaiian Style* had a sneak preview? Lucky fans in Memphis saw the sneak peek on June 9, 1966. The film opened in New York City six days later and opened nationally in July 1966.

- *Paradise, Hawaiian Style* picked up an early honor? The film was chosen "Picture of the Month" by *Seventeen* magazine in June 1966.

- In 1966, *Paradise, Hawaiian Style* grossed $2.5 million? *Variety* ranked the film number forty on their list of top-grossers.

PARADISE, HAWAIIAN STYLE TRIVIA QUIZ

1. Why was Rick Richards fired?

2. What was the motto of Danny Kohana's island charter service?

3. How many children did Danny have?

4. What was Rick's philosophy when doing business with Lani, Pua, Lehua, and Joanna?

5. What product did Mr. Cubberson sell?

6. What group was attending a convention at the Maui Sheraton?

7. How long had Lehua been waiting for her dinner date with Rick?

8. What was Rick's nickname for secretary Judy Hudson?

9. What were the breeds of the four dogs Rick and Joanna transported?

10. What was the name of the dog food given to the dogs aboard the helicopter?

11. What was the name of Mrs. Barrington's chauffeur?

12. What was the name of the restaurant where Rick fought with Judy's date?

13. What was the catchphrase used in the color advertisement for Rick and Danny's charter service?

14. Where did Lani lose the keys to Rick's helicopter?

15. Who was the guest of honor at the Polynesian Welcoming Festival?

SPINOUT

(METRO–GOLDWYN–MAYER, 1966)

PLOT

*E*lvis is a singing race car driver pursued by three marriage-minded women. He wins a race, marries all three, and manages to remain single.

CAST

Elvis Presley	Mike McCoy
Shelley Fabares	Cynthia Foxhugh
Diane McBain	Diana St. Clair
Deborah Walley	Les
Jack Mullaney	Curley
Will Hutchins	Lt. Tracy Richards
Warren Berlinger	Philip Short
Jimmy Hawkins	Larry
Carl Betz	Howard Foxhugh
Cecil Kellaway	Bernard Ranley
Una Merkel	Violet Ranley
Frederic Worlock	Blodgett
Dodie Marshall	Susan

CREW

Joe Pasternak	Producer
Norman Taurog	Director
Theodore J. Flicker and George Kirgo	Screenplay
George Stoll	Music
Jack Baker	Staging of Musical Numbers
The Jordanaires	Vocal Accompaniment
Col. Tom Parker	Technical Advisor

SONGS
"Spinout" • "Stop, Look, and Listen" • "Adam and Evil" • "All That I Am" •
"Never Say Yes" • "Am I Ready" • "Beach Shack" • "Smorgasbord" •
"I'll Be Back"

ELVIS CELEBRATES TEN YEARS IN FILMS

The year *Spinout* was released marked Elvis's tenth year making movies. To celebrate, MGM pulled out all the stops for the *Spinout* publicity campaign.

• Theater managers received press kits containing photos of Elvis, posters, flyers, tabloid heralds, booklets about his gold Cadillac and his acting career.

• Theaters sponsored essay contests on "The Perfect American Male." The best essays won Elvis records as prizes.

• Radio stations received promotional copies of the *Spinout* single and open-ended interviews with Shelley Fabares, Deborah Walley, and Diane McBain.

• Newspaper ads for the film featured high-performance catchphrases: "Hitting the Curves in His Fastest Adventure Yet" and "With His Foot on the Gas and No Brakes on the Fun."

"SPINOUT" ACCELERATES UP THE CHART

The title song to Elvis's 1966 film was written by Sid Wayne, Ben Weisman, and Dolores Fuller. "Spinout" accelerated up *Billboard*'s Hot 100 chart during its seven-week race, shifting into reverse only after it peaked at number forty.

"Spinout," the eight other songs from the film, and three bonus songs ("Tomorrow Is a Long Time," "Down in the Alley," "I'll Remember You") were included on the soundtrack LP. Album buyers also found a special twelve-inch by twelve-inch color photo tucked inside. The LP *Spinout* burned rubber on *Billboard*'s Top LPs chart for thirty-two weeks, hitting a high of number eighteen.

"SPINOUT" FLIP SIDE: "ALL THAT I AM"

The flip side of "Spinout" was the song that Mike McCoy (Elvis) sings to Diana St. Clair (Diane McBain) at the campsite. "All That I Am" was written by Sid Tepper and Roy C. Bennett. On *Billboard*'s Hot 100 chart, the song lingered for eight romantic weeks, peaking at number forty-one. On the Easy Listening chart, "All That I Am" hit number nine.

WHEN LES MEANS MORE

Elvis's costar Deborah Walley played Les, the drummer in the combo, and the character clearly has a crush on her boss. Unfortunately, the boys in the band don't think of Les as a girl. "What am I a hound dog?" she complains at the campsite. In real life, Elvis did not confuse Deborah Walley with a hound dog. In fact, while filming *Spinout*, the pair dated.

Perhaps Elvis first noticed Walley's charms in *Gidget Goes Hawaiian* (1961). Walley replaced Sandra Dee, who had been the screen's first combination of a girl who is not tall yet not a midget (hence Gidget), for this romp in the Islands with James Darren. Walley had roles in other beach flicks, including *Beach Blanket Bingo* (1965), *Dr. Goldfoot and the Bikini Machine* (1965), *Ghost in the Invisible Bikini* (1966), and *It's a Bikini World* (1967).

Her other films include *Bon Voyage* (1962), *Summer Magic* (1963), *The Young Lovers* (1964), *Ski Party* (1965), *The Bubble* (1966), and *Benji* (1974). On television, Walley had a role on the comedy series "The Mothers-in-Law" (1967–1969) in which she played a young newlywed coping with college and in-laws.

DID YOU KNOW THAT...

- The title for Elvis's 1966 film underwent several overhauls before *Spinout* was chosen? Some of the titles considered were *Jim Dandy*, *After Midnight*, *Always at Midnight*, *Never Say No*, and *Never Say Yes*.

- *Spinout* was not the title for the British release of the film? The British title was *California Holiday*.

- Two well-known sites were used for location footage in *Spinout*? The sites were the Ascot Motor Car Racing Ground and Dodger Stadium.

- Two hundred extras were used for the road race scene? The scene also called for twenty-eight supporting actors, fifty cars, and twelve custom racing cars.

- Actor Carl Betz, who played racing car magnate Howard Foxhugh, played Shelley Fabares's father in a popular television series? Betz was best known for his role as Dr. Alex Stone on "The Donna Reed Show" (1958–1966). Fabares played his daughter, Mary, from 1958 to 1963. Betz won an Emmy for his work on the television series "Judd for the Defense" (1967–69). His movies include *The President's Lady* (1953), *Powder River* (1953), *Inferno* (1953), *Vickie* (1953), *Dangerous Crossing* (1953), and *City of Bad Men* (1953).

- Actor Jimmy Hawkins, who played combo member Larry, had a similar role in an earlier Elvis movie? Hawkins played combo member Doc in *Girl Happy* (1965).

- *Spinout* was the last film for actress Una Merkel, who played wealthy matron Violet Ranley? Merkel began her film career in 1920 as a stand-in for Lillian Gish. Merkel advanced to playing her own roles, usually a wisecracking comic foil with a Southern drawl. Her films include *The Fifth Horseman* (1924), *Abraham Lincoln* (1930), *The Maltese Falcon* (1931), *42nd Street* (1933), *Saratoga* (1937), and *Destry Rides Again* (1939). She was nominated for an Academy Award for Best Supporting Actress for her role as Geraldine Page's mother in *Summer and Smoke* (1961).

- Actor Cecil Kellaway, who played wealthy Bernard Ranley, received an Academy Award nomination as Best Supporting Actor for his role as a leprechaun? As the leprechaun in *The Luck of the Irish* (1948), he acted as the conscience

of Tyrone Power. Unfortunately, Kellaway lost the Oscar to Walter Huston for his role in *The Treasure of the Sierra Madre.* Kellaway was known for playing twinkly-eyed, roguish characters. Born in Capetown, South Africa, he began his film career in Australia and came to Hollywood in 1939. His films include *Wuthering Heights* (1939), *Intermezzo* (1939), *The Good Fellows* (1943), *The Postman Always Rings Twice* (1946), *Harvey* (1950), *The Shaggy Dog* (1959), and *Guess Who's Coming to Dinner?* (1967).

- Two members of Elvis's Memphis Mafia had bit parts in *Spinout?* Red West and Joe Esposito played the members of Shorty Bloomquist's pit crew.

- *Spinout* had a sneak preview? The sneak peek was held at the Malco Theatre in Memphis in September 1966, and the film opened nationally in November 1966.

SPINOUT TRIVIA QUIZ

1. What vehicle did Mike McCoy use to tow his race car?

2. What was the name of Mike's combo?

3. How much money did Howard Foxhugh offer the combo to sing for his daughter's birthday?

4. What was the name of the company owned by Howard Foxhugh?

5. What was Cynthia Foxhugh's nickname for her father?

6. What was Les's full first name?

7. How many eggs did Les use in her chocolate mousse?

8. What happened to Philip Short when he became nervous?

9. What was the name of the book Diana St. Clair was researching?

10. Whenever Mike kissed one of his lovely ladies what tune did he hear?

11. Who were the neighbors next door to the Foxhugh residence?

12. What was the name of their butler?

13. What was the name of the car Howard Foxhugh wanted Mike to race for him?

14. How much money had Howard Foxhugh offered to the winner of the race?

15. What was the name of the 250-mile race that Mike won?

24.
EASY COME,
EASY GO

(PARAMOUNT, 1967)

PLOT

*W*ith the help of a go-go dancer and a nightclub owner, former navy frogman Elvis is after sunken treasure. But two pirates—one shapely and the other sinister—are out to beat him to it.

CAST

Elvis Presley .... Ted Jackson
Dodie Marshall .... Jo Symington
Pat Priest .... Dina Bishop
Pat Harrington, Jr. .... Judd Whitman
Skip Ward .... Gil Carey
Elsa Lanchester .... Madame Neherina
Frank McHugh .... Captain Jack
DiKi Lerner .... Zoltan
Jonathan Hole .... Coin Dealer
Sandy Kenyon .... Lt. Marty Schwartz
Reed Morgan .... Lieutenant Tompkins
Mickey Elley .... Lieutenant Whitehead

CREW

Hal B. Wallis .... Producer
John Rich .... Director
Allan Weiss
and Anthony Lawrence .... Screenplay
Edith Head .... Costumes
David Winters .... Staging of Musical Numbers
Joseph J. Lilley .... Scoring and Conducting of Music

The Jordanaires .... Vocal Accompaniment
Col. Tom Parker .... Technical Advisor

SONGS
"Easy Come, Easy Go" • "The Love Machine" • "Yoga Is as Yoga Does" •
"You Gotta Stop" • "Sing, You Children" • "I'll Take Love"

THE LOVE MACHINE AND "THE LOVE MACHINE"

At the Easy Go-Go, Ted Jackson (Elvis) and his shipmates lieutenants Schwartz, Tompkins, and Whitehead meet dancer Jo Symington (Dodie Marshall) through the club's owner, Judd Whitman (Pat Harrington, Jr.). Although Ted is at first attracted to Jo, he soon realizes that there is no chemistry between him and the lovely lady.

"Well," Judd tells him later, "there are other numbers on the wheel of fortune, pal."

"Hey, you still got that thing with the phone numbers on it?" Ted asks.

Judd brings on stage the Love Machine, a giant spinning wheel containing photos of a multitude of girls along with their measurements and phone numbers. While Ted sings the song "The Love Machine," Schwartz (Sandy Kenyon), Tompkins (Reed Morgan), and Whitehead (Mickey Elley) each take a turn spinning the wheel and writing down the pertinent information about the girl who has come up as a match.

"The Love Machine" was written for *Easy Come, Easy Go* by Gerald Nelson, Fred Burch, and Chuck Taylor. Nelson and Burch wrote two other songs for the film: "Sing, You Children" and "Yoga Is as Yoga Does."

The results of the Love Machine matches turn out to be disappointing for Schwartz, Tompkins, and Whitehead, *and* for Ted. As he complains to his buddies the next day: "I think Judd's wheel is rigged. My girl was 38-24-38—it added up to her age."

ELSA LANCHESTER: ACTRESS AND YOGA INSTRUCTOR

To gain more information about the cargo that sunk along with the *Port of Call*, Ted Jackson seeks out the skipper's only living relative, Jo Symington. When Ted arrives at Jo's house, he intrudes upon a yoga class being led by Madame Neherina (Elsa Lanchester).

"Young man, you are causing ripples on the waters of peace and contentment," Madame Neherina admonishes.

"I didn't mean to make waves. I'm looking for somebody," he explains.

"We are all searching for someone, yearning to communicate across a void of spiritual isolation. And what we are concerned with here are the means, and now, young man, either shape up or ship out."

Ted elects to shape up, so he sits on the floor and tries the yoga posture called the Spinal Twist. He fails miserably to achieve the posture, and this leads to his singing an amusing duet of "Yoga Is as Yoga Does" with Madame Neherina.

English-born actress Elsa Lanchester began her career on the London stage. In 1927, at the age of twenty-five, she moved from the stage to the British screen, making a number of films, including *The Private Life of Henry VIII* (1933), *The Ghost Goes West* (1936), and *Rembrandt* (1936). She came to the United States

and divided her time between Broadway and Hollywood. Her American movies include *David Copperfield* (1935), *Naughty Marietta* (1935), *The Bride of Frankenstein* (1935), *The Spiral Staircase* (1946), *The Bishop's Wife* (1947), *Les Miserables* (1952), *Mary Poppins* (1964), *That Darn Cat* (1965), *Murder by Death* (1976), and *Die Laughing* (1980). She received Academy Award nominations for Best Supporting Actress for *Come to the Stable* (1949) and *Witness for the Prosecution* (1957).

Lanchester was married for thirty-three years to British actor Charles Laughton—someone who also had a connection to Elvis.

ELVIS FLASHBACK: SEPTEMBER 9, 1956

Working with Elsa Lanchester on *Easy Come, Easy Go* may have caused Elvis to flash back in memory to the night of September 9, 1956. On that night, when Elvis made his first appearance on "The Ed Sullivan Show," he was introduced by Elsa Lanchester's husband, Charles Laughton.

In August 1956, Ed Sullivan was involved in a head-on automobile accident. He was hospitalized for several weeks and was unable to appear on the September 9 broadcast. Charles Laughton served as substitute host on Sullivan's New York-based television show and introduced Elvis, who was in Hollywood. Elvis sang "Don't Be Cruel" and "Love Me Tender." When Laughton reintroduced Elvis later in the show, Elvis sang "Ready Teddy" and "Hound Dog."

Of the total viewing public, 82.6 percent were tuned in to "The Ed Sullivan Show" (1948–1971) for Elvis's first appearance.

EASY COME, EASY GO EP

The extended-play album *Easy Come, Easy Go* contained all six of the songs from the film. In addition to the commercial releases, there were promotional releases of the EP that heralded Elvis's twenty-third film. On one promo EP, for example, the message that appeared at the top of the label just below RCA Victor proclaimed "RCA Victor presents ELVIS in the original soundtrack recording from the Paramount Picture EASY COME, EASY GO, a Hal Wallis Production."

EASY COME, EASY GO PRESLEY PERPLEXERS

Here and there in Elvis's films are instances that cause the keen-eyed fan to do a double take: minor mistakes resulting from errors in continuity, slips in the editing process, or goofs that are simply unexplainable. Did you catch or miss either of these Presley Perplexers in *Easy Come, Easy Go*?

- Ted Jackson runs into Dina Bishop (Pat Priest) at the Easy Go-Go, and she offers to buy him a drink. While they are chatting at the table, Dina's boyfriend, Gil Carey (Skip Ward), shows up and threatens to start a fight with Ted.

Jo Symington (Dodie Marshall) sees the trouble brewing, so she pulls Ted onto the floor for a dance, then asks him to take her home. Fans can't help but notice the orange-red top that Jo wears during the scene. But in the very next scene, when Ted pulls his car up to Jo's house and helps her out, she is suddenly wearing a white top, white slacks, and a black-and-white striped jacket.

- During the climactic underwater scene, Ted and Gil fight over the sunken chest from the *Port of Call.* Ted fills Gil's wet suit with air, and the scoundrel floats to the surface. In no time at all, Ted brings the chest topside. Along with the audience, he is probably amazed to discover that Gil has reached Dina's boat, shed his wet suit, changed into dry clothes, and dried and styled his hair.

Dodi Marshall and Skip Ward–*Easy Come, Easy Go* quick-change artists!

DID YOU KNOW THAT...

- *Easy Come, Easy Go* was not the original title for Elvis's 1967 movie? Other titles considered were *Port of Call, A Girl in Every Port, Nice and Easy*, and *Easy Does It.*

- In addition to his film work, director John Rich was well known for directing television situation comedies? His television credits include episodes of "I Married Joan" (1952–1955), "Our Miss Brooks" (1952–1956), "Mr. Ed" (1961–1965), "The Dick Van Dyke Show" (1961–1966), "Gilligan's Island" (1964–1967), "Gomer Pyle U.S.M.C." (1964–1970), "That Girl" (1966–1971), "All in the Family" (1971–1983), "The Brady Bunch" (1977), and "Benson" (1979–1986).

- Actress Pat Priest, who played rich girl Dina Bishop, was better known for her role on a monstrously funny television show? Priest played Marilyn, the niece of Herman Munster, on "The Munsters" (1964–1966).

- Actor Pat Harrington, Jr., who played nightclub owner Judd Whitman, was the host of a television quiz show? Harrington was the 1962 host of "Stump the Stars" (1950–1963). He is better known for the role of building superintendent Dwayne Schneider on the television series "One Day At a Time" (1975–1984). Earlier, he had played Pat Hannegan, who married Teresa "Terry" Williams, on "Make Room for Daddy" (1953–1957).

- *Easy Come, Easy Go* was the last film for actor Frank McHugh, who played Captain Jack? During his career, McHugh had roles in more than 150 films, including *Little Caesar* (1930), *The Front Page* (1931), *42nd Street* (1933), *Gold Diggers of 1935* (1935), *The Roaring Twenties* (1939), *Back Street* (1941), *Going My Way* (1944), *It Happens Every Thursday* (1953), *The Last Hurrah* (1958), and *Say One for Me* (1959).

- *Easy Come, Easy Go* earned $1.95 million in 1967? The film ranked number fifty on *Variety*'s list of top-grossing films of the year.

EASY COME, EASY GO TRIVIA QUIZ

1. Near which area did Ted Jackson defuse the old underwater mine?

2. What two items comprised the cargo of the *Port of Call*?

3. Where was Jo Symington's house located?

4. What was Jo's full first name?

5. What reason did Ted give to Jo for his interest in the treasure?

6. How was Jo related to the captain of the *Port of Call*?

7. Where did Ted rent the salvage equipment?

8. Who was the sponsor of Captain Jack's Saturday morning children's program?

9. From what malady did Captain Jack claim to suffer?

10. Who were the two female shipmates on Dina Bishop's boat?

11. Who turned Ted's red convertible into the "first automobile mobile"?

12. What did Dina write on the photo she left on Ted's boat?

13. Of what metal were the pieces of eight made?

14. How much was each coin worth?

15. What was the money from the sale of the treasure used for?

25.

DOUBLE TROUBLE

(METRO–GOLDWYN–MAYER, 1967)

PLOT

*B*andleader Elvis has more than double trouble when a teenage fan falls in love with him. Her guardian vows to break up the romance, thieves hide stolen diamonds in Elvis's suitcase, and it appears that someone is trying to kill him.

CAST

Elvis Presley	Guy Lambert
Annette Day	Jillian (Jill) Conway
John Williams	Gerald Waverly
Yvonne Romain	Claire Dunham
The Wiere Brothers	Themselves
Chips Rafferty	Archie Brown
Norman Rossington	Arthur Babcock
Monty Landis	Georgie
Leon Askin	Inspector De Groote
Stanley Adams	Captain Roach
Walter Burke	Captain's Mate
The G-Men	Themselves

CREW

Judd Bernard and Irwin Winkler	Producers
Norman Taurog	Director
Jo Heims	Screenplay
Jeff Alexander	Musical Score
Col. Tom Parker	Technical Advisor

SONGS
"Double Trouble" • "Baby, If You'll Give Me All Your Love" •
"Could I Fall in Love" • "Long Legged Girl (with the Short Dress On)" •
"City by Night" • "Old MacDonald" • "I Love Only One Girl" •
"There Is So Much World to See"

DASHING DUET: "COULD I FALL IN LOVE"

After his musical set at a London nightclub, Guy Lambert (Elvis) greets Jill Conway (Annette Day). He is attracted to her, yet knows he should put her in a cab and send her home so that he isn't tempted further. Instead, she suggests that they go to his flat.

At the flat, Jill tidies up the apartment a bit and puts the kettle on for tea. Meanwhile, Guy steams on the couch because he had been hoping for a little less conversation and a little more . . . well, you know.

"Guy, would you put something on the record player," Jill calls from the kitchen.

"What a time to dance," he grumbles as he places on the phonograph his own hit recording of "Could I Fall in Love."

Jill joins him on the couch. "Oh, isn't that lovely?" she says as she turns her head toward the phonograph and misses one of Guy's kisses.

"It could have been."

"The music . . . the song. Don't you remember, darling? You said it was our song."

"I did? I did."

"Sing it to me."

"Sing at a time like this?"

"Please. You've no idea what your singing does to me."

As the song plays, and the recorded voice of Guy Lambert sings "Could I Fall in Love," Guy sings a duet with himself.

"Could I Fall in Love" was written for *Double Trouble* by Randy Starr. New York City-born Starr arranged the song "Old MacDonald" for the film as well. Elvis recorded two other songs written by Starr: "The Girl I Never Loved" and "Who Needs Money." Starr teamed up with composer Fred Wise and penned for Elvis "Adam and Evil," "Carny Town," "Datin'," "Kissin' Cousins," and "Look Out, Broadway."

THE LONG AND THE SHORT OF
"LONG LEGGED GIRL (WITH THE SHORT DRESS ON)"

When Guy Lambert and his band perform "Long Legged Girl (With the Short Dress On)," they are on the ship sailing from London to Belgium. Jill Conway hears the band, and it doesn't take her long to find Guy among the shipboard throng, which is a good thing because Guy doesn't take long to sing the song.

Written by J. Leslie McFarland and Winfield Scott, "Long Legged Girl (With the Short Dress On)" has a playing time of one minute, twenty-six seconds, making the tune the shortest Elvis single to hit the Hot 100 chart. When released, the single cruised onto the chart, had a five-week stay, and reached a high of number sixty-three.

DOUBLE TROUBLE MAKES ANNETTE'S DAY

Blue-eyed, red-haired Annette Day made her film debut in Elvis's 1967 film. *Double Trouble* was, in fact, Day's first and only motion picture, and her discovery was the stuff of which Hollywood stories are made.

While browsing in an antique shop on Portobello Road in London, coproducer Judd Bernard was struck by the delicate beauty of the girl behind the counter. He began a conversation. The girl turned out to be Annette Day, daughter of the shop's proprietor. Had she ever appeared in a film, the producer asked. No, she hadn't. Did she have any acting experience at all, perhaps in a local production? No, unfortunately, she didn't. Would she be willing to audition for a part in an upcoming Elvis Presley movie? And the rest, as they say, is history.

DOUBLE TROUBLE LP

The soundtrack album from *Double Trouble* packed all eight songs neatly onto both sides of the disc, and there was enough room to include four bonus songs: "It Won't Be Long," "Never Ending," "Blue River," and "What Now, What Next, Where To." A limited number of original pressings of the LP included a seven-inch-by-nine-inch color photo of Elvis. The album spent a twenty-week vacation on *Billboard*'s Top LPs chart, seeing all the sights as it peaked at number forty-seven.

DOUBLE TROUBLE'S PRESLEY PERPLEXERS

Here and there in Elvis's films are instances that cause the keen-eyed fan to do a double take: minor mistakes resulting from errors in continuity, slips in the editing process, or goofs that are simply unexplainable. Did you catch or miss either of these Presley Perplexers in *Double Trouble*?

* The killer lures Jill Conway to the old, abandoned well in Antwerp with the intention of causing her to fall to her death. Guy Lambert hears her screams and rushes in to confront her attacker. During the scuffle, Guy takes off his blue jacket in order to throw better punches. The battle continues and then ends with the killer himself falling to his death down the shaft of the well. Guy picks up his jacket, leaves with Jill, then does something perplexing. Once on the street, he rolls up the jacket and throws it in a trash can. Was he afraid someone would identify him as having worn the jacket? Did he mistakenly think it was the killer's jacket? Had fashion trends changed that quickly?

* After Claire Dunham (Yvonne Romain) and Gerald Waverly (John Williams) are arrested, Guy pours himself a glass of wine. Jill takes the glass, puts her

arms around Guy and accidentally spills the wine on the back of Guy's red jacket. Viewers can clearly see the stain on his back. However, immediately afterwards, when Guy tussles with the detective from Scotland Yard, the back of Guy's jacket is dry.

DID YOU KNOW THAT...

- *Double Trouble* was not the original title for the film? The working title was *You're Killing Me.*

- The exotic locales in *Double Trouble* were actually filmed at MGM's studios? The crew of *Double Trouble* carefully re-created the cities and seas of Great Britain and Belgium on the back lot in Culver City, California.

- The crew of *Double Trouble* strove for realism on the back lot whenever possible? In fact, during the aboard-ship sequences, complete with windswept, rolling seas, sixteen extras were overcome with "seasickness." They had to be replaced so that filming could resume.

- *Double Trouble* was the second American film for actress Yvonne Romain, who played partner-in-crime Claire Dunham? The first American film for the British-raised actress was *The Swinger* (1966), which starred Ann-Margret. Romain's British films include *Pickup Alley* (1957), *The Curse of the Werewolf* (1961), *Return to Sender* (1963), and *The Brigand of Kandahar* (1965).

- Actor John Williams, who played Uncle Gerald, is known for a role in which he upholds the law? Williams portrayed Inspector Hubbard in *Dial M for Murder* (1954) and re-created the part in stage and television versions. His other well-known films include *Sabrina* (1954), *To Catch a Thief* (1955), *Will Success Spoil Rock Hunter?* (1957), *Witness for the Prosecution* (1957), and *The Young Philadelphians* (1959).

- The Wiere Brothers, who played Belgian detectives, are known as an international trio of slapstick comedians? Harry, Herbert, and Sylvester Wiere had film roles in *Vogues of 1938* (1937), *The Great American Broadcast* (1941), *Hands Across the Border* (1943), *Swing Shift Maisie* (1943), and *Road to Rio* (1947). They brought their zaniness to television in the short-lived comedy series "Oh, Those Bells!" (1962).

- Actor Leon Askin, who played Inspector De Groote, was born in Vienna? He began his career on European stages and in cabarets before coming to the United States in 1940. Askin had roles in a number of films, including *Road to Bali* (1952), *What Did You Do In The War, Daddy?* (1966), and *Young Frankenstein* (1974). He is better known to television audiences for his portrayal of Gen. Alfred Burkhalter, Luftwaffe officer in charge of prison camps, on the series "Hogan's Heroes" (1965–1971).

124 • Poster art for *Double Trouble* showed a double image of Elvis playing his guitar? The ad lines read: "Elvis takes mad mod Europe by song as he swings into a brand new adventure filled with dames, diamonds, discotheques, and danger!"

• Some advertisements for *Double Trouble* erroneously stated that Elvis sang nine songs in the film? Although recorded for *Double Trouble*, the song "It Won't Be Long" was cut.

• *Double Trouble* grossed $1.6 million in 1967? On *Variety's* list of top-grossing films, *Double Trouble* ranked number fifty-eight.

DOUBLE TROUBLE TRIVIA QUIZ

1. What was the number of Guy Lambert's London apartment?

2. What was Jill Conway's home address?

3. In what section of London was Jill's home located?

4. How old was Jill at the beginning of the film?

5. At what time was Guy scheduled to meet Uncle Gerald?

6. Who was the artist of the painting that Guy admired in Uncle Gerald's study?

7. In what Belgian city were Guy and the G-Men scheduled to appear?

8. At what Antwerp theater were Guy and the G-Men scheduled to appear?

9. In what Antwerp hotel were Guy and Jill first registered?

10. What was the address of the Hotel Olympia, where Guy and Jill later stayed?

11. What was their room number at the Hotel Olympia?

12. Jill claimed to have a maiden aunt living in which city?

13. What was the name of the love-starved woman in the Hotel Olympia?

14. To pass the time in the police station, what card game did Guy play with De Groote and three police officers?

15. What was the name of the ship on which Guy and Jill sailed on their honeymoon?

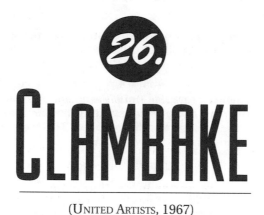

CLAMBAKE

(UNITED ARTISTS, 1967)

PLOT

*7*he son of a rich oilman, Elvis switches identities with a water skiing instructor to discover not only how the other half lives but if he can find a woman who will love him for himself rather than for his money.

CAST

Elvis Presley	Scott Hayward
Shelley Fabares	Dianne Carter
Will Hutchins	Tom Wilson
Bill Bixby	James J. Jamison III
James Gregory	Duster Hayward
Gary Merrill	Sam Burton
Hal Peary	Hal, the Doorman

CREW

Arnold Laven, Arthur Gardner, Jules Levy	Producers
Arthur H. Nadel	Director
Arthur Browne, Jr.	Story and Screenplay
The Jordanaires	Vocal Accompaniment
Col. Tom Parker	Technical Advisor

SONGS

"Clambake" • "Who Needs Money" • "A House That Has Everything" •
"Confidence" • "You Don't Know Me" • "Hey, Hey, Hey" •
"The Girl I Never Loved"

YOU PROBABLY KNOW "YOU DON'T KNOW ME"

Dianne Carter (Shelley Fabares) drops by the ski shop to see how things are going with "Tom Wilson" (Elvis). "Tom" can't resist asking how things are going with Dianne and his rival in romance and in the regatta, James J. Jamison III (Bill Bixby). Dianne has been angling for a marriage proposal from the millionaire, and his popping of the question can't be too far off. This scene ends with "Tom" singing "You Don't Know Me," a song written in 1955 by Eddy Arnold and Cindy Walker.

You probably know "You Don't Know Me" as the tune Ray Charles made a million seller in 1962. His version hit the Hot 100 chart, the Rhythm & Blues chart, and the Easy Listening chart. Prior to the smash by Charles, Eddy Arnold's version scored big on the Country chart, reaching number ten; and Jerry Vale's version performed well on *Billboard*'s Top 100 chart, reaching number fourteen.

Elvis's version of "You Don't Know Me" spent six weeks on the Hot 100 chart and hit its peak at number forty-four. On the Easy Listening chart, the song went to number thirty-four. "You Don't Know Me" was the flip side of "Big Boss Man."

ELVIS'S INJURIES DELAY FILMING

The cast and crew of *Clambake* were scheduled to begin principal filming in early March 1967. Unfortunately, prior to the start date, Elvis tripped over a television cord in the bathroom of his Bel Air home and struck his head in the fall. A visit to the hospital for X-rays revealed no fractures, but doctors did diagnose a severe concussion. Filming was postponed until the last week of March while the King recuperated.

ELVIS AND PRISCILLA MARRY

The filming of *Clambake* ended on April 27, 1967. This was cutting it a bit close since Elvis's next role—that of husband—was scheduled to begin on May 1.

At 3:00 A.M. on May 1, a Lear jet carrying Elvis and Priscilla from Palm Springs touched down in Las Vegas. The groom and his bride were whisked away to the Clark County courthouse to obtain a marriage license. Elvis paid fifteen dollars for the license, which required neither a blood test nor a waiting period. The next stop was the Aladdin Hotel. There Elvis and Priscilla parted company to ready themselves for the ceremony.

Rumors had been swirling among the media that something big was about

to happen. Within a few hours after the purchase of the marriage license, Hollywood gossip columnist Rona Barrett phoned the Presley camp to confirm the rumors that Elvis and Priscilla would be married in Palm Springs.

By 7:00 A.M. the lobby of the Aladdin was alive with reporters and photographers. But their chance to grab the scoop of the year was still several hours away.

At 9:41 A.M., in a second-floor private suite, Nevada Supreme Court Judge David Zenoff began the double-ring wedding ceremony to unite thirty-two-year-old Elvis Presley and twenty-one-year-old Priscilla Beaulieu.

The groom, dressed in black tuxedo pants, and a black brocaded coat and vest, was nervous as he took his place next to Priscilla. She smiled up at him sweetly. The bodice of her white chiffon-over-satin, semifitted, floor-length gown was trimmed with seed pearls and bugle beads. From the back trailed a six-foot train. A double-tiered rhinestone crown with a full veil framed her face, and she carried a white Bible decorated with pink rosebuds. Priscilla's maid of honor was her sister Michelle, and the best men were Joe Esposito and Marty Lacker. Elvis and Priscilla vowed to "love, honor, cherish, and comfort" one another, exchanged rings, and became husband and wife in the simple, eight-minute ceremony.

Following the ceremony, Elvis and Priscilla posed for photographs, then answered questions during a brief press conference. Their reception in the Aladdin Room was a wedding breakfast, which featured a smorgasbord plus a five-foot-high, six-tiered wedding cake, festive with pink-and-white frosting roses. Family, friends, invited reporters, and photographers toasted the newlyweds while a string trio played beautiful ballads.

"Why did you wait this long to get married?" one reporter asked Elvis.

"Well," he began, "I . . . I just thought . . . the life I was living was . . . too difficult, and I decided it would be best if I waited till I . . . I really knew for sure. And now I'm really sure."

Elvis was sure about something else—there would not be much time for a wedding trip. He and Priscilla left the hotel that afternoon and returned to Palm Springs for a four-day honeymoon. Afterwards, the newlyweds flew to Memphis to visit Graceland and the Circle G ranch near Walls, Mississippi, that Elvis had purchased.

Dee Presley, Vernon's second wife, gave a wedding shower for Priscilla, and at the end of May, Elvis and Priscilla held a wedding reception at Graceland for their friends, family, and some fans who had been unable to attend the ceremony in Las Vegas. Then, much too soon, Mr. and Mrs. Elvis Presley headed to Los Angeles. The King was scheduled to begin work on another film.

FANS WHO MISS SPECIAL CLAMBAKE LP CRY "OH SHUCKS"

The soundtrack album from Elvis's 1967 film was snapped up quickly by fans. The LP contained not only the seven tunes from *Clambake* but offered five bonus songs: "Guitar Man," "How Can You Lose What You Never Had," "Big Boss Man," "Singing Tree," and "Just Call Me Lonesome." But fans were snapping up the album for more than just the songs. Included inside the jackets of specially marked albums was a twelve-inch-by-twelve-inch, full-color, autographed photo of Elvis and Priscilla at their wedding. *Clambake* buried itself in the sands of *Billboard*'s Top LPs chart, where it remained for fourteen weeks, topping out at number forty.

CLAMBAKE'S PRESLEY PERPLEXERS

Here and there in Elvis's films are instances that cause the keen-eyed fan to do a double take: minor mistakes resulting from errors in continuity, slips in the editing process, or goofs that are simply unexplainable. Did you catch or miss any of these Presley Perplexers in *Clambake*?

- Scott Hayward (Elvis) and Dianne Carter (Shelley Fabares) share a romantic interlude at the Florida beach, and Scott sings "A House That Has Everything." Apparently the beach they chose had everything, too, including the sun setting in the east over the Atlantic Ocean! This Miami Beach scene was actually filmed in Los Angeles.

- At the end of the film, Scott and Dianne drive from the hotel, discussing Scott's real identity, and making plans to get married. In the background are the beautiful mountains of Miami Beach! This scene, too, was filmed in Los Angeles.

- At the beginning of *Clambake*, Scott stops to get a sandwich, and the camera pans over the service station sign, which heralds "H*e*yward Oil Company." However, at the end of *Clambake*, when Scott shows his driver's license to Dianne, his surname is spelled "H*a*yward."

DID YOU KNOW THAT...

- Two original items were missing from Elvis's twenty-fifth film? The original title, *Too Big for Texas*, was dropped in favor of *Clambake*. The song "How Can You Lose What You Never Had" was originally included in the movie but was axed from the final print.

- Footage from an actual boat race was used in *Clambake*? The action was captured from the Orange Bowl International Power Boat Regatta held at the Marine Stadium in Miami.

- Actor Will Hutchins did not actually sing in the duet with Elvis on "Who Needs Money"? Hutchins's "voice" belonged to Ray Walker of the Jordanaires. Hutchins had a role in an earlier Elvis film, *Spinout* (1966). The actor's television credits include playing Tom Brewster in "Sugarfoot" (1957–1961), Woody Banner in "Hey, Landlord" (1966–1967), and Dagwood Bumstead in "Blondie" (1968–1969).

- Actor Bill Bixby, who played millionaire playboy James J. Jamison III, began his career as a model? That initial exposure led to roles in films such as *Irma La Douce* (1963), *Under the Yum Yum Tree* (1963), *The Kentucky Fried Movie* (1977), *The Incredible Hulk* (1977), and *The Incredible Hulk Returns* (1988).

- Actor James Gregory, who played Duster Hayward, father of Scott and president of Hayward Oil, played another president on a television series? Gregory portrayed President Ulysses. S. Grant in "The Wild, Wild West" (1965–1970). The actor is better known for the roles of Major Duncan, Capt. Wilton Parmenter's superior, on "F Troop" (1965–1967) and of Police Inspector Frank Luger on the television series "Barney Miller" (1975–1982).

- Actor Gary Merrill, who played boat owner Sam Burton, was known for playing the good guy in action movies? His films include *Winged Victory* (1944),

Twelve O'Clock High (1949), *The Human Jungle* (1954), *The Pleasure of His Company* (1961), *Destination Inner Space* (1966), and *Thieves* (1977). Merrill had a memorable role as Bette Davis's husband in *All About Eve* (1950), and soon after the two married in real life.

- Actor Hal Peary, who played Hal the doorman, was at one time responsible for creating a national catchphrase? Peary played Throckmorton P. Gildersleeve, the next-door neighbor of Fibber McGee on the 1930s radio program "Fibber McGee and Molly." Gildersleeve was known for spouting "You're a hard man, McGee," and the phrase swept the country. Peary's character was so popular that the actor was given his own radio program, "The Great Gildersleeve," in 1941. This show is considered one of the first broadcast spinoffs.

- The dolphin that made a cameo appearance in *Clambake* was Flipper? Flipper was actually a female dolphin named Susie. Susie was the star of the television series "Flipper" (1964–1967), which was set in Coral Key Park Marine Preserve in Florida. In the show, Flipper was the pet dolphin of Sandy Ricks (Luke Halpin) and his brother Bud (Tommy Nordon).

- Fans could own a piece of the white suit worn by Elvis in *Clambake*? The suit was cut up, and small pieces were placed in envelopes that were packaged in the four-record boxed set, *Elvis: The Other Sides—Worldwide Gold Award Hits, Volume 2*, released by RCA in 1971.

CLAMBAKE TRIVIA QUIZ

1. What did Scott Hayward order at the snack bar at the service station?

2. How many more payments did Tom Wilson have to make on his motorcycle?

3. At what hotel did Scott and Tom stay?

4. What was the name of James J. Jamison's powerboat?

5. In what business was the Jamison family engaged?

6. From whom did Scott obtain the boat he drove in the regatta?

7. What was the name of Scott's boat?

8. What was the number of Scott's boat?

9. In what field did Scott major in college?

10. What was the name of the protective resin covering that Scott developed and used to coat his race boat?

11. Who said "For Hayward's friends, the elbow bends."

12. How large was the diamond engagement ring promised to Dianne Carter by J. J. Jamison?

13. What were the prizes for winning the Orange Bowl International Power Boat Regatta?

14. What gift did Scott tell Dianne he had received for his twenty-first birthday?

15. According to his driver's license, what was Scott's date of birth?

STAY AWAY JOE

(METRO–GOLDWYN–MAYER, 1968)

PLOT

*B*ronco rider Elvis returns from the rodeo circuit to his Navajo Indian reservation with a small herd of government-provided cattle. If he and his father can raise the herd successfully, the United States government promises to help the rest of the reservation. When the plan fails and it appears that the entire family will go to jail, Elvis comes to the rescue.

CAST

Elvis Presley	Joe Lightcloud
Burgess Meredith	Charlie Lightcloud
Joan Blondell	Glenda Callahan
Katy Jurado	Annie Lightcloud
Thomas Gomez	Chief Lightcloud
Henry Jones	Hy Slager
L. Q. Jones	Bronc Hoverty
Quentin Dean	Mamie Callahan
Anne Seymour	Mrs. Hawkins
Douglas Henderson	Congressman Morrissey
Angus Duncan	Lorne Hawkins
Susan Trustman	Mary Lightcloud
Warren Vanders	Hike Bowers
Dick Wilson	Car Salesman

CREW

Douglas Laurence	Producer
Peter Tewksbury	Director
Michael A. Hoey	Screenplay
Dan Cushman	Novel
Jack Marshall	Music Score

The Jordanaires .... Vocal Accompaniment
Col. Tom Parker .... Technical Advisor

SONGS
"Stay Away" • "Stay Away, Joe" • "Lovely Mamie" • "Dominick" •
"All I Needed Was the Rain"

"STAY AWAY"

Sid Tepper and Roy C. Bennett based their composition "Stay Away" on the melody of "Greensleeves." Elvis sings "Stay Away" over the opening credits of his 1968 film.

The single couldn't stay away from *Billboard*'s Hot 100 chart. The release lingered for five weeks, peaking at number sixty-seven.

"LOVELY MAMIE

Joe Lightcloud (Elvis) sings just a few seconds of "Lovely Mamie" in *Stay Away, Joe*. The tune for the song was "Alouette," a traditional French Canadian folk song. Although "Lovely Mamie" does appear on some bootleg albums, RCA has not released the song.

STAY AWAY, JOE: A NOVEL IDEA

Elvis's twenty-sixth film was based on the best-selling book *Stay Away, Joe* by Dan Cushman. The novel was a Book-of-the-Month Club selection for April 1953 and earned both praise and damnation from the critics:

- Clarence Gorchels, writing for *Library Journal*, reported: "A boisterously funny story. No matter that the book has no 'message' or noble theme, for the author has created a small masterpiece of facile narration and comic characterization. Warmly recommended for adults with a ready sense of humor."

- Edward Weeks, writing for *Atlantic*, reported: "Since no one in the book except Mary has ever taken a bath, done a day's work, or spoken a grammatical word, the story has what you might call atmosphere. Which would be all very well if it had native charm too, or more than one sympathetic character, or momentum. But in spite of the fact that hell pops all the time, I only get an impression of frantic random action. The author has not enough control of the story to make it funny, and I get very tired of the dialect, the beer, and the dirt."

- The *New Yorker* reported: "The characters are all from comic books but are not comic, the humor is broad, the laughter is empty, the setting is drab, there is noise but no spirit, and every element of humanity is missing."

- Rose Feld, writing for the *New York Her-*

ald Tribune, reported: "This rocky, rough-slabbed creature chiseled by Mr. Cushman is hardly lovable as a character, but he is real and alive and as amusing as a lumbering bear. Whatever his isms—and they include lechery and drink and cheating—there is no trace of evil or malice in the man. There are moments indeed when the reader will join . . . in defending him against his women folk."

ELVIS AS JOE LIGHTCLOUD: A GOLDEN TURKEY TO SOME

In their 1980 book *The Golden Turkey Awards,* authors Harry and Michael Medved took Elvis to task for his portrayal of Native American Joe Lightcloud. The authors wrote: "In responding to *Stay Away, Joe* we can only echo the terse but eloquent statement of countless Hollywood Indians over the years: 'Ugh!'"

Elvis was nominated for a Golden Turkey Award in the category of "The Most Ludicrous Racial Impersonation in Hollywood History." The other nominees in the category were:

- Robby Benson portraying a Chicano in *Walk Proud* (1979).

- Marlon Brando portraying an Okinawan in *The Teahouse of the August Moon* (1956).

- Charles Mack and George Moran portraying Black Americans in *Hypnotized* (1933).

- And the winner of the dubious award was—not Elvis, but Marlon Brando.

DID YOU KNOW THAT...

- Location filming took place in Arizona? Cast, crew, and cameras worked near Sedona and Cottonwood, Arizona. Near Sedona, the crew built a Navajo Indian reservation for use during filming.

- Extras were recruited for the all-night party scenes? One hundred thirty-nine members of the Navajo Indian Reservation near Tuba City appeared in the film.

- Actor Burgess Meredith, who played Joe Lightcloud's father, Charlie, has acted in more than sixty motion pictures? Meredith's credits include *Of Mice and Men* (1939), *The Story of GI Joe* (1945), *Joe Butterfly* (1957), *Advise and Consent* (1962), and *There Was a Crooked Man* (1970). He was nominated for an Academy Award as Best Supporting Actor for his work in *The Day of the Locust* (1975) and *Rocky* (1976). Television audiences remember Meredith as Martin Woodbridge, the principal at Jefferson High School, on the series "Mr. Novak" (1963–1965) and as the Penguin on the series "Batman" (1966–1968).

- Actress Katy Jurado, who played Joe Lightcloud's step-mother, Annie, limped in some scenes of *Stay Away, Joe?* She had broken several bones in her foot a few days before the start of filming. She kept this news from the director and producer, removed the foot cast when filming began, and explained that the limp was part of the character she was playing.

- Actress Joan Blondell, who played gun-toting mama Glenda Callahan, played no-nonsense characters in two television series? Blondell played saloon owner

Lottie Hatfield on "Here Come the Brides" (1968–1970) and Peggy Revere, owner of the Revere Secretarial School, on "Banyon" (1972–1973). Her film credits include *The Public Enemy* (1931), *Gold Diggers of 1937* (1936), *Topper Returns* (1941), *A Tree Grows in Brooklyn* (1945), *The Corpse Came COD* (1947), *Will Success Spoil Rock Hunter?* (1957), *The Cincinnati Kid* (1965), *Support Your Local Gunfighter* (1971), and *The Woman Inside* (1981). She was nominated for an Academy Award as Best Supporting Actress for her work in *The Blue Veil* (1951).

- Actor Dick Wilson, who played the car salesman from whom Joe Lightcloud bought his red convertible, was a pitchman on a well-known television commercial? Wilson played Mr. Whipple the grocer on the "Please don't squeeze the Charmin" commercials.

- None of the fun was missing from *Stay Away, Joe*, but one of the songs was? "Goin' Home" was written for the film by Joy Byers but was cut from the final print.

- The advertising lines for *Stay Away, Joe* were as outrageous as the character Elvis played? Some of the lines were: "Elvis goes West . . . and the West goes wild!" "He's playing Indian—but he doesn't say 'How' . . . he says 'When!'" "Elvis is kissin' cousins again—and also friends, and even some perfect strangers!"

STAY AWAY, JOE TRIVIA QUIZ

1. How many heifers did Joe Lightcloud receive from Congressman Morrissey?

2. How did Joe arrive at his family's homestead?

3. What congressional district did Congressman Morrissey represent?

4. How much money did Joe contribute towards the beer for the party?

5. What happened to the young bull that Joe received from the congressman?

6. What did Joe trade for the red convertible?

7. How old was Mamie Callahan?

8. What was Callahan's?

9. Who was Dominick XII?

10. From whom did Joe acquire Dominick?

11. What did Joe not know about Dominick?

12. What was the first improvement Annie Lightcloud made as a result of selling cows?

13. Who was called "The Pride of Calgary, Cheyenne, and Madison Square Garden"?

14. From which rodeo chute did Dominick and Joe burst forth?

15. How many head of cattle did Joe buy with his winnings?

28.

SPEEDWAY

(METRO–GOLDWYN–MAYER, 1968)

PLOT

*W*hen his tax returns are audited by the Internal Revenue Service, stock-car racing champion Elvis finds that he owes big money to the government. A lovely IRS agent succeeds not only in collecting a portion of the back taxes but putting a lien on his heart as well.

CAST

Elvis Presley	Steve Grayson
Nancy Sinatra	Susan Jacks
Bill Bixby	Kenny Donford
Gale Gordon	R. W. Hepworth
William Schallert	Abel Esterlake
Victoria Meyerink	Ellie Esterlake
Ross Hagen	Paul Dado
Carl Ballantine	Birdie Kebner
Poncie Ponce	Juan Medala
Harry Hickox	The Cook
Christopher West	Billie Joe
Mary Ann Ashman	Miss Charlotte Speedway 100
Charlotte Considine	Lori
Sandy Reed	Race Announcer

CREW

Douglas Laurence	Producer
Norman Taurog	Director
Phillip Shuken	Screenplay
Jeff Alexander	Music Score

The Jordanaires .... Vocal Accompaniment
Col. Tom Parker .... Technical Advisor

SONGS
"Speedway" • "Let Yourself Go" • "Your Time Hasn't Come Yet, Baby" •
"He's Your Uncle, Not Your Dad" • "Who Are You? (Who Am I)?" •
"There Ain't Nothing Like a Song"

NANCY SINATRA: THOSE PIPES ARE MADE FOR SINGING

Nancy Sinatra first met Elvis on March 3, 1960, a snowy and windswept day that brought a plane from Frankfurt, Germany, to McGuire Air Force Base in New Jersey at 6:30 A.M. Among the GIs that poured through that plane's doorway and down the stairs was Sgt. Elvis Presley, home for good, at last. Part of the welcoming party that greeted the returning soldier was Nancy Sinatra. She presented to him a box of dress shirts that were a present from her father, Frank Sinatra.

Nancy next caught up with Elvis in late March 1960 when they were in Miami at the Fontainebleau Hotel rehearsing for and then taping a Frank Sinatra–Timex TV special, "Welcome Home, Elvis." Broadcast on May 12, 1960, the special featured Elvis singing "Fame and Fortune," "Stuck on You," and in a duet with Ol' Blue Eyes, the Sinatra hit "Witchcraft." In turn, Frank Sinatra sang Elvis's hit "Love Me Tender," with Elvis adding the harmony. Frank and Nancy Sinatra sang a duet of "You Make Me Feel So Young." The special marked Nancy's national television debut.

After her 1960 marriage to singer Tommy Sands (a former client of Col. Tom Parker), Nancy abandoned show business, but when they divorced in 1965, she resumed her career. Her first three records—"Like I Do," "Tonight You Belong to Me," and "Think of Me"—were hits in Europe and South Africa but not in the United States. Nancy's 1966 release "These Boots Are Made for Walkin'," written by Lee Hazlewood, marched up *Billboard*'s Hot 100 chart to number one and became a gold record. Global sales totaled nearly four million copies. In 1966, Nancy followed up this success with another gold record, "Sugartown," which was also written by Hazlewood.

Nancy and Hazlewood teamed up in 1967 and 1968 and created four hit duets, "Summer Wine," "Jackson," "Lady Bird," and "Some Velvet Morning." The year 1967 also brought Nancy her third gold record for the duet with her father that went to number one, "Somethin' Stupid." Other songs that Nancy recorded include "How Does That Grab You, Darlin'?" "Sugar Town," "Love Eyes," "You Only Live Twice" (from the James Bond film), "Lightning's Girl," and "Tony Rome."

During the filming of *Speedway* there

were rumors that Nancy and Elvis were involved in an affair. Nancy quashed the gossip when she gave a baby shower for Priscilla.

In August 1969, Elvis, Priscilla, Vernon, and Dee Presley were in the audience for Nancy's opening at the Las Vegas International Hotel. Her shows there featured not only her greatest hits but the last of her songs to make the charts in 1969, "God Knows I Love You," "Here We Go Again," and "Drummer Man."

"LET YOURSELF GO"

When the house band finishes playing a lively dance number, master of ceremonies Birdie Kebner (Carl Ballantine) takes to the stage with an announcement.

"It's entertainment time here at the Hangout," he says "and you all know the rules. When I hit you with the light, you gotta get up and do somethin'. If you don't, we do somethin' to you." He then focuses a car headlight on Steve Grayson (Elvis) and declares "You're on!"

Steve protests, but the band begins playing, the audience starts applauding, so he decides to give a musical love lesson by singing "Let Yourself Go."

"Let Yourself Go" was composed for *Speedway* by Joy Byers, and Elvis's single release of the song jumped onto *Billboard*'s Hot 100 chart. However, the song enjoyed but a five-week excursion on the chart, hitting only as high as number seventy-one. "Let Yourself Go" was the flip side of another song from *Speedway*, "Your Time Hasn't Come Yet, Baby."

THE LITTLE GIRL HAS MARRIAGE ON HER MIND

Steve Grayson first spots her snitching six giant-sized hot dogs from the snack area of the Hangout. He soon discovers that Ellie Esterlake (Victoria Meyerink) has "borrowed from the cook while he wasn't looking" not only the hot dogs but potato chips, cole slaw, three colas, and one diet cola to feed her hungry sisters and her father, Abel.

Race car driver Abel Esterlake (William Schallert) has a bad leg that keeps him from working. As a result, he and his daughters live a hand-to-mouth existence in an old station wagon that doesn't start. Steve is so moved by the family's desperate circumstances that he gives them money, a month's worth of groceries, and a brand-new car. The Esterlakes, especially Ellie, are overwhelmed by his generosity, .

"You know something, Mr. Steve? I wish I were big enough to marry you," she tells him.

That leads Steve to sing "Your Time Hasn't Come Yet, Baby," a song about childhood, growing up, and knowing when it's time to walk down the aisle.

"Your Time Hasn't Come Yet, Baby" was written by Joel Hirschhorn and Al Kasha. Elvis's single release had a seven-week engagement on the Hot 100 chart, where it peaked at number seventy-two. The song performed a bit better on the Country chart. There it reached number fifty.

SPEEDWAY LP

The cover of the *Speedway* soundtrack album featured seven action closeups of Elvis and a bold notice that was intended to rev up reaction from fans: "Special in This Album—Nancy Sinatra singing "Your Groovy Self."

Fans found an eight-inch-by-ten-inch color photo inside the album plus all the songs from the movie on side one of the LP, including "There Ain't Nothing Like a Song," Elvis's duet with Nancy Sinatra.

The first track on side two was Sinatra's solo tune, "Your Groovy Self," followed by five bonus songs: "Five Sleepy Heads," "Western Union," "Mine," "Goin' Home," and "Suppose." Three of the bonus songs—"Five Sleepy Heads," "Western Union," and "Suppose"—had been intended for use in the movie but had been cut.

The inclusion of the Sinatra song marked the first time a solo by another artist appeared on a regular RCA Elvis album. The soundtrack achieved another milestone, too, since it was the last Elvis LP released in both monaural and stereo. During a thirteen-week race on *Billboard*'s Top LPs chart, the *Speedway* soundtrack braked in at a high of number eighty-two.

DID YOU KNOW THAT...

- *Speedway* was not the original title for Elvis's 1968 movie? Other titles considered were *Guitar City*, *So I'll Go Quietly*, and *Pot Luck*.

- Parts of *Speedway* were filmed on location? Ten cameras were on location at Charlotte Speedway in North Carolina to film the Charlotte 500 race.

- Director of Photography Joseph Ruttenberg was nominated for ten Academy Awards for Best Cinematography? Of the ten nominations, he won four Oscars for his work on *The Great Waltz* (1938), *Mrs. Miniver* (1942), *Somebody Up There Likes Me* (1956), and *Gigi* (1958).

- Seven professional stock-car racers played themselves in *Speedway*? The opening credits mention Buddy Baker, Dick Hutcherson, Tiny Lund, Roy Mayne, Richard Petty, G. C. Spencer, and Cale Yarborough.

- Actor William Schallert, who played Abel Esterlake, father of the motherless Esterlake brood, portrayed fathers in two television series? Schallert had the roles of Martin Lane, father of Patty, on "The Patty Duke Show" (1963–1966) and Carson Drew, father of Nancy, on "The Nancy Drew Mysteries (1977–1978). His film credits include *Riot In Cell Block 11* (1954), *Written on the Wind* (1956), *The Incredible Shrinking Man* (1957), *Lonely Are the Brave* (1962), *In the Heat of the Night* (1967), *Charley Varrick* (1973), and *Twilight Zone—The Movie* (1983).

- Actor Bill Bixby, who played friend and manager Kenny Donford, was a friend to an extraterrestrial on a popular television series? Bixby played newspaper reporter Tim O'Hara, who befriended a Martian who crash landed on Earth on the series "My Favorite Martian" (1963–1966). Bixby also had starring roles on "The Courtship of Eddie's Father" (1969–1979), "The Magician" (1973–1974), "The Incredible Hulk" (1978–1982), and "Goodnight, Beantown" (1983–1984).

- Singer-actress Nancy Sinatra was not the first choice for the role of IRS agent Susan Jacks? The part was initially offered to British singer Petula Clark, but she decided against accepting the role. Sinatra made her screen debut in the 1964 movie *For Those Who Think Young.* Her other movie credits include *Get Yourself a College Girl* (1964), *Marriage on the Rocks* (1965), *Ghost in the Invisible Bikini* (1966), *The Last of the Secret Agents?* (1966), *The Oscar* (1966), and *The Wild Angels* (1966).

- The real name of actor Gale Gordon, who played IRS investigator R. W. Hepworth, is Charles T. Aldrich, Jr.? Gordon has distinguished himself as an actor in movies and on television. His film credits include *Here Come the Nelsons* (1952), *Rally 'Round the Flag, Boys* (1958), *Don't Give Up the Ship* (1959), and *All in a Night's Work* (1961). On television, Gordon played principal Osgood Conklin on "Our Miss Brooks" (1952–1956), Mr. Heckendorn, the apartment building superintendent on "Make Room for Daddy" (1953–1957), George Wilson's brother John on "Dennis The Menace" (1959–1963), banker Theodore J. Mooney on "The Lucy Show" (1961–1968), and Harrison Otis Carter, brother-in-law of Lucille Carter (Lucille Ball) on "Here's Lucy" (1968–1974).

- Actor Ross Hagen, who played rival driver Paul Dado, made his film debut in *Speedway?* Hagen was known for his role as game hunter Bert Jason on the television series "Daktari" (1966–1969).

- When Burt Mustin, who played the janitor in the coffee shop, made *Speedway*, he was eighty-three years old? He made his screen debut at the age of sixty-seven in *Detective Story* (1951) and went on to capture roles in *Raintree County* (1957), *Rally 'Round the Flag, Boys* (1958), *Son of Flubber* (1963), *The Thrill of It All* (1963), *Sex and the Single Girl* (1964), *Cat Ballou* (1965), *The Cincinnati Kid* (1965), *The Reluctant Astronaut* (1967), and *Baker's Hawk* (1976). On television, he is best remembered for the role of Gus, the old fire chief, on "Leave It to Beaver" (1957–1963).

- *Speedway* reached number forty on the *Variety* list of top-grossing films for 1968? *Speedway* earned $3 million for the year.

SPEEDWAY TRIVIA QUIZ

1. What was the number of Steve Grayson's race car?

2. What was the number of rival Paul Dado's race car?

3. Paul Dado kissed a rabbit's foot for luck before the race. What did Birdie Kebner kiss for luck for Steve?

4. What interest rate did Abel Esterlake promise to pay back on the money Steve gave him?

5. What was the total amount Steve won at the Charlotte Speedway 250 race?

6. What was the name of the restaurant at which Lori the carhop worked?

7. What was the name of the church at which Lori and her fiance were married because of Steve's financial help?

8. What was the amount of Steve's income tax deduction for air that was subsequently disallowed?

9. After the audit, what was the amount that Steve owed to the government?

10. How much was Steve given as a weekly allowance?

11. What was the name of Kenny Donford's bookie?

12. What was the nickname of the mobile home shared by Steve and Kenny?

13. What was Paul Dado's qualifying time for the World 600?

14. Why did Steve have trouble making speed in the World 600?

15. How much of Steve's third-place winnings went to the government towards his back taxes?

29. LIVE A LITTLE, LOVE A LITTLE

(METRO–GOLDWYN–MAYER, 1968)

PLOT

*A*s a photographer with two full-time jobs—one at a staid advertising agency and the other at a girlie magazine—Elvis finds little time to live or love until he falls for a kookie cutie who changes his mind about the single life.

CAST

Elvis Presley	Greg Nolan
Michele Carey	Bernice
Don Porter	Mike Lansdown
Rudy Vallee	Louis Penlow
Dick Sargent	Harry
Sterling Holloway	Milkman
Celeste Yarnall	Ellen
Eddie Hodges	Delivery Boy
Joan Shawlee	Robbie's Mother
John Hegner	Robbie

CREW

Douglas Laurence	Producer
Norman Taurog	Director
Michael A. Hoey and Dan Greenburg	Screenplay
Billy Strange	Music Score
Col. Tom Parker	Technical Advisor

SONGS

"Wonderful World" • "Edge of Reality" • "A Little Less Conversation" •
"Almost in Love"

ELVIS'S LIVE A LITTLE, LOVE A LITTLE DREAM IS ON THE "EDGE OF REALITY"

Elvis sang "Edge of Reality" in the surrealistic dream sequence in *Live a Little, Love a Little*. Written by Bill Giant, Bernie Baum, and Florence Kaye, the song failed to chart but appeared on the "Bubbling Under" chart at number one hundred twelve. "Edge of Reality" was the flip side of "If I Can Dream," the song Elvis used to end his December 3, 1968, NBC television special, "Elvis."

For the special, Colonel Parker had urged Elvis to conclude the program with a Christmas song, but producer Steve Binder had a better idea. He wanted Elvis to end the show with a song that made a statement. Binder encouraged Elvis to listen to a new composition written for the occasion by the choral director of the special, W. Earl Brown. Brown played "If I Can Dream" for Elvis, who asked to hear it again and then again. Brown played the song six times for Elvis, who at last said "I'll do it, I'll do it."

"If I Can Dream," backed with "Edge of Reality," was released by RCA before the debut of the special. After the special, "If I Can Dream" acted as a wake-up call for fans, who rushed to record stores to purchase copies of the single release. The song was on *Billboard*'s Hot 100 chart for thirteen weeks where it topped out at number twelve.

LET'S TALK ABOUT "A LITTLE LESS CONVERSATION"

At the poolside party at the home of boss number one, Mike Lansdown (Don Porter), Greg Nolan (Elvis) spies beautiful guest Ellen (Celeste Yarnall). He romances her by singing "A Little Less Conversation."

"A Little Less Conversation" was written by guitarist and composer Billy Strange and country singer and composer Mac Davis. The song talked its way onto *Billboard*'s Hot 100 chart for a four-week chat, where it reached number sixty-nine.

In October 1955, fourteen-year-old Mac Davis saw Elvis perform on the same bill with Buddy Holly at the Cotton Club in Lubbock, Texas. In the 1960s and 1970s, Davis composed songs for major artists, including Elvis. "In the Ghetto" and "Don't Cry, Daddy" were two songs written by Davis that went gold for Elvis.

Billy Strange wielded his mean guitar for the Ventures and Duane Eddy, and also played guitar on a number of Elvis's recording sessions. For *Live a Little, Love a Little*, Strange was the musical director.

Mac Davis and Billy Strange cowrote other songs for Elvis, including "Clean Up Your Own Back Yard," "Charro," "Nothingville," and "Memories."

"ALMOST IN LOVE"

The flip side of "A Little Less Conversation" was "Almost in Love," written by Rick Bonfa and Randy Starr. "Almost in Love" barely made *Billboard*'s Hot 100 chart. After a brief two-week stay, the song only reached number ninety-five.

"Almost In Love" and "A Little Less Conversation" were both featured on the LP *Almost In Love*.

FRIEND AND FAN: DIRECTOR NORMAN TAUROG

Live a Little, Love a Little was the last Elvis film directed by friend and fan Norman Taurog. The eight other Elvis films that Taurog directed were *GI Blues* (1960), *Blue Hawaii* (1961), *Girls! Girls! Girls!* (1962), *It Happened at the World's Fair* (1963), *Tickle Me* (1965), *Spinout* (1966), *Double Trouble* (1967), and *Speedway* (1968).

One of Elvis's favorite directors, Taurog was not only a colleague but a friend and fan as well. In fact, Taurog and his wife presented Elvis and Priscilla a yellow bassinet to celebrate the birth of Lisa Marie. When asked about working with the King, Taurog once said "I was always proud of his work, even if I wasn't too proud of the scripts. I always felt that he never reached his peak."

Norman Taurog began his film career in 1913 as a juvenile actor before making a switch to directing in 1919. Between 1919 and 1928, he directed 275 two-reel silent films, then began to concentrate on full-length talkies.

He scored his first hit in 1931 with *Skippy*, a film in which his six-year-old nephew Jackie Cooper starred. As a result of his work, Taurog received an Academy Award for Best Director and established a reputation as a director skilled at working with child actors. This reputation led to his directing *The Adventures of Tom Sawyer* (1938) with Tommy Kelly and Ann Gillis, *Mad about Music* (1938) with Deanna Durbin, and *Boys' Town* (1938) with Mickey Rooney.

Other films that bear Taurog's directorial imprint include *Young Tom Edison* (1940), *Girl Crazy* (1943), *The Hoodlum Saint* (1946), *Words and Music* (1948), and *That Midnight Kiss* (1949).

In the 1950s, producer Hal Wallis engaged Taurog to direct a series of movies starring Jerry Lewis and Dean Martin, including *Jumping Jacks* (1952), *The Stooge* (1952), *You're Never Too Young* (1955), and *Pardners* (1956). Then, between 1960 and 1968, Wallis asked Taurog to turn his attention to directing Elvis.

Live a Little, Love a Little marked Taurog's last association with Elvis and the director's retirement from filmmaking. Taurog died on April 7, 1981, at the age of 82.

THEY <u>REALLY</u> WANT HIS AUTOGRAPH

During the filming of *Live a Little, Love a Little*, cast, crew, and cameras were working on the street in downtown Los Angeles. Two elderly ladies in the crowd of watching fans caught sight of *him* and rushed through the security barriers. Elvis soon found himself flat on the pavement, but the senior citizens weren't after the King. They had trampled Elvis in an effort to get autographs from costar Rudy Vallee.

Rudy Vallee was born Hubert Prior Vallee in 1901 and began his entertainment career in 1920 as a self-taught saxophonist. He adopted the first name Rudy from Rudy Wiedoeft, a saxophonist that Vallee admired.

To pay his way through college, Vallee played in college bands and, for a different vocal sound, sang through a cheerleader's megaphone. In 1928, he formed his own band and became a popular crooner in nightclubs, on the vaudeville circuit, and on radio. As a number one radio and movie attraction throughout the 1930s and 1940s, Vallee was known for his salutation "Heigh-ho, everybody" and the theme song "My Time Is Your Time." His early films include *Sweet*

Music (1935), *Gold Diggers in Paris* (1938), *Time Out for Rhythm* (1941), and *The Palm Beach Story* (1942).

In 1949, Vallee began a new career as a nightclub comedian, which he continued for the next twelve years. He then reprised his acting career by accepting roles in summer-stock productions, Broadway plays, television series, and Hollywood films. He is best remembered to younger audiences as the preposterous corporation president in the film *How to Succeed in Business without Really Trying* (1967), a role he created in the 1962 musical. On television, he is known for the role of criminal Lord Marmaduke Ffogg on "Batman" (1966–1968).

In 1962, Vallee told a reporter for *Show Business Illustrated* that "I'll be front page news until the day I die." He remained popular with his fans and active in show business until his death on July 3, 1986.

DID YOU KNOW THAT...

- The screenplay for *Live a Little, Love a Little* was based on a novel by script cowriter Dan Greenburg? *Kiss My Firm But Pliant Lips* was Greenburg's first novel. He is also the author of *How to Be a Jewish Mother*, *What Do Women Want?*, and *Confessions of a Pregnant Father*.

- The fight scene in the newspaper pressroom was filmed at an actual newspaper office? The location was the *Hollywood Citizen–News*, and three newspaper employees—Joe Diannito, Russ Alexander, and Leon Brunelle—had small parts in the scene.

- Albert, the Great Dane, was played by Brutus? In real life, Brutus was Elvis's dog, one of a pair that he owned. The other Great Dane was named Snoopy; however, there is no evidence to suggest that during filming Snoopy served as a stand-in for Brutus.

- Vernon Presley had a bit part in *Live a Little, Love a Little*? Elvis's father could be seen as an extra sitting at a table. Vernon had previously appeared as an extra in *Loving You* (1957).

- Actor Dick Sargent, who played lovesick Harry, is better known as the husband of a television witch? Sargent replaced Dick York as Darrin Stevens on the popular series "Bewitched" (1964-1972), starring Elizabeth Montgomery as Samantha Stevens. Sargent's other television credits include "Hazel" (1961–1966), "The Tammy Grimes Show" (1966), and "The Dukes of Hazzard" (1979–1985).

144 • The voice of actor Sterling Holloway, who played Truman the Milkman, is as well known as his distinctive face? He was the voice of Winnie the Pooh and also lent his voice for characters in *Dumbo* (1941), *Bambi* (1942), and *Jungle Book* (1967). His long career spanned silent films, talkies, and television. On television he played Waldo Binny, friend of Chester A. Riley on "The Life of Riley" (1953–1958), Sorrowful Joe, the worst jinx of the 101st Fort Apache Cavalry on "The Adventures of Rin Tin Tin" (1954–1964), and first mate Buck Singleton on "The Baileys of Balboa" (1964–1965).

• Actor Eddie Hodges, who played the delivery boy, made his movie debut in a film starring Frank Sinatra? In *A Hole in the Head* (1959), Hodges played Sinatra's son, and the pair sang the Academy Award-winning song "High Hopes." Hodges scored two top-twenty songs in the 1960s: "I'm Gonna Knock on Your Door" and "(Girls, Girls, Girls) Made to Love." His other film roles include *The Adventures of Huckleberry Finn* (1960), *Advise and Consent* (1962), *Summer Magic* (1963), *C'mon, Let's Live A Little* (1967), and *The Happiest Millionaire* (1967).

LIVE A LITTLE, LOVE A LITTLE TRIVIA QUIZ

1. What name did Bernice first give to Greg Nolan?

2. What were Albert the Great Dane's sleeping accommodations?

3. For which dairy did Truman the Milkman work?

4. According to Woodrow the delivery boy, what was his regular line of work?

5. What were Harry's favorite foods?

6. What take-out food did Greg bring home to the recuperating Bernice?

7. Who were the partners in Creative Advertising?

8. On what floor was Creative Advertising located?

9. What was the name of the magazine run by Mike Lansdown?

10. What healthful cocktail did Mike Lansdown call "good for the liver"?

11. What was the name of the mermaid model Greg photographed?

12. What kind of stew did Bernice serve to Harry and Greg?

13. What was Greg's home address?

14. What was the ratio of women to men at Lansdown's pool party?

15. Where did Greg find runaway Bernice?

30.

CHARRO!

(NATIONAL GENERAL PICTURES, 1969)

PLOT

Reformed gunslinger Elvis is framed by the leader of an outlaw gang for murder and the theft of a valuable cannon owned by the Mexican government.

CAST

Elvis Presley	Jess Wade
Ina Balin	Tracey Winters
Victor French	Vince Hackett
Solomon Sturges	Billy Roy Hackett
James Sikking	Gunner
James Almanzar	Sheriff Dan Ramsey
Barbara Werle	Sara Ramsey
Lynn Kellogg	Marcie
Paul Brinegar	Opie Keetch
Harry Landers	Heff
Tony Young	Lieutenant Rivera
Charles H. Gray	Mody
Rodd Redwing	Lige
Garry Walberg	Martin Tilford
Duane Grey	Gabe
J. Edward McKinley	Henry Carter
John Pickard	Jerome Selby

CREW

Harry A. Caplan	Executive Producer
Charles Marquis Warren	Producer
Charles Marquis Warren	Director
Charles Marquis Warren	Screenplay
Col. Tom Parker	Technical Advisor

"CHARRO"

Elvis sings "Charro" over the opening credits of his 1969 film. *Charro!* was a departure from other Elvis films in that the movie featured no other songs by the King. Written by Billy Strange and Mac Davis, "Charro" was released in March 1969 as the flip side of "Memories."

PREVIEWS AND PUBLICITY TRIPS

Although *Charro!* opened nationwide on March 13, 1969, fans caught sneak peeks of Elvis's twenty-ninth movie in specially planned previews throughout the South. The governors of Oklahoma, Texas, and Louisiana declared "*Charro!* Day" to celebrate the previews in their states, and twenty-five cities held "*Charro!* Girl" contests. To enhance those publicity efforts, National General Pictures dispatched two contingents of *Charro!* actors to those states to make appearances and to attend the previews.

MOVIE MAKING TRIPLE THREAT: CHARLES MARQUIS WARREN

Charles Marquis Warren was a *Charro!* triple threat, serving as producer, director, and writer of the screenplay for Elvis's twenty-ninth film.

Warren began writing and directing films in the 1940s. Some of the films he wrote include *Beyond Glory* (1948), *Streets of Laredo* (1949), *Oh! Susanna* (1951), *Pony Express* (1953), *Day of the Evil Gun* (1968). He wrote and directed *Little Big Horn* (1951), *Hellgate* (1952), *Arrowhead* (1953), *Ride a Violent Mile* (1957), and *Desert Hell* (1958). Warren directed *Seven Angry Men* (1955), *Back from the Dead* (1957), *Blood Arrow* (1958), and *Cattle Empire* (1958).

He brought his talents to television where he produced and directed the series "Gunsmoke" (1955–1975) and "Rawhide" (1959–1966).

CHARRO!'S MAN OF MUSIC: HUGO MONTENEGRO

The man who scored and conducted all the music for *Charro!* (except for the title song) was composer, arranger, and conductor Hugo Montenegro.

Born and raised in New York City, Montenegro served two years in the navy, where he gained experience arranging for service bands. In 1955, he began a thirteen-year career in the record industry. Although the music albums he made were good, he never had a hit, but he was in demand as staff manager to André Kostalanetz and as arranger/conductor for Harry Belafonte.

A move to California introduced Montenegro to the film industry, and he wrote and conducted the scores for *Hurry Sundown* (1967), *The Ambushers* (1968), *Lady in Cement* (1968), *The Wrecking Crew* (1969), *The Undefeated* (1969), *Viva Max!* (1969), *Tomorrow* (1972), and *The Farmer* (1977).

In 1968, Montenegro had a million-selling, number two hit with the theme from the 1967 Italian-made Western film *The Good, the Bad, and the Ugly*, starring Clint Eastwood. The tune was composed by Ennio Morricone, and with Montenegro's skill and the unique sound of his orchestra and chorus, the single,

"The Good, the Bad, and the Ugly," remained on the United States charts for twenty-two weeks. In Britain, the instrumental was number one for four weeks and spent twenty-four weeks on the charts.

Montenegro's striking work on "The Good, the Bad, and the Ugly" subsequently influenced the music he created for *Charro!* The use of unusual instruments such as the ocarina, electric violin, piccolo trumpet, and electronic harmonica brought the background music of *Charro!* to the foreground and created an unforgettable score.

DID YOU KNOW THAT...

- Location filming of *Charro!* took place near Apache Junction, Arizona? Cast and crew worked in and around the Superstition Mountains. Interiors were filmed at the Samuel Goldwyn studios in Hollywood.

- *Charro!* was not the original title for Elvis's 1969 film? *Come Hell, Come Sundown* was one title that was considered early in production.

- *Charro!* was the only movie in which Elvis wore a beard throughout? One scene in *Live a Little, Love a Little* showed a fuzzy-faced Elvis with Michele Carey, but he quickly vanquished those whiskers with a straight razor. In all of his other films, he was clean shaven.

- Poster art for *Charro!* featured Elvis's bearded face? Advertising lines declared "On his neck he wore the brand of a killer. On his hip he wore vengeance" and "A different kind of role . . . a different kind of man."

- Actress Ina Balin, who played saloon owner Tracey Winters, was selected International Star of Tomorrow in 1961 by the Hollywood Foreign Press Association? Balin's films include *Black Orchid* (1959), *From the Terrace* (1960), *The Comancheros* (1961), *The Young Doctors* (1961), *The Patsy* (1964), *The Greatest Story Ever Told* (1965), *Run Like a Thief* (1967), *The Projectionist* (1971), *The Don Is Dead* (1973), and *The Comeback Trail* (1974).

- Actor Victor French, who played outlaw gang leader Vince Hackett, was on the right side of the law in two television series? French played CONTROL Agent 44 on "Get Smart" (1965–1970) and police chief Roy Mobey on "Carter Country" (1977–1979). French is best remembered for the role of Isaiah Edwards on "Little House on the Prairie" (1974–1982), "Little House: A New Beginning" (1982–1983), *Little House: Look Back to Yesterday* (1983), and *Little House: Bless All the Dear Children* (1984). He also played Mark Gordon, the earthly sidekick of angel Jonathan Smith (Michael Landon) on "Highway to Heaven" (1984–1988).

- Actor Paul Brinegar, who played Opie Keetch, is best known for working with Clint Eastwood in an early television Western series? Brinegar co-starred with Eastwood on the long-running series "Rawhide" (1959–1966), which featured Brinegar as Wishbone, the cook. Brinegar had roles on other television series such as "The Life and Legend of Wyatt Earp" (1955–1961) and "Lancer" (1968–

1971). His films include *The Gal Who Took the West* (1949), *Storm Warning* (1951), *Here Come the Nelsons* (1952), *Cattle Empire* (1958), *High Plains Drifter* (1973), and *Chattanooga Choo Choo* (1984).

- Actor James Sikking, who played outlaw Gunner, portrayed a loose-cannon police officer on a television dramatic series? Sikking had the role of Sgt. Howard Hunter on "Hill Street Blues" (1981–1987). Sikking's movie credits include *Von Ryan's Express* (1965), *The New Centurions* (1972), *The Terminal Man* (1974), *The Electric Horseman* (1979), and *Ordinary People* (1980).

- Actor Solomon Sturges, who played Billy Roy Hackett, brother of Vince Hackett, is the son of director Preston Sturges? Preston Sturges directed a number of classic Hollywood films, including *Sullivan's Travels* (1941) and *The Miracle of Morgan's Creek* (1944). Solomon Sturges made his film debut in *Charro!* and went on to play a role in *The Working Girls* (1973).

CHARRO! TRIVIA QUIZ

1. What did Jess Wade order at the cantina?

2. How long had it taken Jess to ride to the cantina?

3. How much money was Jess carrying when he was searched by Billy Roy Hackett?

4. Of what metals was the Victory Gun made?

5. What was the value of the Victory Gun?

6. What was the historical significance of the Victory Gun?

7. Who was the member of the Hackett gang who was shot in the neck during the theft of the Victory Gun?

8. How did Vince Hackett insure that Jess would be implicated in the theft?

9. What was the reward offered by the Mexican government for the capture of Jess Wade and the return of the Victory Gun?

10. In what town was Dan Ramsey the sheriff?

11. How long had Ramsey been sheriff?

12. Where did Jess find the key to Tracey Winters's room?

13. What was Jess looking for in Tracey's room?

14. Who removed the bullets from Ramsey's chest?

15. By what time of day had Vince Hackett ordered that Billy Roy be released?

The Trouble with Girls

(Metro–Goldwyn–Mayer, 1969)

PLOT

*A*s the manager of a chautauqua company in 1927, Elvis has his hands full of trouble with girls: one is a union organizer and the other murdered the local pharmacist.

CAST

Elvis Presley	Walter Hale
Marlyn Mason	Charlene
Nicole Jaffe	Betty
Sheree North	Nita Bix
Edward Andrews	Johnny
John Carradine	Mr. Drewcott
Mr. Morality	Vincent Price
Anissa Jones	Carol Bix
Joyce Van Patten	Maude
Pepe Brown	Willy
Dabney Coleman	Harrison Wilby
Bill Zuckert	Mayor Gilchrist
Anthony Teague	Clarence
Med Flory	Constable
Kevin O'Neal	Yale man
Frank Welker	Rutgers man
John Rubinstein	Princeton man
Chuck Briles	Amherst man
Linda Sue Risk	Lily-Jeanne Gilchrist

CREW

Lester Welch .... Producer
Peter Tewksbury .... Director
Arnold Peyser and Lois Peyser .... Screenplay
Mauri Grashin .... Story
Day Keene and Dwight Babcock .... Novel
Billy Strange .... Music Score
Col. Tom Parker .... Technical Advisor

SONGS
"Swing Down, Sweet Chariot" • "The Whiffenpoof Song" •
"Violet (Flower of NYU)" • "Clean Up Your Own Backyard" •
"Sign of the Zodiac" • "Almost"

THE TROUBLE WITH <u>THE TROUBLE WITH GIRLS</u>

What started as a good idea in 1959, took ten years to get to the silver screen. Here is the troubled history of *The Trouble with Girls*.

- June 1959: The Hollywood trade papers announce that Don Mankiewicz plans to write a screenplay for a film to be titled *Chautauqua*. Mankiewicz will base his screenplay on an unpublished story by Mauri Grashin, Day Keene, and Dwight Babcock.

- December 1960: Glenn Ford is tapped to star in *Chautauqua*, which will be produced by Edmund Grainger.

- February 1961: Elvis is selected to costar in *Chautauqua*, along with Glenn Ford, Hope Lange, and Arthur O'Connell.

- May 1961: Valentine Davies is now writing the screenplay for *Chautauqua*, with production set to begin in the fall.

- July 1961: Glenn Ford is out, and Elvis is in as star of *Chautauqua*, with Edmund Grainger producing. The screenplay is now being written by William Wister Haines, based on a published novel by Day Keene and Dwight Babcock.

- August 1964: Elvis is out, and Dick Van Dyke is in as star of *Chautauqua*. The screenplay is now being written by Blanche Hanalis, based on Gay MacLaren's book, *Merrily We Roll Along*.

- November 1964: Blanche Hanalis bites the dust as writer of the screenplay in favor of Richard Morris.

- May 1965: Metro–Goldwyn–Mayer sells the rights to *Chautauqua* to Columbia Pictures. Elliott Arnold is selected as scriptwriter for the film, which will be produced by Sol C. Siegel. *Chautauqua* is renamed *Big America*.

- April 1968: Metro–Goldwyn–Mayer regrets having sold *Big America*, buys back the rights, retitles the property *Chautauqua*, and states that Elvis will definitely be the film's star.

- October 28, 1968: Production on *Chautauqua* begins, with Peter Tewksbury directing and Lester Welch producing. The screenplay is written by Arnold Peyser and Lois Peyser. Their script is based on a story by Mauri Grashin and a novel by Day Keene and Dwight Babcock.

- December 16, 1968: Filming of *Chautauqua* is completed.

- September 1969: *Chautauqua* opens nationally with the title and subtitle *The Trouble with Girls (And How to Get into It)*. This was the only Elvis movie to have a subtitle.

LEARN A BIT ABOUT CHAUTAUQUA

According to the narrator of *The Trouble with Girls*: "The really big event of the year in thousands of towns like Radford Center, Iowa, was the traveling chautauqua troupe that was coming to town with its silver-tongued orators and exciting entertainers." The chautauqua troupe headed by Walter Hale (Elvis) was an offspring of the chautauqua movement, a system of popular adult education that was born in Chautauqua, New York, in 1873.

The movement began as an idea proposed at a Methodist Episcopal camp meeting by two men—Dr. John H. Vincent, secretary of the Methodist Sunday School, and Lewis Miller, a businessman active in church affairs. The idea was to train Sunday school teachers during the summer in an attractive area. By 1874, their religious education program was launched, and teachers of all Protestant denominations gathered that August at Lake Chautauqua for ten days filled with lectures, conferences, and recreation.

Gradually, the program broadened to include general education, popular entertainments, and directed home study. The success of New York's annual assembly inspired other cities across the United States to start their own "chautauquas" based on the original. The popularity of those local programs led to the development of traveling chautauquas that began criss-crossing the country in the early 1900s, bringing speakers, musicians, plays, operas, and a host of other intellectual and cultural opportunities to isolated communities.

After 1924, the number of traveling chautauquas began to decline because of the public's growing interest in films and radio. The flickering images of early television signaled that the era for chautauqua programs had passed. The original Chautauqua center still exists and continues adult education activities today.

THE TROUBLE WITH GIRLS'S PRESLEY PERPLEXERS

Here and there in Elvis's films are instances that cause the keen-eyed fan to do a double take: minor mistakes resulting from errors in continuity, slips in the editing process, or goofs that are simply unexplainable. Did you catch or miss any of these Presley Perplexers in *The Trouble with Girls*?

- As the film opens, the narrator sets the time of the movie's action in 1927 and mentions that during that year "Janet Gaynor won the first Oscar." Janet Gaynor was indeed the first actress to capture an Academy Award, winning that first Oscar for her work in three films: *Seventh Heaven* (1927), *Sunrise* (1927), and *Street Angel* (1928). However, the first Academy Award ceremony was not held until May 16, 1929.

- Frank Welker, the college man in the Rutgers sweater, does a terrific Donald Duck impression in one scene. However, Donald Duck was not introduced to the world until 1936, when he appeared in a Walt Disney short called *Orphans' Benefit.*

- Walter Hale and his football team won their game by a score of 110 to 97. Thankfully, no one was injured because heads were protected by plastic football helmets. However, according to the College Football Hall of Fame, leather helmets were in use in 1927. Plastic football helmets were not marketed until the 1950s and not in general use until the 1960s.

DID YOU KNOW THAT...

- The parade sequence in *The Trouble with Girls* featured 450 extras? Of that number, 100 extras were children. The scene also called for fifty vintage automobiles, ten vintage trucks, two fire engines, and a steam-driven train.

- For the role of Charlene, the piano player and union steward in *The Trouble with Girls*, singer Bobbie Gentry was first considered? Actress Marlyn Mason won the role and made her film debut.

- Actor Dabney Coleman, who played pharmacist Harrison Wilby, portrayed another terrible boss in a film that starred a country singer? Coleman played the role in *9 to 5*, which starred Dolly Parton. The actor's other film credits include *Downhill Racer* (1969), *Cinderella Liberty* (1973), *The Towering Inferno* (1974), *North Dallas Forty* (1979), *Tootsie* (1980), and *On Golden Pond* (1981).

- Actor John Carradine, who played chautauqua performer Mr. Drewcolt, had a distinguished film career beginning in the 1930s? Carradine's films included *The Invisible Man* (1933), *The Garden of Allah* (1936), *Drums along the Mohawk* (1939), *The Grapes of Wrath* (1940), *House of Frankenstein* (1944), *Around the World in 80 Days* (1956), *The Adventures of Huckleberry Finn* (1960), *Terror in the Wax Museum* (1973), and *The Ice Pirates* (1984). On television, Carradine played Mr. Gateman, Herman's employer, on "The Munsters" (1964–1966) and the grandfather of Jason McCord on "Branded" (1965–1966).

- Actor Vincent Price, who played chautauqua lecturer Mr. Morality, is known for his work in horror films? His films included *The Invisible Man Returns* (1940), *Abbott and Costello Meet Frankenstein* (1948), *House of Wax* (1952), *The House on Haunted Hill* (1958), *The Tingler* (1959), *Tales of Terror* (1962), *Scream and Scream Again* (1970), and *Bloodbath at the House of Death* (1984).

- *The Trouble with Girls* was the only motion picture for juvenile actress Anissa

Jones, who played singer and dancer Carol Bix? Jones was best known for her portrayal of Buffy Davis on the television series "Family Affair" (1966–1971).

- Actress Sheree North, who played Nita Bix, the love interest of Harrison Wilby, is known for portraying the girlfriend of a character on a popular television series? North played Charlene McGuire, the girlfriend of Lou Grant, on "The Mary Tyler Moore Show" (1970–1977). North's film credits include *Excuse My Dust* (1951), *How to Be Very Very Popular* (1955), *The Lieutenant Wore Skirts* (1956), *Madigan* (1968), *Charley Varrick* (1973), and *Rabbit Test* (1978).

- The versatile voice of Frank Welker, the man in the Rutgers sweater, has been used for hundreds of cartoon characters for Hanna–Barbera Productions? Welker supplied the voice of Freddy in "Scooby-Doo, Where Are You?" (1969–1974. Welker's other cartoon television credits include "Wheelie and the Chopper Bunch" (1974–1975), "Jabberjaw" (1976–1978), "Buford and the Ghost" (1979), "Flintstone Family Adventures" (1980–1981), "The Flintstone Funnies" (1981–1984), and "Jim Henson's Muppet Babies" (1984).

- Actor John Rubinstein, who played the man in the Princeton sweater, is the son of famed pianist Arthur Rubinstein? An accomplished composer as well as an actor, John has appeared in a variety of movies, including *Journey to Shiloh* (1965), *Getting Straight* (1970), *The Candidate* (1972), and *Daniel* (1983). His television credits include the series "Family" (1976–1980), in which he played Jeff Maitland, and "Crazy Like a Fox" (1984–1986), in which he played Harrison K. Fox.

- MGM property man Bob Murdock was in the money in *The Trouble with Girls?* Murdock made the three, brand-new one-hundred-dollar bills that Walter Hale handed to Charlene (Marlyn Mason) during the last scene in the film. Murdock was also responsible for making $10 million for *Where Were You When the Lights Went Out?* (1968) and $2 million for *The Split* (1968).

- Advertising lines for *The Trouble with Girls* hinted at an updated image for Elvis? Lines included "This Is Elvis '69—His New Look" and "The Chautauqua Circuit and Where It Led."

THE TROUBLE WITH GIRLS TRIVIA QUIZ

1. What distinguished Walter Hale as the manager of the chautauqua troupe?

2. What did Walter give to Willy for wearing a button advertising the chautauqua?

3. What song did Carol and Willy perform during auditions for the children's play?

4. What was the number on the jersey that Walter wore in the football game?

5. How did Betty remember the names of guests at the hotel?

6. On what day was the lecture "From Cannibalism to Culture" offered?

7. What was the name of the ballet company that performed at the chautauqua?

8. In what opera company was Olga Prchlik the featured mezzo-soprano?

9. What did Harrison Wilby suggest that Carol and Willy buy from his drugstore?

10. What type of grease did Maude use before her swim?

11. What was Maude's time in swimming the English Channel?

12. Who was the chautauqua troupe member accused of murdering Harrison Wilby?

13. What was the next stop for the chautauqua troupe?

14. For how long had Charlene studied law?

15. How did Walter get Charlene to return to the troupe?

CHANGE OF HABIT

(UNIVERSAL, 1969)

PLOT

*D*octor Elvis devotes his life to ghetto patients in an understaffed clinic. When three nuns are sent by the church to help him, the lives of all four change in ways they could not have imagined.

CAST

Elvis Presley	Dr. John Carpenter
Mary Tyler Moore	Sister Michelle Gallagher
Barbara McNair	Sister Irene Hawkins
Jane Elliot	Sister Barbara Bennett
Leora Dana	Mother Joseph
Edward Asner	Lieutenant Moretti
Robert Emhardt	The Banker
Regis Toomey	Father Gibbons
Doro Merande	Rose
Ruth McDevitt	Lily
Richard Carlson	Bishop Finley
Nefti Millett	Julio Hernandez
Laura Figueroa	Desirée
Lorena Kirk	Amanda Parker
Virginia Vincent	Miss Parker
David Renard	Colom
Ji-Tu Cumbuka	Hawk
Bill Elliott	Robbie
Rodolfo Hoyos	Mr. Hernandez

CREW

Joe Connelly	Producer
William Graham	Director
James Lee, S. S. Schweitzer, and Eric Bercovici	Screenplay
William Goldenberg	Music
Col. Tom Parker	Technical Advisor

SONGS
"Change of Habit" • "Rubberneckin'" • "Have a Happy" • "Let Us Pray"

CHECKIN' OUT "RUBBERNECKIN'"

As Sister Michelle (Mary Tyler Moore), Sister Irene (Barbara McNair), and Sister Barbara (Jane Elliot) approach the Washington Street Clinic, they hear loud singing coming from an upstairs apartment.

"Music to exorcise evil spirits by," Sister Irene suggests.

Incognito in civilian attire, the nuns enter the building, find the door to the clinic apparently locked, and ring the doorbell. Dr. John Carpenter (Elvis)—the guitar-playing, evil-spirit exorcist—comes down the stairs and gets a good look at the new nurses who will be working with him in the clinic.

The song that Dr. Carpenter had been singing in his apartment with a group of teenagers from the neighborhood was written by Dory Jones and Bunny Warren. "Rubberneckin'" had a five-week stopover on *Billboard*'s Hot 100 chart, hitting only as high as number sixty-nine. "Rubberneckin'" was released as the flip side of "Don't Cry Daddy."

CHANGE OF HABIT BASED ON REAL LIFE NUN

The fictional Sister Michelle Gallagher was a psychiatric social worker with a degree in speech therapy. Michelle thought she could help Julio Hernandez (Nefti Millet) with his speech impediment. The character of Sister Michelle was loosely based on a real-life nun, Sister Mary Olivia Gibson.

Sister Mary was in charge of the speech clinic at Maria Regina College in Syracuse, New York. In her work with children who had speech problems, Sister Mary employed many of the same approaches that Sister Michelle used with her patients, including love and patience.

CHANGE OF HABIT'S PRESLEY PERPLEXER

Here and there in Elvis's films are instances that cause the keen-eyed fan to do a double take: minor mistakes resulting from errors in continuity, slips in the editing process, or goofs that are simply unexplainable. Did you catch or miss this Presley Perplexer in *Change of Habit?*

• During the opening credits of the film, the nuns cross a busy street as a bus passes by. On the side of the bus is a sign advertising a Los Angeles radio station, KDAY. Although *Change of Habit* was filmed in Los Angeles, the setting for the movie is New York City.

DID YOU KNOW THAT...

• Elvis was signed for the role of Dr. John Carpenter in January 1969? Mary Tyler Moore had been signed in October 1968. The film went into production in March 1969.

• Most of the location filming for *Change of Habit* took place in the area of Fifth and Main streets in downtown Los Angeles? Interior scenes were shot on stage D at Universal Studios.

• Actress Mary Tyler Moore is known for playing perky characters in two television series? Moore portrayed Laura Petrie on "The Dick Van Dyke Show" (1961–1966) and Mary Richards, associate producer for WJM-TV news on "The Mary Tyler Moore Show" (1970–1977). Her other television credits include "Richard Diamond, Private Detective" (1957–1960), "Mary" (1978), and "The Mary Tyler Moore Comedy Hour" (1979). In addition to appearing in *Change of Habit*, her film credits include *X-15* (1961), *Thoroughly Modern Millie* (1967), *Don't Just Stand There* (1968), *What's So Bad about Feeling Good?* (1968), *Ordinary People* (1980), and *Six Weeks* (1982).

• Actress Barbara McNair, who played Sister Irene Hawkins, began her career as a singer? In the 1960s, McNair performed in nightclubs in Las Vegas, New York City, and Miami Beach and cut two albums for Motown, *Here I Am* (1967) and *The Real Barbara McNair* (1970). She starred in her own weekly television program of music and songs, "The Barbara McNair Show" (1969). Acting skills that she had honed on Broadway in the late fifties, she eventually brought to Hollywood. In 1968, she portrayed a nightclub singer in *If He Hollers, Let Him Go*, during which she appeared nude. Film stills of Barbara in the buff were run in *Playboy*. McNair's other films include *Spencer's Mountain* (1963), *Stiletto* (1969), *They Call Me MISTER Tibbs!* (1970), and *The Organization* (1971).

• Actress Jane Elliot who played Sister Barbara Bennett, made one other film after *Change of Habit?* There was a soap opera quality to *One Is a Lonely Number* (1972) that perhaps opened doors for Elliot on television soap operas. She played spoiled, money-hungry Tracy Quatermaine on "General Hospital" from 1978 to 1980 and schizophrenic Carrie Todd on "The Guiding Light" from 1981 to 1982.

158

- Actor Robert Emhardt, who played the Banker, had a less menacing role in an earlier Elvis film? Emhardt portrayed Mr. Maynard, the cook at Grogan's Gaelic Garden, in *Kid Galahad* (1962). Emhardt's other film credits include *The Iron Mistress* (1952), *3:10 to Yuma* (1957), *Wake Me When It's Over* (1960), *The Group* (1966), *Where Were You When the Lights Went Out?* (1968), *Lawman* (1971), *Scorpio* (1973), *The Seniors* (1978), and *Forced Vengeance* (1982).

- Actor Regis Toomey, who played parish priest Father Gibbons, had been active in movies since the 1920s? He made close to two hundred films, including *Alibi* (1929), *The Big City* (1937), *Northwest Passage* (1940), *They Died with Their Boots On* (1941), *The Big Sleep* (1946), *Show Boat* (1951), *Guys and Dolls* (1955), *Voyage to the Bottom of the Sea* (1961), and *Won Ton Ton, the Dog Who Saved Hollywood* (1976).

- Actor Edward Asner, who played Lieutenant Moretti, was later reunited with Mary Tyler Moore on her successful 1970s television series? Asner played Lou Grant, cantankerous WJM-TV news producer (and Mary's boss) on "The Mary Tyler Moore Show" (1970–1977). When the show ended, Asner's character was spun off into a new series, "Lou Grant" (1977–1982), in which he played the irascible city editor of the *Los Angeles Tribune*. Asner was an alumnus from an earlier Elvis film. In *Kid Galahad* (1962), he played Frank Gerson, an assistant district attorney from Manhattan.

- Two songs recorded for *Change of Habit* were eliminated from the film? "Let's Be Friends" and "Let's Forget about the Stars" were not used but do appear on Elvis's *Let's Be Friends* LP.

- Actress Mary Tyler Moore was awarded a dubious distinction for her role as Sister Michelle Gallagher? In 1981 Harry and Michael Medved, authors of *The Golden Turkey Awards*, named the actress as the winner of the "Ecclesiastical Award for the Worst Performance by an Actor or Actress as a Clergyman or Nun." That award notwithstanding, Moore has been honored by the entertainment industry with more prestigious awards. She was named to the Television Hall of Fame in 1985 and has received several Emmy and Golden Globe awards throughout her career.

CHANGE OF HABIT TRIVIA QUIZ

1. What was the address of Dr. John Carpenter's clinic?

2. What was the name of the business next door to the clinic?

3. What organization sent the nuns to work in the clinic?

4. What were Sister Barbara's credentials?

5. What were Sister Irene's credentials?

6. What was the length of the nuns' assignment at the clinic?

7. Where was John Carpenter from originally?

8. How long had Father Gibbons been a priest at the parish?

9. To what order did Michelle, Irene, and Barbara belong?

10. What was the name of the market picketed by Sister Barbara?

11. Who was the sergeant in John Carpenter's army unit to whom he owed his life?

12. How much did Sister Irene borrow from the Banker?

13. Of whom was San Juan de Chequez the patron saint?

14. On what date did the nuns schedule the street fiesta?

15. Who attacked Sister Michelle after the fiesta?

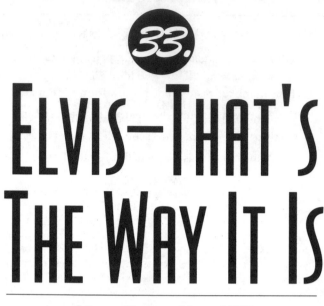

ELVIS–THAT'S THE WAY IT IS

(METRO–GOLDWYN–MAYER, 1970)

STORYLINE

*I*n this documentary, Elvis prepares for his triumphant opening night at the International Hotel in Las Vegas.

CREW

Herbert F. Soklow .... Producer
Denis Sanders .... Director
Lucien Ballard .... Director of Photography
Henry Berman .... Editor
Dale Hutchinson .... Unit Production Manager
John Wilson .... Assistant Director
Larry Hadsell and Lyle Burbridge .... Sound Recording
George Folsey, Jr. .... Associate Film Editor
Bill Belew .... Designer of Elvis's Wardrobe
Col. Tom Parker .... Technical Advisor
George L. Parkhill .... Coordinator for RCA Records
Joe Guercio .... Orchestra Conductor

TECHNICAL ASSISTANTS

Richard Davis | Tom Diskin
Joe Esposito | Lamar Fike
Felton Jarvis | Jim O'Brien
Al Pachucki | Bill Porter
Sonny West

ELVIS'S MUSICIANS

James Burton	Glen Hardin
Charlie Hodge	Jerry Scheff
Ronnie Tutt	John Wilkinson

BACKGROUND VOCALISTS

Millie Kirkham	The Sweet Inspirations
The Imperials	

SONGS
(in alphabetical order)
"All Shook Up" • "Blue Suede Shoes" • "Bridge over Troubled Water" •
"Can't Help Falling in Love" • "Crying Time" • "Heartbreak Hotel"
"How the Web Was Woven" • "I Just Can't Help Believin'" • "I've Lost You"
"Little Sister" • "Love Me Tender" • "Mary in the Morning" • "Mystery Train" •
"The Next Step Is Love" • "One Night" • "Patch It Up" • "Polk Salad Annie" •
"Stranger in the Crowd" • "Suspicious Minds" • "Sweet Caroline" •
"That's All Right (Mama)" • "Tiger Man" • "What'd I Say" • "Words" •
"You Don't Have to Say You Love Me" • "You've Lost That Lovin' Feelin'"

"MYSTERY TRAIN" / "TIGER MAN"

Over the opening credits of *Elvis—That's the Way It Is*, Elvis sings a medley of "Mystery Train" and "Tiger Man" accompanied by the screaming voices of thousands of fans.

Herman (Little Junior) Parker and Sam Phillips wrote "Mystery Train," and Parker recorded the song in 1953. Elvis recorded his version of "Mystery Train" for Sun Records in July 1955. RCA reissued the song in November 1955, and by December "Mystery Train" was climbing *Billboard*'s Country Disc Jockey chart. The song peaked at number eleven.

Joe Hill Louis and Sam Burns wrote "Tiger Man," and Louis recorded the song in 1952. Elvis sang "Tiger Man" in a number of concerts, usually teaming the rousing song with "Mystery Train." When the December 1968 television special "Elvis" was rebroadcast in August 1969, "Tiger Man" was used in place of "Blue Christmas." In *Elvis—That's The Way It Is*, "Tiger Man" is sung not only over the opening credits but also during Elvis's performance at the International Hilton. Cameras also captured fans doing their version of "Tiger Man" at the Fifth Annual Elvis Presley Appreciation Society Convention in Luxembourg.

"ALL SHOOK UP"

"All Shook Up" was inspired by a chance remark made to song writer Otis Blackwell in 1956. At the time, Blackwell was in the office of Shalimar Music when one of the owners of the company, Al Stanton, walked by shaking a bottle of Pepsi-Cola. "Why don't you write a song called 'All Shook Up'?" Stanton said. The rest, as they say, is musical history.

The song inspired by a bottle of pop and recorded by Elvis in 1957 had fans so shook up that "All Shook Up" debuted on *Billboard*'s Top 100 chart at number twenty-five. Three weeks later, the song zoomed to number one and refused to budge for the next eight weeks. "All Shook Up" spent a total of thirty weeks on the chart and did well on other charts, too. The song hit number three on the Country Best-Seller Chart and soared to number one on both the Country Juke Box chart and the Rhythm & Blues chart. "All Shook Up" crowned the British charts at number one for seven weeks.

Later, two young British songwriters drew inspiration from "All Shook Up" when they began to write the lyrics to "She Loves You." Elvis had sung "Yeah, yeah" in "All Shook Up," and John Lennon and Paul McCartney added "Yeah, yeah, yeah" to the lyrics of their 1963 hit.

"HEARTBREAK HOTEL"

The inspiration for "Heartbreak Hotel" was heartbreaking and tragic.

In the fall of 1955, Tommy Durden saw a headline in the *Miami Herald* that asked: "Do You Know This Man?" A photograph of a male suicide victim accompanied the headline, as well as an article that related the scant facts about the case. When discovered, the man carried no personal papers but did leave a note that read "I walk a lonely street." Miami police were seeking friends or family members who could identify the body.

Intrigued by the words of the note and inspired to use them in a blues song, Durden called his collaborator, Mae Axton. After relating the story and sharing his idea for a song, Durden hurried over to Axton's house, and within twenty minutes the pair wrote "Heartbreak Hotel."

Elvis heard and loved a demo of the song in November 1955 but didn't record "Heartbreak Hotel" until January 1956. The song was the second one he recorded for RCA ("I Got a Woman" was the first) but the first single released by the record company, and "Heartbreak Hotel" became Elvis's first number one single.

During its twenty-seven-week stay on *Billboard*'s Top 100 chart, *Heartbreak Hotel* was number one for seven weeks. The song hit number one on the Country Best-Seller chart, the Country Juke Box chart, the Country Disc Jockey chart, and scored a high number five on the Rhythm & Blues chart. "Heartbreak Hotel" was the second song in history ("Blue Suede Shoes" by Carl Perkins being the first) to hit all three *Billboard* charts (Top 100, Country, Rhythm & Blues), and Elvis was off and running with his first million seller.

AND THE VERDICT FROM THE CRITICS

Elvis—That's the Way It Is opened nationally on November 11, 1970. Here's what some of the critics had to say:

Dawn A. Lospaluto of the *Newark Evening News* wrote: "Director Denis Sanders and cinematographer Lucien Ballard have created a very engaging picture. If you're an Elvis fan already, you'll love it. If you're not, you just might end up being one."

Henry S. Resnik of *Saturday Review* wrote: "Elvis is magnificent, more powerful than ever . . . still one of the most compelling of all rock performers."

Howard Thompson of *The New York Times* wrote: "The powerhouse drive that used to flair about wildly is shrewdly disciplined and siphoned until it explodes into his extraordinary sense of rhythm. Tired? Elvis? He's ferocious."

DID YOU KNOW THAT...

- The working title of the documentary was *Elvis*? The credits of the film indicate that the official title is *Elvis: That's the Way It Is*.

- Shooting the documentary began in July 1970? The camera crew captured Elvis's rehearsals at MGM in July then shot footage of his shows at the International Hotel in August and of his concert at the Veterans Memorial Coliseum in Phoenix.

- Director Denis Sanders won two Academy Awards for Best Documentary? He received the honors for *A Time Out of War* (1954) and *Czechoslovakia, 1968* (1970).

- The documentary showed Elvis and Joe Esposito riding around the studio lot on a red tandem bicycle? Elvis later donated the tandem to his fans, and the bicycle was raffled off for charity at the Fifth Annual Elvis Presley Appreciation Society Convention in Luxembourg.

- According to the documentary, stalwart fans Sue Wiegert and Cricket Mendell were introduced to one another outside of Graceland by Vernon's brother Vester Presley? The two met in 1967 and teamed up to travel together to Memphis, Los Angeles, Las Vegas, Houston or wherever else Elvis could be found.

- Fans Bob Neal and his fiancée Nancy were planning to be married in October 1970 but moved the date of their wedding to August? They were shown in the documentary exchanging vows at the Cupid Wedding Chapel in Las Vegas. The Neals then celebrated their nuptials by attending Elvis's concert.

- Mother-and-daughter Elvis fans were spotted and interviewed for *Elvis— That's the Way It Is*? The middle-aged daughter related that "Mother does like it when he moves. She doesn't like it when they shoot him only from the waist up and he stands too still. Mother likes a lot of action, and I must admit I do, too. He sends my Phi Beta Kappa key ajangling!"

- The International Hotel billed Elvis's third month-long appearance as an "Elvis Summer Festival"? To celebrate, there was a wide array of Elvis merchandise available: photographs, books, posters, scarves, stuffed toys, and white Styrofoam skimmers with colorful bands.

- Before entering the Showroom, Rona Barrett said of Elvis "I think he's one of the wildest guys around."? Other celebrities captured in the documentary were Juliet Prowse, Xavier Cugat, Charo, Norm Crosby, Dale Robertson, Cary Grant, and Sammy Davis, Jr.

- Doc Pomus and Mort Shuman wrote "Little Sister"? Elvis's single release of "Little Sister" entered *Billboard*'s Hot 100 chart in August 1961, climbed as high as number five, and had a total chart stay of thirteen weeks.

- "One Night" charted on *Billboard*'s Hot 100, the Country chart, and the Rhythm & Blues charts? The song, written by Dave Bartholomew and Pearl King, hit number four, number twenty-four, and number ten, respectively when released in October 1958.

- Elvis wiped his face on a fan's table napkin after singing "Polk Salad Annie"? The song was written by Tony Joe White, who had a number eight hit on *Billboard*'s Hot 100 chart with the song in 1969. "Polk Salad Annie" has been featured on live Elvis LPs but was not released as a single.

- "Suspicious Minds" had the longest running time of any Elvis number one record? The song was written by Mark James, and the version recorded by Elvis runs four minutes, twenty-two seconds. "Suspicious Minds" was number one on *Billboard*'s Hot 100 chart for one week and spent a total of fifteen weeks on the chart. In a 1987 *USA Today* telephone poll, fans named "Suspicious Minds" as their favorite Elvis song.

- The closing title credit differed from the opening title credit? The film closed with the title *Elvis—That's the Way It WAS*.

ELVIS–THAT'S THE WAY IT IS TRIVIA QUIZ

1. Who said "Good morning, Hollywood camera."?

2. During rehearsal, for which song did Elvis need the sheet music?

3. Who sent this telegram to Elvis: "Here's hoping you have a very successful opening and that you break both legs."?

4. What was the winning number in the raffle for Elvis's red tandem bicycle?

5. What color did Elvis substitute for the word blue in the song "Blue Suede Shoes"?

34.
ELVIS
ON TOUR

(Metro–Goldwyn–Mayer, 1972)

STORYLINE

*T*his documentary captures Elvis on tour across the United States, blends film footage from his early days, and shares behind-the-scenes moments with the King of Rock and Roll.

CREW

Pierre Adidge and Robert Abel	Producers
Pierre Adidge and Robert Abel	Directors
Robert Thomas	Director of Photography
Col. Tom Parker	Technical Advisor
Joe Guercio	Orchestra Conductor
Jackie Kahane	Onstage Comedian
Barry Adelman and Barry Silver	Writers for Jackie Kahane
Bill Belew	Designer of Elvis's Wardrobe
Tom Diskin	Stage Supervision

MUSICIANS WITH ELVIS

James Burton • Glen Hardin • Charlie Hodge • Ronnie Tutt • Jerry Scheff • John Wilkinson

BACKGROUND VOCALISTS

J. D. Sumner and the Stamps Quartet • The Sweet Inspirations • Kathy Westmoreland

ASSISTANTS TO ELVIS

James Caughley • Joe Esposito • Lamar Fike • Marvin Gambill • Vernon Presley • Jerry Schilling • Red West • Sonny West

SONGS

"Johnny B. Goode" • "See See Rider" • "Polk Salad Annie" • "Separate Ways" •
"Proud Mary" • "Never Been to Spain" • "Burning Love" • "Don't Be Cruel" •
"Ready Teddy" • "That's All Right (Mama)" • "Lead Me, Guide Me" •
"Bosom of Abraham" • "Love Me Tender" • "Until It's Time for You to Go" •
"Suspicious Minds" • "I, John" • "Bridge over Troubled Water" •
"Funny How Time Slips Away" • "An American Trilogy" • "Mystery Train" •
"I Got a Woman"/"Amen" • "A Big Hunk o' Love" • "You Gave Me a Mountain" •
"Lawdy Miss Clawdy" • "Can't Help Falling in Love" • "Memories"

"THAT'S ALL RIGHT (MAMA)"

"That's All Right (Mama)" was Elvis's first hit for Sun Records. The song was released on July 19, 1954, sold nearly twenty thousand copies, and was a top-five hit on the Memphis record charts.

Elvis performed "That's All Right (Mama)" on his October 2, 1954, appearance on the Grand Ole Opry and on his October 16, 1954, appearance on the "Louisiana Hayride." Elvis's Sun recording of the song was used in the *Elvis on Tour* documentary.

"SEPARATE WAYS"

"Separate Ways" was written by Red West and Richard Mainegra shortly after Elvis and Priscilla separated. Elvis recorded the personally painful song in March 1972. Released in November 1972, "Separate Ways" stayed on *Billboard*'s Hot 100 chart for twelve weeks and peaked at number twenty.

"BURNING LOVE"

Elvis recorded "Burning Love" in March 1972. The song was written by Dennis Linde, born in Abilene, Texas, who also contributed his guitar skills to the recording session. When released in August 1972, "Burning Love" caught fire and blazed for fifteen weeks on *Billboard*'s Hot 100 chart. The song smoldered at number two but was kept out of the number one spot by Chuck Berry's "My Ding-a-Ling."

"AN AMERICAN TRILOGY"

Houston-born songwriter Mickey Newbury arranged three traditional songs, "Dixie," "The Battle Hymn of the Republic," and "All My Trials," into a medley called "An American Trilogy." Newbury recorded the medley in 1971 for Elektra, and his version peaked at #26 on *Billboard*'s Hot 100 chart.

• Although there is controversy surrounding its authorship, "Dixie" was popularized in 1859 by Dan Emmett, who first performed the song in a New York City minstrel show. Introduced to the South in 1860, the song became popular during the Civil War. In April 1865, President Abraham Lincoln asked the Union Army band to play "Dixie" when he received word of General Lee's surrender at Appomattox.

- Author and abolitionist Julia Ward Howe was urged by the Rev. James Freeman Clarke to write new lyrics for the song "John Brown's Body." Howe put pen to paper in December 1861, and the words tumbled out onto the page. She sold the poem to the *Atlantic Monthly* for five dollars. Her editor suggested the title "The Battle Hymn of the Republic" and published the piece in February 1862.

- The author of "All My Trials" is unknown.

Elvis incorporated "An American Trilogy" into some of his 1970s concerts. In fact, his version of the medley, which was released in April 1972, was recorded from his February 17, 1972, performance at the Las Vegas Hilton. "An American Trilogy" stayed for six weeks on *Billboard*'s Hot 100 chart where it peaked at number sixty-six.

"MEMORIES"

Billy Strange and Mac Davis wrote "Memories" for Elvis, which he introduced during his 1968 television special, "Elvis." When released in March 1969, the song entered *Billboard*'s Hot 100 chart, stayed for seven weeks, and peaked at number thirty-five. On the Country chart, "Memories" hit a high of number fifty-six, and on the Easy Listening chart, the tune peaked at number seven. "Memories" is heard over the closing credits of *Elvis on Tour*.

DID YOU KNOW THAT...

- Producers/directors Pierre Adidge and Robert Abel were experienced with making rock-umentaries? In 1971, they had produced the acclaimed *Joe Cocker: Mad Dogs and Englishmen*.

- Cameras rolled during Elvis's fifteen-city tour in April 1972? He began the tour in Buffalo, New York, on April 5 and ended the tour in Albuquerque, New Mexico, on April 19.

- Although Elvis disliked interviews, he granted one to Adidge and Abel during the production of *Elvis on Tour*? In May 1972, Elvis sat in a small dressing room at MGM with Jerry Schilling, Red and Sonny West, Joe Esposito, and Charlie Hodge, and for two hours shared his life story with Adidge and Abel.

- Film director Martin Scorsese worked on *Elvis on Tour*? Scorsese was the montage supervisor. The critically acclaimed director counts among his film credits *Taxi Driver* (1976), *Raging Bull* (1980), *The King of Comedy* (1983), *The Color of Money* (1986), *The Last Temptation of Christ* (1988), *GoodFellas* (1990), *Cape Fear* (1991), and *The Age of Innocence* (1993).

- "See See Rider" was a song Elvis used to begin many of his concerts in the 1970s? In the 1920s, Big Bill Broonzy wrote and recorded the song as "C. C. Rider." The title was a slang term for country circuit preacher.

- "Bosom of Abraham" was sung backstage, but Elvis did not sing lead? Charlie Hodge sang lead while Elvis sang bass, with vocal accompaniment by the Stamps. In June 1971, Elvis recorded "Bosom of Abraham" (written in the late 1940s by William Johnson, George McFaddan, and Ted Brooks), which was the flip side of "He Touched Me." By accident, RCA issued nearly ten thousand copies of the record before discovering that both sides played at $33^1/_3$ RPM rather than 45 RPM. The copies were withdrawn from sale, and the problem was corrected.

- "Funny How Time Slips Away" was written by Willie Nelson? Nelson wrote the song in only ten minutes while enroute to work in 1961. "Funny How Time Slips Away" was included on several Elvis LPs but was not released as a single.

- "I Got a Woman" was the first song Elvis recorded for RCA? The song was released as a single in 1956 but failed to chart. Elvis favored this song, written by Ray Charles in 1954, in a medley with "Amen" during his 1970s concerts.

- Elvis recorded "A Big Hunk o' Love" in June 1958 while on leave from the army? When released a year later, the song went all the way to number one on *Billboard*'s Hot 100 chart. "A Big Hunk o' Love" was at the top spot for two weeks and spent a total of fourteen weeks on the Hot 100. On the Rhythm & Blues chart, the song hit number ten and had a seven-week reign.

- *Elvis on Tour* was number thirteen on *Variety*'s weekly list of top-grossing movies? During the film's first weekend of release to 187 theaters in 105 cities, *Elvis on Tour* grossed $494,270.

- *Elvis on Tour* won a Golden Globe award in 1973? Elvis was in Las Vegas when the awards banquet was held in the Hollywood Palladium. He watched the show on his bathroom television and was thrilled when he learned that the members of the Hollywood Foreign Press Association had voted *Elvis on Tour* as the Best Documentary of the year.

ELVIS ON TOUR TRIVIA QUIZ

1. For which song did Elvis require sheet music?

2. What Southern city presented to Elvis the key to the city during his April 1972 tour?

3. Which two songs from "The Ed Sullivan Show" were shown as clips?

4. Which song sung by Elvis was a million-selling hit in 1969 for Creedence Clearwater Revival?

5. Which song sung by Elvis was a hit in 1969 for Frankie Laine?

THE ELVIS MASTER QUIZ

*n*ow that you have immersed yourself in Elvis's thirty-three movies, test yourself to see what you *really* know about the King of Rock and Roll. Successfully completing the following Elvis master quiz earns you a Ph.D.D. (Perfect Hound Dog Designation) in Presleyana. But more about the rewards later. First, use page 175 to record your answers to The Encyclopedic, Panoramic Elvis Presley Mega-Monster Movie Trivia Challenge. Then, compare your responses to the answers on pages 182 to 183. Next, see page 185 for information on receiving a diploma that proves you are truly an Elvis expert!

SECTION ONE: TAKING CARE OF BUSINESS

The following questions relate to jobs held by characters played by Elvis in his films.

1. What was Clint Reno doing when his brothers returned from the war?

2. What song did Deke Rivers sing on stage at Community Fair Night in Longhorn, Texas?

3. What was the first release of Laurel Records, the company owned by Vince Everett and Peggy Van Alden?

4. At what Bourbon Street nightclub did Danny Fisher work sweeping floors before school?

5. What was the nickname of Tulsa McLean's tank crew?

6. How did Pacer Burton and his family make their living?

7. How much did Rolfe Braxton first offer as a weekly salary to Glenn Tyler to

work in the health tonic business?

8. What was the name of the travel agency started by Chad Gates after his marriage to Maile Duval?

9. When Toby Kwimper was elected sheriff, at what time did he suggest that the gambling trailer close for the evening?

10. What was the amount of the purse for the boxing match between Kid Galahad and Ezzard Bailey at the Capitol Casino?

11. What was the name of the couple Ross Carpenter escorted on his charter fishing boat?

12. What was the company for which Mike Edwards dusted potatoes?

13. At what hotel did Mike Windgren replace El Trovador as a cabaret singer?

14. What was Josh Morgan's air force rank?

15. In front of which hotel was the finish line of the Las Vegas Grand Prix race in which Lucky Jackson came in first?

16. How long did Charlie Rogers work at Carver's Combined Shows?

17. What was the name of the Fort Lauderdale nightclub where Rusty Wells and his combo played?

18. In what cabin did Lonnie Beale stay in while working at the Circle Z?

19. What was the name of the act that Johnny Tyronne brought to the Galaxy Hotel in Las Vegas?

20. What was the name of the riverboat on which Frankie and Johnny were performers?

21. What was the name of the helicopter charter service operated by Rick Richards and Danny Kohana?

22. What was the number on the side of Mike McCoy's 427 Cobra race car?

23. What job did Ted Jackson perform while in the navy?

24. What was the name of Guy Lambert's band?

25. What was the amount of the tip Scott Hayward received from J. J. Jamison to fix the binding on his water ski?

26. In which three locations had Joe Lightcloud excelled as a bronco rider?

27. What was the total amount Steve Grayson won in the Charlotte 100?

28. What was Greg Nolan's monthly salary at both Creative Advertising and *Classic Cat Magazine*?

29. Who appointed Jess Wade the deputy sheriff of Rio Seco?

30. In what year did Walter Hale's chautauqua troupe visit Radford Center, Iowa?

31. What were the office hours at Dr. John Carpenter's Washington Street Clinic?

32. Where did Elvis say, "If the songs don't go over, we can do a medley of costumes."

SECTION TWO: DUELING DIALOGUE

Each of the following are dialogue pairs, presenting an Elvis costar's line and Elvis's response. Identify the film from which each example of dueling dialogue is taken.

33. Costar: "Your matador is waiting for you back there."
Elvis: "And the stubborn burro is out here."

34. Costar: "The cannibals are complaining that their mattresses are too lumpy."
Elvis: "I told 'em to quit eatin' 'em."

35. Costar: "In over one thousand years no leader of the Assassins has ever violated a promise."
Elvis: "Well, it's nice to know you're doing business with such a reputable firm."

36. Costar: "This is Tatum territory, Yankee. Now take your gas buggies and skeedaddle off of Pappy's mountain."
Elvis: "That's no way to be greetin' kinfolks."

37. Costar: "How dare you think such cheap tactics would work with me."
Elvis: "That ain't tactics, honey. That's just the beast in me."

38. Costar: "There's something else I want."
Elvis: "Well, do you want to tell me now or should I wait 'til after you get it."

39. Costar: "You know, you didn't fail because your marks were bad. Mr. Evans said you failed because of your attitude. He said anybody that disagreed with you got a punch in the mouth. Is that what I brought you up to do, to fight?
Elvis: "No, paw, that's not what you brought me up to do, but I stopped listening to you. I ran out of other cheeks."

40. Costar: "The roads are so icy. Wouldn't it be better if we just waited a few days?"
Elvis: "Bikinis may go out of style."

41. Costar: "Want to drink on it?"
Elvis: "Not unless yours is a Mickey."

42. Costar: "You sure Frankie walked out on you?"
Elvis: "I can still feel her farewell message."

43. Costar: "Jo. She's kind of a beatnik, isn't she?"
Elvis: "Well, if that means happily broke and full of all kind of crazy principles, that's what she is."

44. Costar: "This is hard, rough work—on second thought, forget it, you might be too soft for real work."
Elvis: "Just a minute. All right. But I'm not going to go biting the heads off any chickens."

45. Costar: "I bought this dress to welcome you home. It's the first time I've worn it."
Elvis: "You know something? On you, wet is my favorite color."

46. Costar: "You're beginning to irritate me."
Elvis: "Murder is an irritating business."

47. Costar: "I'd like you to check my motor. It whistles."
Elvis: "I don't blame it."

48. Costar: "I'll bet you're a marvelous lover."
Elvis: "I'm representing the United States in the Olympics."

49. Costar: "Hey, it must be Daddy. He's come to rescue us."
Elvis: "Yeah, I think I'm gonna need rescuing after he gets here."

50. Costar: "I want him loose."
Elvis: "You want? I'll tell you what you get. That cannon back in Mexico where it belongs and you in a Mexican court tellin' how you stole it and why you did this."

51. Costar: "That's the first time Dado's beat your time all year."
Elvis: "Oh, he doesn't get the checkered flag yet."

52. Costar: "Hello. I was looking for you."
Elvis: "I can't help you, Banker. I'm not a veterinarian."

53. Costar: "You say you are not our enemy then you must be friend. Will you ride with us?"
Elvis: "You have many warriors. One more warrior's not important."

SECTION THREE: LEADING LADIES WHO'S WHO

Match the leading lady in column 1 with the role she played as an Elvis leading lady in column 2.

Column 1	Column 2
54. Ursula Andress	A. Mamie Callahan
55. Ann-Margret	B. Dianne Carter
56. Ina Balin	C. Charlene
57. Joan Blackman	D. Jillian Conway
58. Annette Day	E. Margarita Dauphin
59. Quentin Dean	F. Maile Duval
60. Shelley Fabares	G. Susan Jessup
61. Joan Freeman	H. Holly Jones
62. Dolores Hart	I. Cathy Lean
63. Anne Helm	J. Lili
64. Hope Lange	K. Rusty Martin
65. Dodi Marshall	L. Cathy Reno
66. Marlyn Mason	M. Princess Shalimar
67. Mary Ann Mobley	N. Irene Sperry
68. Joan O'Brien	O. Jo Symington

69. Debra Paget	P. Diane Warren
70. Juliet Prowse	Q. Tracey Winters

SECTION FOUR: MINOR CHARACTER MATCH

Match the minor character and the actor or actress who played the role in column 1 with the name of the Elvis movie in which he or she appeared in column 2.

Column 1	Column 2
71. Cully (Harry Morgan)	R. *Blue Hawaii*
72. Davis (Rafer Johnson)	S. *Frankie and Johnny*
73. Sunny Daze (Nita Talbot)	T. *Girl Happy*
74. Mike Gavin (Neville Brand)	U. *Kid Galahad*
75. Frank Gerson (Ed Asner)	V. *Kissin' Cousins*
76. Lorraine (Maureen Reagan)	W. *Love Me Tender*
77. Estelle Penfield (Merry Anders)	X. *Spinout*
78. Ping Pong (Guy Lee)	Y. *Tickle Me*
79. Philip Short (Warren Berlinger)	Z. *Wild in the Country*

SECTION FIVE: WHO SAID IT?

Using the following list of Elvis characters, decide who spoke these lines of movie dialogue.

Lonnie Beal	Steve Grayson	Tulsa McLean
Pacer Burton	Walter Gulick	Greg Nolan
Dr. John Carpenter	Walter Hale	Clint Reno
Ross Carpenter	Scott Hayward	Rick Richards
Mike Edwards	Toby Kwimper	Deke Rivers
Vince Everett	Guy Lambert	Jess Wade
Danny Fisher	Joe Lightcloud	Rusty Wells

80. "I got plans for what I intend to do, and it's not stopping punches with my head."

81. "Last one out of the water is a papaya picker."

82. "When we go into battle, I will think of my mother and of how Two Moons tried to help her, and I will be strong . . . very strong."

83. "You've got a cannon pointing at your heads, and you're willing to let a bunch of riff-raff make you crawl."

84. "Whoa! . . . Brett . . . Vance . . . They told us you were dead!"

85. "I don't want things easy. I want to be able to make my own mistakes and work 'em out."

86. "One of the bulls decided I was sitting on him too long, so he decided to sit on me."

87. "I just don't know how to tear up a handshake."

88. "Nolan is here with the truth."

89. "You know, there might come a time we'll remember this as the day that I started out with a broken leg and thanks to you ended up strapped in a nose cone."

90. "I've been alone all my life. I need somebody."

91. "Okay, fellas. Recess is over. We're down here on a babysittin' job."

92. "I asked for three hard-nosed nurses, and they send me Park Avenue debutantes."

93. "Well, the botherin' part's all right, but I ain't gonna marry no girl and build no house just so I can be bothered regular."

94. "Romancing a girl is a hobby not a business."

95. "It's talent that talks. The kid's really great."

96. "I don't take handouts from anybody. I don't want to be kept."

97. "Would you give the trio a five-minute break? They're boring holes in the back of my neck."

98. "Oh, you stay off the track. I got enough competition as it is."

99. "Holy cow! I forgot the bull!"

100. "Well I never heard of anybody paying money to hear a guitar player."

ANSWER SHEET FOR
THE ELVIS MASTER QUIZ

1.	26.	51.	76.
2.	27.	52.	77.
3.	28.	53.	78.
4.	29.	54.	79.
5.	30.	55.	80.
6.	31.	56.	81.
7.	32.	57.	82.
8.	33.	58.	83.
9.	34.	59.	84.
10.	35.	60.	85.
11.	36.	61.	86.
12.	37.	62.	87.
13.	38.	63.	88.
14.	39.	64.	89.
15.	40.	65.	90.
16.	41.	66.	91.
17.	42.	67.	92.
18.	43.	68.	93.
19.	44.	69.	94.
20.	45.	70.	95.
21.	46.	71.	96.
22.	47.	72.	97.
23.	48.	73.	98.
24.	49.	74.	99.
25.	50.	75.	100.

SCORING THE ELVIS MASTER QUIZ

Award yourself one point for each correct answer. Then, total the number of correct answers to determine your overall score. Next, check your overall score with the list below to determine any special Elvis honors that can be added to your diploma.

60 – 69 = Passing. Congratulations!

70 – 79 = One Teddy Bear (with distinction)

80 – 89 = Two Teddy Bears (with great distinction)

90 – 100 = Three Teddy Bears (with highest distinction)

The 8 1/2-by-11-inch diploma you'll receive is pink with black lettering (Elvis's favorite colors in the 50s) and suitable for framing. What a terrific way to showcase your Elvis expertise! Complete and mail the following form to receive your Ph.D.D. in Presleyana. And congratulations! The King would be proud!

ANSWERS TO MOVIE TRIVIA QUIZZES
LOVE ME TENDER

1. Lieutenant • 2. Randall • 3. East Texas • 4. Georgia • 5. A bonnet • 6. Twenty dollars • 7. Three months • 8. In the barn • 9. Cathy Reno • 10. Two hundred dollars • 11. Martha Reno • 12. Ten years • 13. Jethro • 14. Hannah's Mill • 15. 1843

LOVING YOU

1. Highway Beverage • 2. Eighteen dollars plus tips • 3. Jim Tallman • 4. Rough Ridin' Ramblers • 5. Longhorn, Texas • 6. A guitar • 7. Wayne • 8. The Grand Theatre • 9. *Dallas Chronicle* • 10. Carl Meade • 11. Fifty percent • 12. Farmingdale • 13. Joseph • 14. Jimmy Tompkins • 15. KTED

JAILHOUSE ROCK

1. Twenty-one • 2. Fouteen months • 3. "Breath of a Nation" • 4. Mary Jane Hamilton • 5. Club La Florita • 6. About twenty dollars • 7. Geneva Records • 8. Mickey Alba • 9. Laurel Records • 10. Nine percent • 11. Cy's Pet Shop • 12. A Cadillac • 13. Twelve years old • 14. Climax Studios • 15. 1313

KING CREOLE

1. Royal High School • 2. A quart of ice cream • 3. Regal Pharmacy • 4. 29 Royal Street • 5. Charles Street • 6. Shark, Sal, and Dummy • 7. George • 8. Eighty-five dollars a week • 9. Three • 10. Twenty years • 11. The Best Legs in the State of Maine • 12. Dr. Cabot • 13. Father Franklin • 14. A switchblade knife • 15. It had been Ronnie's theme song.

GI BLUES

1. The Three Blazes • 2. Three hundred dollars • 3. The Chili Parlor • 4. Papa Mueller • 5. At a gas station in Oklahoma • 6. Lili • 7. Alaska • 8. Cafe Europa • 9. His grandmother, a full-blooded Cherokee Indian. • 10. Milan, Italy • 11. Seventy-six • 12. Heidelberg • 13. Tiger • 14. 2:30 A.M. • 15. Cookey, Mac, and Harvey

FLAMING STAR

1. A shaving mirror • 2. Angus Pierce • 3. Will Howard • 4. The village of the white settlers • 5. She was his niece. • 6. "The thin woman who deserted her own people"

• 7. More than twenty years • 8. A shotgun and a pound of black powder • 9. Two Moons • 10. Dred Pierce • 11. One of the two trappers • 12. She believed the vision meant that death was near. • 13. Dottie • 14. He was hit with a spear in his left thigh and with an arrow in his right shoulder. • 15. Pacer Burton

WILD IN THE COUNTRY

1. Comic books • 2. Almost nine years old • 3. Old Seminole Tonic • 4. $12.50 • 5. High Tension Grove • 6. A salesman • 7. Rosy • 8. A heart condition • 9. A guitar • 10. Paul • 11. Phil Macy • 12. Professor Larson • 13. Cherry • 14. Six dollars • 15. Carbon monoxide poisoning in her garage

BLUE HAWAII

1. Eddie • 2. United Airlines • 3. She caught him kissing a flight attendant. • 4. Two years • 5. Hooky-Hooky Day • 6. Duke • 7. Chadwick • 8. Great Southern Hawaiian Fruit Company • 9. Daddy • 10. Atlanta • 11. Fifteen years • 12. Seventeen • 13. Perfume and a peignoir • 14. Mai-Tai • 15. Gates of Hawaii

FOLLOW THAT DREAM

1. A candy bar to share • 2. During his first judo lesson in the army • 3. $63.80 • 4. A fender from his father's Oldsmobile • 5. Six months • 6. A diaper pin • 7. A toilet and cheap lumber • 8. Ninety-two dollars • 9. Nineteen years old • 10. Two thousand dollars • 11. He recited the multiplication tables. • 12. Arthur King • 13. State Welfare Supervisor • 14. Blackie and Al • 15. 9:00 A.M.

KID GALAHAD

1. Orth Van & Storage • 2. The Catskills • 3. Lowbridge, Kentucky • 4. The motor pool • 5. One hundred fifty dollars • 6. Five dollars a round • 7. Dolly Fletcher • 8. Prohosko's Repair Shop • 9. Albany, New York • 10. White with a green waistband • 11. Lew Nyack • 12. Milton's Meadows • 13. Henry's Hamburger Haven • 14. Eighteen hundred dollars • 15. Church of St. Stanislaus

GIRLS! GIRLS! GIRLS!

1. *Kingfisher* • 2. *Westwind* • 3. Mariners • 4. 7:30 P.M. • 5. Paradise Cove • 6. Ross shelled peas; Laurel cleaned shrimp. • 7. Wesley Johnson • 8. Chicago • 9. In a

millinery shop • 10. 136 Bay Street, Apartment 3 • 11. Salt • 12. Skipper • 13. One ton, twenty pounds • 14. Ten thousand dollars • 15. When white spots appeared in Kapoo's eyes, it meant rain.

IT HAPPENED AT THE WORLD'S FAIR

1. Bessie • 2. Four hundred dollars • 3. 3820 Maple Street • 4. Seven hundred dollars • 5. A ukelele • 6. Tiger • 7. Ninety-nine cents • 8. Sue-Lin had a stomachache. • 9. Barney Thatcher • 10. Century 21 Estates • 11. Twenty-five cents • 12. Space Medicine Program • 13. Twelve hundred dollars • 14. In the Dream Car Exhibit • 15. Furs

FUN IN ACAPULCO

1. The Harkins • 2. Armando, Pedro, Pablo, Sam • 3. El Torito's • 4. One peso • 5. Tequila • 6. In front of the church in the plaza • 7. El Trovador • 8. Chapultepec Room • 9. Two dollars • 10. Tampa, Florida • 11. 136 feet • 12. Fifty percent • 13. Princess • 14. The Cassanova of the North • 15. The Flying Windgrens

KISSIN' COUSINS

1. Operation Big Smokey • 2. F-84 • 3. The Shooting Star aerobatic team • 4. Hidden Rock, North Carolina • 5. Seven • 6. Euphrasia Morgan • 7. A nylon stocking • 8. Hezekiah • 9. Porcupine Flats • 10. 36-22-35 • 11. Blue Quail • 12. Howlin' Devils Gorge • 13. Checkers • 14. Mountain Maiden's Breath • 15. One thousand dollars

VIVA LAS VEGAS

1. Mr. Swanson • 2. Baker's Grand Prix Garage • 3. Seven • 4. Twenty-two • 5. Sons of the Lone Star State • 6. The Flamingo Hotel • 7. Her father helped build Hoover Dam. • 8. She wanted to buy a boat for her father. • 9. Cal Howard • 10. Potato chips • 11. A silver dollar • 12. Heads • 13. A silver trophy and an all-expenses-paid, two-week honeymoon in Las Vegas. • 14. A pool table • 15. He crashed after his left rear tire blew.

ROUSTABOUT

1. Lou, the owner of Mother's Tea House • 2. Six dollars • 3. Phoenix • 4. The palmistry tent • 5. Estelle • 6. He was the knife thrower. • 7. Thirty-eight • 8. To-

peka, Kansas • 9. Seventy-five cents • 10. He waited for small carnivals to die and then bought them. • 11. Carver's Combined Shows • 12. $300 (Charlie wanted $400; he and Carver agreed on $350.) • 13. Waterford County Tigers • 14. Forty miles per hour • 15. One thousand dollars

GIRL HAPPY

1. 77 Club • 2. Seadrift Motel • 3. Five • 4. Betsy and Laurie • 5. Music • 6. Mr. Penchill, the manager • 7. Playing bridge • 8. Michigan State, MIT, Harvard University, Vassar, Wellsley, Smith, Brown • 9. BVD • 10. Princeton • 11. At the Coral Pier • 12. Kit Kat Club • 13. "Drop Dead" • 14. Lipstick • 15. Chicken and champagne

TICKLE ME

1. Zuni Wells • 2. The Corral • 3. Circle Z • 4. Yogurt Gulch • 5. Swimming instructor • 6. Five hundred dollars per week • 7. Silverado • 8. Dolly D • 9. One hundred thousand dollars in twenty-dollar Double Eagle gold coins • 10. Milk • 11. A luau • 12. King Canute • 13. Thunderbolt • 14. Martin Woodruff • 15. In Durango's Place

HARUM SCARUM

1. Istanbul • 2. Taj • 3. Mountains of the Moon • 4. "Oh Noble Client" • 5. Guild of Marketplace Thieves • 6. Ten thousand dollars • 7. The summer palace • 8. Yani • 9. Sheik El-Hussein • 10. Arabian • 11. Palace of the Jackals • 12. Bakir Oil Company • 13. Fifty thousand • 14. Sari and Yussef • 15. Zacha

FRANKIE AND JOHNNY

1. SS *Mississippi Queen* • 2. A lucky rabbit's foot • 3. He rubbed a horseshoe. • 4. Five • 5. Chesay • 6. Singing Queen of the Riverboats • 7. One • 8. Thirteen • 9. Two hundred dollars • 10. Madame Pompadour • 11. Colonial House • 12. Cully • 13. Two and five • 14. Blackie • 15. A cricket

PARADISE, HAWAIIAN STYLE

1. He was caught kissing a stewardess during a flight. • 2. "We Fly You Anywhere" • 3. Five • 4. "You scratch my back, and I'll scratch yours." • 5. Alligator shoes • 6.

The Society for the Prevention of Cruelty to Alligators • 7. Two years • 8. Friday • 9. Irish setter, basset hound, poodle, and collie • 10. Bowser Biscuits • 11. Ruggles • 12. Colonel's Plantation Steak House • 13. "Come Fly with Us" • 14. Moonlight Beach • 15. Donald Belden

SPINOUT

1. 1929 Duesenberg • 2. 1 Plus 2 + 1/2 • 3. $5,000 • 4. Foxhugh Motors • 5. Foxy • 6. Lester • 7. Eight • 8. He fainted. • 9. *The Perfect American Male* • 10. "The Wedding March" • 11. Mr. and Mrs. Bernard Ranley • 12. Blodgett • 13. Fox 5 • 14. Fifty thousand dollars • 15. Santa Fe Road Race

EASY COME, EASY GO

1. Rocky Point • 2. Coffee and pieces of eight • 3. Near the end of Silver Canyon • 4. Josephine • 5. He told her he was writing a book on shipwrecks. • 6. She was his granddaughter. • 7. From Captain Jack's Marine Equipment • 8. Zelda's Cornmeal Mush • 9. "Hydrophobia" - fear of water • 10. Vicki and Mary • 11. Zoltan • 12. "Finders Keepers, Lover" • 13. Silver • 14. Thirty cents each • 15. Down payment on an arts center

DOUBLE TROUBLE

1. B6 • 2. 311 Surrey Road • 3. St. John's Wood • 4. Seventeen • 5. Around two o'clock • 6. Constable • 7. Bruges • 8. Olympia Theater • 9. Hotel Victoria • 10. 89 Parkstrasse • 11. Five • 12. Stockholm • 13. Gerda • 14. Draw poker • 15. SS *Damocles*

CLAMBAKE

1. Ham on rye and a cup of coffee • 2. Three • 3. The Shores Hotel • 4. *Scarlet Lady* • 5. The Jamison family manufactured erotic pajamas, "Jamison's Jammies." • 6. Sam Burton • 7. *Raw-Hide* • 8. ninety-nine • 9. Engineering • 10. GOOP (glycol oxyoxynoic phosphate) • 11. Paul the bartender at the Shores Hotel • 12. About five carats • 13. The Governor's Trophy and ten thousand dollars • 14. An oil well • 15. February 23, 1940

STAY AWAY, JOE

1. Twenty • 2. He rode the bull. • 3. The twenty-third • 4. One hundred dollars • 5. Bronc Hoverty barbecued the bull. • 6. His horse, Old Gray • 7. Nineteen • 8. The

grocery store and tavern owned by Glenda Callahan • 9. A champion bull • 10.
Hike Bowers • 11. Dominick had never been ridden. • 12. She bought a toilet. •
13. Joe Lightcloud • 14. Number four • 15. One hundred

SPEEDWAY

1. 6 • 2. 43 • 3. A real rabbit • 4. Eight percent • 5. Ninety-five hundred dollars • 6.
Drive-In A Go Go • 7. West Hill Community Church • 8. Forty-five hundred dol-
lars • 9. $145,000 • 10. One hundred dollars • 11. Mr. Tillman • 12. The Trailer
Trap • 13. 35.10 seconds • 14. Abel Esterlake was asleep in the back seat. • 15.
$170

LIVE A LITTLE, LOVE A LITTLE

1. Alice • 2. He slept in a baby crib in his own room. • 3. Purple Valley Dairies • 4.
Sanitary engineer • 5. Egg rolls and hot dogs • 6. Fried chicken • 7. Radlin, Kernig,
Canford, and Penlow • 8. Twenty-one • 9. *Classic Cat Magazine* • 10. Wheat germ
and clam juice cocktail • 11. Sally • 12. Beef and beer stew • 13. 211 Lookout
Mountain Drive • 14. Five to one • 15. At the beach

CHARRO!

1. Tequila • 2. A day and a half • 3. Six dollars • 4. Solid gold over bronze, decorated with silver • 5. One hundred thousand dollars • 6. The Victory Gun fired the
last shot against Emperor Maximilian, which freed Mexico from his rule. • 7.
Norm • 8. He burned a wound on Jess's neck with a red-hot brand. • 9. Ten thousand dollars • 10. Rio Seco • 11. Twelve years • 12. In a flower pot in the hallway •
13. His gun and holster • 14. Opie Keetch • 15. Sundown

THE TROUBLE WITH GIRLS

1. Walter Hale wore a white suit. • 2. A silver dollar • 3. "The Darktown Strutters'
Ball" • 4. 11 • 5. She associated each name with an animal. • 6. July 14 • 7. The
Imperial Russian Ballet Troupe • 8. The Metropolitan Opera • 9. A box of fireworks • 10. Axle grease • 11. Fourteen hours, twenty-one minutes • 12. Clarence
• 13. Gilroy, Iowa • 14. Six months • 15. He reported to the police that she was a
thief, and they put her on the chautauqua train that was heading out of town.

CHANGE OF HABIT

1. 934 Washington Street • 2. Gonzales and Green, Morticians • 3. Catholic Action Committee • 4. She was a laboratory technician. • 5. She was a registered nurse with a degree in public health. • 6. Two months • 7. Shelby County, Tennessee • 8. Forty-three years • 9. The Order of Little Sisters of Mary • 10. Ajax Market • 11. Cal Edwards • 12. One hundred dollars • 13. Patron saint of Caribbean fishermen • 14. August 3 • 15. Julio

ELVIS–THAT'S THE WAY IT IS

1. Elvis • 2. "I Just Can't Help Believin'" • 3. Tom Jones • 4. 350 • 5. White

ELVIS ON TOUR

1. "Burnin' Love" • 2. Roanoke, Virginia • 3. "Don't Be Cruel" and "Ready Teddy" • 4. "Proud Mary" • 5. "You Gave Me a Mountain"

ANSWERS TO THE ELVIS MASTER QUIZ

1. Plowing the fields • 2. "(Let's Have a) Party" • 3. "Treat Me Nice" • 4. Gilded Cage • 5. Pretty Boy II • 6. They were ranchers. • 7. Ten dollars • 8. Gates of Hawaii • 9. ll:00 P.M. • 10. $750 • 11. Mr. and Mrs. Morgan • 12. Greater Washington Produce Company • 13. The Acapulco Hilton • 14. Second Lieutenant • 15. The Horseshoe Hotel • 16. Three weeks • 17. Sandbar Club • 18. 7A • 19. Harem of Dancing Jewels from the Near East • 20. SS *Mississippi Queen* • 21. Danrick Airways • 22. ll • 23. He was an explosive-ordnance disposal man. • 24. The G-Men • 25. Ten dollars • 26. Calgary, Cheyenne, and Madison Square Garden • 27. Seventy-seven hundred dollars, (purse was seventy-five hundred dollars and lap money was two hundred) • 28. One thousand dollars at each firm • 29. Sheriff Dan Ramsey • 30. 1927 • 31. 8:00 A.M. to 5:30 P.M. • 32. Backstage at the International Hotel • 33. *Fun in Acapulco* • 34. *The Trouble with Girls* • 35. *Harum Scarum* • 36. *Kissin' Cousins* • 37. *Jailhouse Rock* • 38. *Spinout* • 39. *King Creole* • 40. *Girl Happy* • 41. *Girls! Girls! Girls!* • 42. *Frankie and Johnny* • 43. *Easy Come, Easy Go* • 44. *Roustabout* • 45. *Blue Hawaii* • 46. *Double Trouble* • 47. *Viva Las Vegas* • 48. *Live a Little, Love a Little* • 49. *Paradise, Hawaiian Style* • 50. *Charro!* • 51. *Speedway* • 52. *Change of Habit* • 53. *Flaming Star* • 54. E • 55. K • 56. Q • 57. F • 58. D • 59. A • 60. B • 61. I • 62. G • 63. H • 64. N • 65. O • 66. C • 67. M • 68. P • 69. L • 70. J • 71.

S • 72. Z • 73. T • 74. W • 75. U • 76. V • 77. Y • 78. R • 79. X • 80. Walter Gulick • 81. Rick Richards • 82. Pacer Burton • 83. Jess Wade • 84. Clint Reno • 85. Scott Hayward • 86. Lonnie Beal • 87. Danny Fisher • 88. Greg Nolan • 89. Mike Edwards • 90. Deke Rivers • 91. Rusty Wells • 92. Dr. John Carpenter • 93. Toby Kwimper • 94. Tulsa McLean • 95. Walter Hale • 96. Ross Carpenter • 97. Guy Lambert • 98. Steve Grayson • 99. Joe Lightcloud • 100. Vince Everett

BIBLIOGRAPHY

The author wishes to thank the following sources, which were invaluable during the writing of *Reel Elvis!*.

Aylesworth, Thomas G., and John S. Bowman. *The World Almanac Who's Who of Film*. New York: World Almanac, 1987.

Benton, Thomas Hart. *An American in Art*. Lawrence, Kans.: The University Press of Kansas, 1969.

Brooks, Tim. *The Complete Directory of Prime Time TV Stars, 1946–Present*. New York: Ballantine Books, 1988.

Current Biography. New York: The H. W. Wilson, Co.

Dundy, Elaine. *Elvis and Gladys*. New York: Macmillan Publishing Co., 1985.

Halliwell, Leslie. *Halliwell's Filmgoer's and Video Viewer's Companion*. Ninth edition. New York: Charles Scribner's Sons, 1988.

Heitland, Jon. *The Man from U.N.C.L.E. Book*. New York: St. Martin's Press, 1987.

Hirschhorn, Clive. *The Hollywood Musical*. London: Octopus Books, 1981.

Hopkins, Jerry. *Elvis*. New York: Simon & Schuster, 1971.

———. *Elvis: The Final Years*. New York: Berkley Books, 1983.

Katz, Ephraim. *The Film Encyclopedia*. New York: Thomas Crowell Publishers, 1979.

Lichter, Paul. *The Boy Who Dared to Rock: The Definitive Elvis*. New York: Galahad Books, 1982.

Lloyd, Ann, and Graham Fuller. *The Illustrated Who's Who of the Cinema*. New York: Macmillan Publishing Co., 1983.

McNeil, Alex. *Total Television: A Comprehensive Guide to Programming from 1948 to the Present*. New York: Penguin Books, 1991.

Marsh, Dave. *Elvis*. New York: Rolling Stone Press/Quadrangle/The New York Times Book Co., Inc., 1982.

The Marshall Cavendish Illustrated History of Popular Music. Freeport, N.Y.: Marshall Cavendish Corporation, 1990.

Medved, Harry, and Michael Medved. *The Golden Turkey Awards*. New York: Perigee Books, 1980.

Mitz, Rick. *The Great TV Sitcom Book*. New York: Perigee Books, 1983.

Murrells, Joseph. *Million Selling Records from the 1900s to the 1980s: An Illustrated Dictionary*. New York: ARCO Publishing Co., Inc., 1984.

Nash, Jay Robert, and Stanley Ralph Ross. *The Motion Picture Guide*. Chicago, Illinois.: Cinebooks, Inc. 1986.

The New York Times Film Reviews. New York: The New York Times Company, 1970.

184 Pareles, Jon, and Patricia Romanowski, editors. *The* ROLLING STONE *Encyclopedia of Rock and Roll.* New York: Rolling Stone/Summit Books, 1983.

Presley, Priscilla Beaulieu. *Elvis and Me.* New York: G. P. Putnam's Sons, 1985.

Ragan, David. *Who's Who in Hollywood 1900–1976.* New Rochelle, N.Y.: Arlington House Publishers, 1976.

Schemering, Christopher. *The Soap Opera Encyclopedia.* New York: Ballantine Books, 1985.

Shale, Richard, compiler. *Academy Awards.* New York: Frederick Ungar Publishing Co., 1982.

Stetler, Susan L., editor. *Almanac of Famous People.* Detroit, Mich.: Gale Research, 1989.

Terrace, Vincent. *The Encyclopedia of Television Programs 1947–1976.* New York: A. S. Barnes and Co., 1976.

Torgoff, Martin, editor. *The Complete Elvis.* New York: Delilah Books, 1982.

VARIETY's *Who's Who in Show Business.* New York: R. R. Bowker, 1989.

Vellenga, Dirk, with Mick Farren. *Elvis and the Colonel.* New York: Delacorte Press, 1988.

Wakeman, John, editor. *World Film Directors.* New York: The H. W. Wilson Co., 1987.

Walter, Claire. *Winners: The Blue Ribbon Encyclopedia of Awards.* New York: Facts on File, Inc., 1978.

West, Richard. *Television Western: Major and Minor Series, 1946–1978.* Jefferson, N.C.: McFarland and Company, Inc., 1987.

Who's Who in Entertainment 1989–1990. Wilmette, Ill.: Marquis Who's Who, 1988.

Worth, Fred L., and Steve D. Tamerius. *Elvis: His Life from A to Z.* Avenel, N.J.: Outlet Book Company, a Random House Company, 1992.

Zmijewsky, Steven, and Boris Zmijewsky. *Elvis: The Films and Career of Elvis Presley.* New York: Carol Publishing Group, 1983.

APPLICATION FOR ELVIS DEGREE

Name _____

Street, route, or p.o. box_____Apt. #_____

City _____ State_____ Zip_____

Phone _____

    I have completed the Elvis Master Quiz and achieved a score of ____, which entitles me to a Ph.D.D. in Presleyana. Please add any special Elvis honors that I have earned.

    I have enclosed a self-addressed, stamped envelope with first-class postage so that I can receive my degree in a Memphis flash!

    Please mail this form and your self-addressed, stamped envelope to:

Pauline Bartel, President
The University at Taylor
Post Office Box 491
Waterford, NY 12188-0491